MOLOKAI

MOLOKAI

THE STORY OF
FATHER DAMIEN

HILDE EYNIKEL

**Translated from the Dutch original
by Lesley Gilbert**

ALBA·HOUSE   NEW·YORK
SOCIETY OF ST. PAUL, 2187 VICTORY BLVD., STATEN ISLAND, NEW YORK 10314

First published in Great Britain in 1999

10 9 8 7 6 5 4 3 2 1

British Library Cataloguing in Publication Data
A record for this book is available from the British Library

ISBN 0 340 71419 0

Library of Congress Cataloging-in-Publication Data

Eynikel, Hilde.
 Molokai: the story of Father Damien / Hilde Eynikel.
  p. cm.
 ISBN: 0-8189-0872-6 (pbk.)
 1. Damien, Father (1840-1889). 2. Catholic Church—Hawaii—Clergy—
Biography. 3. Missionaries-Hawaii—Biography. 4. Missionaries—
Belgium—Biography. I. Title.
 BX4705.D25E854 1999
 266'.2'092-dc21   99-11593
 [B]   CIP

Typeset by Avon Dataset Ltd, Bidford-on-Avon, Warks

Printed and bound in Great Britain by
Clays Ltd, St Ives plc

Hodder and Stoughton Ltd
A Division of Hodder Headline PLC
338 Euston Road
London NW1 3BH

Contents

Introduction   vii
1 Growing Up in Tremelo (*1840–1858*)   1
2 Entry into the Order of the Sacred Hearts (*1859*)   17
3 Sudden Departure for Hawaii (*1863–1864*)   27
4 Consecration as Priest in Honolulu (*1864*)   37
5 Working on an Active Volcano (*1864–1865*)   49
6 Kohala-Hamakua (*1865–1868*)   55
7 Eruption of the Volcano (*1868*)   65
8 The Decision (*May 1873*)   73
9 Accepted (*May 1873–January 1874*)   85
10 Two Priests Vie for the Leper Settlement
   (*February 1874–August 1877*)   107
11 War with Burgerman over the Leper Settlement
   (*October 1877–August 1880*)   135
12 A Royal Honour (*August 1880–October 1881*)   155
13 Nursing Sisters Invited to the Settlement
   (*January 1882–November 1883*)   167
14 Damien a Leper (*January 1884–January 1885*)   181
15 Damien Officially Segregated
   (*February 1885–June 1886*)   199
16 Triumph in Honolulu (*July–December 1886*)   213
17 Dispute about the Money from London
   (*January 1887–May 1888*)   227
18 Damien's Companion, Louis-Lambert Conrardy,
   The Healthy Priest (*May–November 1888*)   259
19 The Franciscan Nuns (*November 1888–February 1889*) 275
20 Nunc Dimittis (*February–April 1889*)   293
21 After Damien (*1889–1995*)   307

Introduction

A bronze statue of Father Damien, representing Hawaii, stands tucked away in the Capitol in Washington D.C. The 'leper priest' is portrayed as a sturdy peasant, as I remember him from school and hearsay. When untangling Damien from the man of legend I gradually discovered a much greater man. Two incidents made me take up this challenge.

In 1992 I found myself confronted with the ugly face of leprosy when making a report on Mother Theresa in Calcutta. A few months later Richard Marks, a cured 'leper', showed me Kalaupapa on Molokai, Hawaii, where Father Damien lived and died. He shared his pain, loneliness and revulsion, and then asked me as an author and historian to write a book on Damien in which the 'exiles' would be treated fairly. Though he insisted that he did not mind being called a 'leper', I understood how much this stigmatising denomination hurts. Over the years I befriended the small community at Kalaupapa, and I thank them for the full support they gave our crew when we were shooting the movie *Father Damien*. They allowed their ravaged faces and deformed hands to be filmed, hoping it would help fundraising for programs to eradicate leprosy in Third World countries, where it remains a scourge. In the Indian province of Bihar, 100,000 new cases are confirmed yearly.

Out of respect I will refer to persons afflicted with Hansen's disease whenever possible as 'patients', 'exiles' or 'deportees'. Damien called himself sarcastically the 'leper priest', but when speaking to the British painter Edward Clifford he used 'sick people, segregated persons'.

When researching Damien I felt blessed as the archives of

Damien's Congregation, the Sacred Hearts of Jesus and Mary (Picpus), are situated opposite the school in Leuven, Belgium, that my sons were attending. Less helpful was the fact that I was allowed to work on excerpts of letters only, while the original documents remained in a concrete vault. All other biographers had suffered the same restrictions. However, I did get access to the original testimonials in the Archiepiscopal archives in Mechelen, Belgium. Based on this information I wrote a first biography in Dutch.

After the publication of that book I was granted unrestricted access to the archives. I hesitated to accept the offer, but then I remembered what the dying Damien had written to his Anglican friend Edward Clifford: 'During your long travelling road homewards, please do not forget that narrow road we both have to walk carefully, so as to meet together at the home of our common and eternal Father.' A bigot would believe that only Catholics go to heaven. Yet Robert Louis Stevenson had described Damien as 'a European peasant, dirty, bigoted, untruthful, unwise, tricky but superb with generosity, residual candor and fundamental good humor. A man with all the grime and paltriness of mankind, but the saint and hero all the more for it.' How could Damien have been a peasant, when his parents and brothers and sisters all attended prestigious boarding-schools? Curiosity won.

Two vault-like rooms in the basement of the convent in Leuven contained wall-high shelves stacked with letters, diaries, testimonials, invoices . . . Most were originals, some xeroxes. I introduced each document into a database, organised by AskSam software. The same procedure was used for documents I found in the Archives of the State of Hawaii in Honolulu, in Mechelen, from privately owned sources and from oral information given by both patients and the De Veuster family. At times I introduced information twice. When, for instance, Damien referred to his youth, I filed it at the date when it happened and also at the time it was written about.

When analysing the resource material, I realised how special Damien was. This book is not meant to be a hagiography, but Damien stands central. He appears to have been a likeable man, intelligent, practical, sharp, stubborn, open-minded, forgiving, with a good sense of humour and a quick temper. Most of all he was an original thinker, quite ahead of his time, and he had the rare gift of empathy. To confirm the historicity of this 'new Damien', I presented this biography for a Ph.D. at the Catholic University of Leuven and was granted the degree *cum magna laude*.

I was given all the help an author can hope for from the Picpus Congregation. Descendants of Damien's brothers and many Hawaiians, including patients, supported this project. No attempt was made to censure or to control my work. Father Paul Macken ss cc has saved me from many inaccuracies.

The last note Damien wrote has a smudge of blood on it. In it Damien asks the settlement physician Dr Swift for help. 'If possible can you please come over, I have some intestinal trouble in the lower bowel, and oblige your weak friend. Jobo Puhomia has been spitting blood from yesterday morning. Please, spare a moment to go and see him at the second house after that of Jack Lewis and oblige your friend. P.S. in the same house you will find the dying woman I spoke to you about last night.' This note is typical of Damien, who worried about his fellow-sufferers much more than about himself.

I

Growing Up in Tremelo
(1840–1858)

Damien seldom referred to his family in his correspondence. He asked after family and friends but he did not reminisce. Nevertheless it is clear who were for him the two people for whom he felt the greatest affection: his brother Auguste, later Fr Pamphile, and his sister Pauline, later Sr Alphonse. Together they had endured the treatment of their mother Cato. She was no God-fearing farmer's wife, gathering her eight children around her every evening by the hearth to read from the big book of lives of the saints. She did do so occasionally, but in general she was a harpy, a shrew or – as it was whispered in Tremelo – a 'witch'.

Background and Youth

Joseph de Veuster was born into a lower middle-class family of tradesmen-farmers in the community of Tremelo, near Leuven in Flanders, the Dutch-speaking area of Belgium, on 3 January 1840. His parents, Franciscus or Frans de Veuster and Anne-Catherine Wouters, familiarly known as Cato, were first cousins, and Joseph was the seventh of their eight children. The child was baptised on the day of its birth and given the single baptismal name of Joseph.

Joseph, who was familiarly known as Jef, was an active child, who often refused to do his mother's bidding. She always got the upper hand, however, and the outcome was often a sore bottom.

Cato de Veuster was a hot-tempered woman, who could be violent with her children. In 1842, she had a violent altercation with her eldest child, Eugénie, and the outcome was that Eugénie and her sister, Constance, who was next in age, were packed off to the Ursuline Convent in Tildonk. When the summer holidays came, Eugénie refused to return to the family home. She was sixteen and had decided to take the veil. She became Sr Alexis of the Sacred Hearts and went to the Netherlands to teach as a missionary. When the school holidays were over, Constance followed her sister to the convent in the Netherlands.

In his earliest years, Jef spent a good deal of time with his paternal grandfather, Hendrik de Veuster, along with his two cousins, Henri Vinckx and Félix de Veuster, who were roughly his age. They went on lengthy walks over the De Veusters' extensive property. Almost everyone in the village worked for the family. Frans alone had seventeen people in his service. Hendrik would show the children the marvels of nature. He would point out which berries were poisonous and which leaves to use to soothe nettle stings. He showed them how to break up the heavy wet soil so that flax could be sown, and sometimes he took them to visit the shepherds, who knew a lot about animals. Hendrik advised the boys to be sensible and listen to them. The boys did so, because, if they were good, they were allowed to ride the old nags, in which the family traded. The foreman went about the neighbourhood buying them up and the beasts were then put out to grass on the pasture around the village, until the time came for their bones to be boiled down to glue. Jef found this perfectly normal. He just wanted to ride. Leaning forward, clasping the beast's back firmly between his legs, he would cling on to its mane. If he was lucky, the horse would then gallop at full speed through the fields.

A Lively Outdoor Child

Hendrik's death in June 1845 brought an end to this happy period. Jef, who was five and a half, grieved for his grandpa and found consolation with Tiske Vie the shepherd, with whom he spent more and more time. The shepherd taught him how to tend the animals and summoned him if a sheep was ready to lamb. Jef spent so much time with the shepherd that he was given the nickname 'shepherd boy'.

As soon as he was out of Cato's hearing, the deeply devout Tiske would let forth a stream of oaths and obscenities. The children would giggle. More exciting were Tiske's ghost stories. He showed them the trees where will-o'-the-wisps, the souls of unbaptised children, hovered. They were told to place their clogs with the tips facing the door, otherwise the Moor would get them. Sometimes Tiske would take them up close to Peter Hoeylichen's hovel. That showed you were really brave, because that man was a sorcerer and no mistake. If you paid him well, he would curse your enemy and then he would get sick and die. He read about sorcery and witchcraft. The children avoided that particular topic, because it was whispered that Cato was a witch. After all, she could read Gothic type in that big book of saints' lives. The other children teased the De Veusters that only witches could decipher it.

Jef could not understand this, because there were stories of saints in the book, such as how the wise, learned priest, Pamphilus, became a martyr. Each chapter began with twelve illustrations. Jef liked the story of the twins Cosmas and Damien, doctors who did many good deeds and died as martyrs. Later on Cato taught the children to read Gothic type themselves, so that she could get on with darning socks.

No one in the village questioned Cato's industry. On her good days, she would sing, but, so the gossip ran in the village, those were the days when the gin bottle was less full than usual. She sang songs about Napoleon and about her time in Rebecq, where she had gone to school, when life had been unclouded. Before bedtime, Cato would go up to the attic to fetch an apple for each of the four younger children – Mieke, born in 1844, had now grown into a sturdy little girl. They sat down together in front of the fire to eat their apple and then she would pack the whole brood off to bed, first making the sign of the cross lovingly on each forehead.

During his earliest childhood years, Jef lived the outdoor life with great intensity. He helped on the farm, although his help was not always appreciated. When he could, he would go jauntily into Janneke Roef's carpentry workshop. From the moment Jef stepped over the threshold, the whole hamlet would hold its breath, because soon the cry would ring out, 'Be off! you're blunting my tools.' Jef would run off to the other carpenter who was called Masfel. He learned how to make bricks and roof tiles from Jan Feyaerts, nicknamed Cross-eyed, who was a notorious drunkard.

When it was mealtime, or if there was a special job to be done, Cato would sound a cowhorn. Standing, she would recite the *Benedictus*. Only when she had said 'Amen' – the only word most people understood – were they allowed to help themselves to stew from the big pot. Meanwhile Frans sat in the best room, eating alone at a small table, unless he had an important guest or the two eldest sons Léonce and Gérard were home from school, for the men were allowed to eat from the 'good dinner service'.

On Sundays, the whole family would go to mass in Werchter. Cato walked ahead with the children along the towpath by the Dijle. She had a rosary in her powerful hands and rattled off the prayers. The children followed her and had to repeat certain passages. She stopped saying the rosary when they got to the outskirts of Werchter, because then she started looking at the houses. If she saw anyone doing any work whatever, she would fuss about breaking the Sabbath, which was Devil's work. Foolish people like that would never prosper. In the church, Cato sat proudly in her own seat with its nameplate. She looked around and took note of new clothes, furtive looks, anyone with a hangover. The children sat either side of her. Frans usually fell asleep during the sermon. Cato would purse her lips at this and dig him in the ribs to wake him. She got really angry if he snored. After mass, he would go to the inn, while Cato marched home with the children. All the way home, the children had to answer questions about the sermon.

Once home, she would prepare Sunday lunch but no one was allowed to sit down until Frans returned. Tipsy, he ate alone at his table and then went and sat in his chair by the stove and dozed off. Cato would try to wake him for evensong, because they had agreed to take it in turns to take the children. Usually, however, she was unable to arouse him from his fuddle and had to take them to church herself. In the evening, the parents read the newspapers. Cato rarely went to mass in the week, except on special holidays, such as 4 December, the saint's day of St Barbara, the patron saint of Ninde, the hamlet in which the De Veusters lived.

Jef did not go to school in Tremelo because the schoolmaster was a tippler. He followed his brother and sister to Master Bols's school in Wezchtea, even though this meant that he sometimes missed days in the winter, because the road was flooded. Bols was a supporter of the Flemish Movement for the promotion of Dutch language and culture and consequently he was in favour of Dutch as the medium of instruction. He prepared his lessons thoroughly, was strict and demanding but also fair. Master Bols did not find Jef a well-behaved pupil. Jef often had to sit at the front of the class with the dunce's cap on. He frequently arrived late, for the towpath along the Dijle held too many temptations. He would stop to catch sticklebacks or shy stones over the water or, in the winter, go skating. Sometimes he would swim naked with the other children, girls included.

In the summer, Jef and Loike, an orphan, had to take black bread with apple sauce and jugs of buttermilk to the girls who had been taken on to pick clover. He enjoyed this, because you could really tease the girls. Food was no problem in the summer, but by the end of the winter, the animals were thin and there was an acute shortage of fresh vegetables. Fortunately, coster-mongers came with salted fish, which had to be soaked for ages until it was edible. Apart from in Lent, though, the wealthy farmers lived well, because they were well organised. Once a week Rik Claes would slaughter a pig at one of the farms. He cut up the meat, made sausages and collected the blood and boiled it to make black pudding. He then divided the meat between a number of baskets that different farmers had sent.

A Visit From Eugénie

One day, when Jef was seven, his sisters Eugénie, Louise, Alexis and Constance paid a visit to the house. For hours, Eugénie wafted through the room. In an accent that showed traces of French and Dutch, she preached to them about spiritual values, heavenly bliss and missionary work. The younger children stared at the nun in awe, because she presented them with a vision of heavenly bliss. As she left, Eugénie leaned toward the four youngest children and declared unambiguously and command-ingly that one day 'their turn' would come. Then she got into the coach.

Constance had finished her education and Cato insisted that she remain at home, casually brushing aside her declared calling. The young woman retreated into gloomy silence and the other children could see that she was unhappy. The sense of heavenly bliss that Eugénie had given them was so great that they wanted to imitate it. On the way to school nine-year-old Auguste suggested that they 'play monastery and convent'. Pauline thought this a great idea. She got one or two other children to come to the woods. There they spent the whole day playing missionaries. Eleven-year-old Pauline prayed aloud in a sort of pseudo-French. Auguste closed his eyes, absorbed in faith. Jef was not sure what to do and pretended to be Master Bols. He made the other children kneel 'in the corner' and put leaves on their heads in place of a dunce's cap. At midday they got hungry. They had thrown their bread into the Dijle as a mortification. It was too early to go home and too late to go to school. Around five o'clock they got frightened. Their parents would have found out by now that they had played truant. Cato would beat them. Suddenly they just wanted to be ordinary children again. They had heard Cato and other mothers calling them. Children who had gone to school got a smack. They cried but you did not tell on your friends. The group suspected that men were searching the river. A farm hand suggested having a look in the lovers' wood. Everyone laughed at him because they were too young and there were too many of them, but he decided to go anyway and there he found them. With a great grin, he announced their impending punishment. That night there were many wailing children in the village.

Was this the first sign of a religious calling? Perhaps. It was certainly a clear sign of the impression Eugénie's visit had made on Pauline, Auguste and Jef. They believed that 'their turn' would come. Perhaps the religious life was the ultimate refuge, for Cato was becoming increasingly intemperate. When she was in one of her moods, the children would hide beneath the pack-bridge over the river Laak, which joined the Dijle near their home. Cato always knew where to find them and yet they were safe. As their stoutly built mother lumbered her way down the steep embankment, they would flee in the other direction.

Jef was not an easy child. He was stubborn and given to getting into a paddy. When he really got beside himself, he would shut himself in the attic and stand on the trapdoor yelling angrily, 'Sakkerdepei!' He had no idea that this was a Flemish distortion of a French oath. Sometimes he would get into such a rage that Cato had to throw water in his face. Jef was a daredevil, who would climb up and sit astride the ridge of the roof. He loved to trot around on a saddleless horse and was always the first to volunteer if a wasps' nest had to be smoked out.

It was also fun to jump on to the platform of a fast-driven cart. You had to be nimble and, above all, keep your cool. One day, when Jef was still very young, the children were at this game again. The carter shouted, 'Don't do that!' but that was precisely what made it so exciting. Jef jumped but he missed the wooden edge of the tailboard. He was thrown forward and his face went into the mud. The carter pulled on the reins, the horses whinnied and shied up and the wheels crunched over Jef's back. He received a severe blow to the head. Only then did the cart come to a standstill. The carter ran towards the boy who lay motionless in the mud. 'Call mistress De Veuster!' he cried. The children ran to Ninde and quickly returned with the anxious farmer's wife. Her Jef was already lying on the platform of the cart. He was alive but looked very pale.

For several days he lay in bed in the best room, because sunlight gave him a headache. The doctor prescribed rest, not only for his head but for his back, because that was where the cart had run over him. Jef was a healthy boy and he recovered quickly but he had back pain for the rest of his life as a result. The sight in one eye was also damaged and he had to wear glasses.

Death on Christmas Eve

In 1847 the relative calm of Jef's youth was disturbed by death. In December, his younger sister Marieke became ill and died on Christmas Eve. The shutters were closed and a large white cross was painted on the door because of the contagion. Neighbours paid their respects from a distance. Cholera had reached the village and Marieke was one of its first victims. On Christmas Day, a Saturday, there were no burials, nor on the following day, Sunday. Emergency measures had not yet been introduced.

It was the boys' task to bear the body to the church in Tremelo on a canopied bier. Jef was a sturdy boy of nearly eight and he too would play his part. Adults did not belong in this tragic procession. Only Cato, an ominous figure in a hooded cape, accompanied them. The boys carefully bore the body outside, feet first, otherwise the little girl's ghost would remain to haunt them. The wasted child was not heavy, but it was difficult to walk through the clammy rain and heavy mud. In the distance they could hear the tolling of the bell known as 'Little-one-death'. At the lychgate, old Fr Scheys was waiting for them, ready quickly to say the Mass of the Angels. Marieke was buried under the cross close to the church. Then the family went to drown its sorrows at the inn.

Marieke's death on 24 December 1847 was the sixty-eighth of that year. By 6 January, in Tremelo, forty people had already died in six days. The year 1848 was a difficult one in rural Flanders, as it was throughout Europe, most notably, of course, in Ireland. Prolonged wet weather caused the failure both of the grain harvest and the potato crop. Damien was to remember all his life the scenes of suffering created by the food shortage.

Jef was confirmed on Palm Sunday, 13 April 1851. Full of pride, he sat on the box in his new suit and shoes. Pauline was missing from his confirmation party because she had already been at boarding school in the Netherlands for two years. Auguste stole the limelight: in the autumn, he was going off to study at the Minor Seminary in Mechelen and he trumpeted the news among the guests.

After Auguste had gone, Jef remained behind like an only child. Léonce, Gérard and Constance were living at home, but they were grown up. Pauline and Eugénie were in Uden in North Brabant and Auguste was in Mechelen. Jef was counting the days until he too could go to Mechelen. It was not so much that he was bored. He swam long distances and in the winter he skated with his brothers: Léonce was more lithe and Gérard faster, but Jef took risks. When the winters were really freezing, he would get as far as Battel, beyond Mechelen.

On one occasion he found that the ice was soft. It was the end of the winter and there was spring in the air. Suddenly, he heard the children shouting, 'Baaske is drowning!' He ran back and saw water splashing in a new grey hole in the swelling ice. He ordered them to hold on to his feet, lay down on the ice and crawled forward cautiously on his belly over the ice toward the hole. He looked into the water that was speckled with ice, saw nothing at first and then the red flash of a jacket. He stuck his arm in the water and was able to catch the boy by the hair and drag him out of the water. Cautiously, he dragged the child to the bank. The others took off their jackets and cardigans, removed the drowning child's clothes and rubbed him warm. Baaske survived.

No Studies (1854–1856)

In the summer of 1854, Jef passed his elementary school certificate. It was normal for the De Veuster children to continue their education, Jacob's children as well as Frans's. Jef's sisters went to the Ursulines, Léonce and Gérard had studied at the Institution Solvay in Rebecy, like their parents, and Auguste and his cousins were at the prestigious Minor Seminary in Mechelen.

Jef thought he also had the right to further education. It was true that he had often been made to wear the dunce's cap, but that was because he was over-active. He was not as clever as Master Bols's own sons, but he was certainly capable of learning. Yet he, alone of all the De Veuster children, had to remain at home. The family was certainly not in financial difficulties. Frans had savings of BF1,105 in 1854. Was it that Master Bols gave negative advice? or that Cato could not bear to let her son go? Perhaps they feared that the Minor Seminary, which provided training for the priesthood, would not only give Auguste – who, as everyone said, was a born priest – but Jef as well, a religious calling. He would be the fifth of the seven surviving children with a religious vocation.

In April 1854, Jef's eldest sister, Eugénie, died of typhus. His sister Pauline, who was studying in the same convent at the time, was with her. In 1856, Pauline took the veil, although she was not convinced that she had a religious calling.

Jef was still wearing a mourning armband when he finished school. Disappointed that he was the only child who would not learn French, he looked down on the responsible tasks he was given in the business. He had to pay the staff, using the money that was hidden under the drying pine cones in the summer. He was allowed to take the reins of the horses for his brother Léonce, who said the rosary during long trips. Jef admired him because he knew by heart all of the mysteries of the rosary. He was jealous when he heard Léonce conducting transactions in French.

Jef felt like a stupid clodhopper, but not on Saturday evenings when he went out with the young folk from the village. Together they would set off for a fair, but on the way couples would drop out of the group to go courting. Jef became a member of the St Sebastian's Guild, shouldered a crossbow and sang along at the annual festival. After mass on Sundays, he went to the inn and played 'bonnets', a game of chance. At other times, he would go to the inn with friends, where, pipe in hand, beer or gin on the table, he would listen to the tales being told.

In this way he was learning a lot more than he could have done at school, everyone assured him. Even so, he was very jealous of Auguste, the brilliant student, who was considering joining a missionary order to the Sandwich Islands in the South Pacific. In the school library, he had found a small, recently published book by a French priest, Frézal Tardieu, the superior of the Collèges des Missions Etrangères (College of Foreign Missions) in nearby Leuven.

The Order of the Sacred Hearts of Jesus and Mary – Studies After All (1856–1857)

In the nineteenth century, the cult of the Sacred Hearts of Jesus and Mary was extremely widespread. Many new orders took up this symbolism in their name.

In 1857 Frans and Cato urged even more strongly that Auguste should enrol at the university to study medicine or law, but the young man, who was approaching twenty, wished to enter the monastery at Leuven. Cato protested. He was too young, he must study first, or work for a few years, then perhaps he could join the order. Already, he was in a position to earn BF1,000 a year. This made Auguste angry and he asked if his parents needed the money. They did not. They should go with him to the monastery and see for themselves. They could make their views known after that.

Cato, Frans and Auguste went down a cobbled street behind the town hall in Leuven to St Michael's Church, then they went down an alley. An over-ornate gate seemed to announce a wealthy monastery but within they were as poor as church mice. In a bare room, sitting on hard seats, the De Veusters stared at empty walls. The superior, a Frenchman and the author of the book, was a sweet but odd man, with an over-large forehead, receding dark hair and intelligent eyes. Frézal Tardieu stooped as he walked, as if he were prematurely aged. Auguste had hoped for enthusiasm but received criticism. 'His soutane is green,' Cato complained. 'Why do you have to choose a poor monastery?' She had already given two children to the Church. Eugénie had died of poverty and malnourishment. It was fortunate that she had been able to restrain Constance. She could not persuade Auguste, however: he had only one aim. He wanted to teach poor but gifted children, visit prisoners and help the poor. He wanted to join the Order on a symbolic date, 9 October, his twentieth birthday. He did so and took the name Brother Pamphile.

Jef followed all of this at a distance. He sat at home listening to the rows and his mother's grumblings. He watched her dealing out blows and feared becoming trapped in that stifling environment, like his brothers Léonce and Gérard and his sister Constance – and at least they could still read French books.

When Jef's frustrations burst out in a blazing row, Cato and Frans decided to send him to the Ecole Commerciale (Business School) in the little Walloon town of Braine-le-Comte, close to Rebecq, where they themselves had studied. It was indeed unfair that he should be the only De Veuster not to learn French. Joseph Vrancken, a distant relation, was at school there. The fees were BF1 per day plus extras. Dirt cheap it was not, but M. Derue-L'Hoir provided a good education. Jef would then be able to go on with his education in Antwerp. A few days later, Jef sat on the box next to his father, wearing a starched white shirt, leather shoes and a bowler hat. He was happy. At last he was going to get to the same level as his brothers, cousins and friends.

The fun ended at the school gate. The building itself was a disappointment. Jef had expected a sort of Institution Solvay, a majestic Ursuline school like Tildonk or a grand Minor Seminary. Even the poor Sacred Hearts monastery in Leuven was more imposing than this building. In the school itself, he did not understand a word that was said. He sat in the class as though he were deaf and dumb and felt like a clodhopper. His Walloon fellow-students called him a Flemish peasant and laughed at him because he knew no French. Jef did not accept this, called them names back and lashed out at them. This led to a fight and his new trousers got torn. The eighteen-year-old did not dare to write home about this, but he did tell them about the pestering, in a childish-sounding letter in French. Gradually, the teasing subsided, because anyone who snapped at him got a hard rap with his ruler. Jef quickly gained a reputation as a bully.

He had to keep up with virtually all the subjects in a new language and he had to change everything he already knew. He had to reshape the beautiful round letters he had learned from Master Bols into a fashionable sloping, elongated hand. He had to copy the words '*lamentation*', '*mutuelle*' and '*amitié*' for hours on end.

He wanted to catch up with what he had missed and even during the Sunday walks he would ask his Walloon fellow-students to spell the names of things they saw for him. Jef had a good memory and his French improved quickly. He did a lot of exercises, even during the lengthy meals. He filled up exercise books, constantly needed new books, pens and paper, asked his parents for money and admitted that his trousers were torn.

The Calling (1858)

Jef regretted that he was not at home at Whitsun to see his sister Pauline, who was visiting her parents. Jef wanted to see her in her nun's habit but, more than that, he wanted to discuss his calling with her. Ought they to take the same road together? So he did make the journey to Tremelo, spent a long time talking to her and realised that her turn was already come. He, as the youngest, was the only one who still had to take the step.

Back in Braine-le-Comte he copied sentences such as '*Les maladies de l'âme sont difficiles à guérir*' ('Ills of the soul are difficult to cure'). He could do it almost perfectly and no longer needed to excuse himself for his many errors in his subsequent letters. By July, he was almost certain that 'his turn' had come. He was not looking forward to the holidays, because that meant six weeks of speaking Dutch and forgetting his French. He wrote to Auguste about his calling and this problem with his studies. Auguste – Br Pamphile – spoke to his superior Frézal about the possibility of allowing Jef to spend his holidays in the monastery. Pamphile also mentioned cautiously, in passing, that Jef suspected he had a religious calling.

The only thing Jef asked his parents for was clothes, because washing was only done every six weeks at school and not every two weeks as it was at home. He begged for news of Pauline. Had she made her decision? In his next letter he switched to his native language in an access of emotion. He was clearly confused and anxious and alluded to a calling; his turn was coming quite quickly. He received clothes and also a letter from Pauline, which was of greater interest to him. She had now become a nun and he wrote, '*Quel bonheur pour elle, chers parents*' ('What a joy for her, dear parents'). Then he continued in Dutch:'She has had the good fortune to complete the most difficult task facing us in this world. I hope that it will now be my turn, beloved parents, to choose the way I wish to follow. Would it be impossible for me to follow your son Pamphile?' Jef had put his most important message on paper.

The holidays began on 15 August. When Jef informed his parents of his plan to spend the holidays with Pamphile in the monastery in Leuven, there was a row and he left.

He worked hard at his French in the monastery, but that was not his chief preoccupation. He wanted to experience monastic life and found that it suited him. He especially enjoyed the peace and quiet and dreamt of joining a contemplative order, like the Trappists. Father Superior Frézal advised him to complete his studies at Braine-le-Comte. He could easily start learning Latin and Greek after that. He was too clever simply to become a canon and, without knowledge of those three languages, without a certificate of secondary education, he had no chance of becoming a priest.

In October, the new school year began with a retreat, led by a Redemptorist, an Order that had been founded by St Alfonso Maria Liguori, as a preaching order. Their sermons were notorious for their severity: the aim was to rekindle religious fervour by preaching hell-fire and damnation. This the preacher did from the pulpit of St Géry's Church in Braine-le-Comte. The dark, romanesque space resounded to the anathemas. Jef got the message that, if he were not to follow his calling, he would burn in hell and whoever tried to stand in his way would burn along with him.

He was susceptible to this language, but not yet completely certain of his decision concerning his future. Time and again he prayed until late in the night and discussed the problem with Joseph Vrancken and the headmaster of the school. He was still toying with the idea of becoming a Trappist. He did not write to his parents about this, but he did do so to Pauline and Pamphile, who encouraged him. Pamphile would even be able to arrange that, if he entered, Jef would not have to start out as a laybrother but as a canon, a position between that of laybrother and the highly educated priest. He could be a teacher and prepare the mass. In exceptional circumstances, he would even be able to fulfil the function of deacon.

On 1 December, he wrote home that he would remain in Tremelo for eight days after New Year. It was an extremely loving letter, in which he thanked Cato and Frans for all their favours and the opportunities they had given him: '*Je ne saurais assez vous prouver ma reconnaissance pour tous les bienfaits dont vous m'avez comblés [sic] dès ma plus tendre enfance.*' ('I shall never be able sufficiently to demonstrate my gratitude to you for all the kindness you have heaped on me from my earliest years'). Once again he made no mention of his calling. He did do so on Christmas Day, however, for now he had made up his mind: he intended to enter the Order of the Sacred Hearts in the New Year. His parents must not try to prevent him. If they did so, he would obey them but, in that case, he would not be doing God's will and would burn in hell; they, too, would be punished with the torments of hell. The letter was hard and bitter. Here is an extract:

I do not believe that you will refuse me, since it is God who calls me to do this and him I must obey, for by refusing to allow your child to obey the will of God in the assumption of this state, you would show yourselves completely lacking in gratitude to him, who might punish you for it with the torments of hell, and I also might commit the irreparable error of losing the calling for which he has intended me from my childhood, and so be eternally damned.

On New Year's Day in Tremelo, Jef read aloud the customary letter in which he gave thanks to his parents. Two days later, on his nineteenth birthday, a year younger than Pamphile to the day, he entered the monastery. Father and son took the train to Leuven without speaking. Frans nevertheless made him aware that he did not agree with his decision, but arguing against it was pointless.

They walked together along the broad avenue to the town hall of Leuven. In front of the baroque St Michael's Church, Frans took his leave. He had one last thing to say, at once a message, a plea and an order. He would take the last train home. If Jef reconsidered, they could travel together.

Frans waited in the station. Finally, he got into the last train alone.

2

Entry into the Order of the Sacred Hearts (1859)

The First Weeks

Joseph de Veuster entered the Order on his nineteenth birthday. His daily routine was the same as it had been in the summer holidays. He was still only the guest of the Order. The master of novices, Caprais Verhaeghe, had to determine during the first four weeks whether the young man could adapt to a strict and monotonous regime. Jef wore his own clothes and was still known as M. Joseph, but a religious name was already under consideration. He was thinking of Damien, the young doctor his mother had read to him about from the book in Gothic type. Auguste had chosen the name Pamphile in recollection of another of these stories. St Damien had suffered martyrdom together with his brother Cosmas in the fourth century.

The monastic day began early, but Jef would rise promptly and was not given to dozing during the meditations in chapel. He followed morning prayers attentively, not staring around distractedly during mass, and maintained the required silence during breakfast. Classes in Holy Scripture were given in poorly heated rooms, but Jef made no complaint. He listened attentively to the letters from missionaries that were read aloud during the midday meal.

The recreation period was the only moment Pamphile had to speak to Jef. In these moments the elder De Veuster attempted to persuade his brother to become a missionary, since this was a most valuable form of service. Giving and helping were prescribed by the Benedictine rule, which was the one followed by the Sacred Hearts Order. Jef thought that he ought first to complete his novitiate. For this, he had to attend classes all afternoon and prayer at the fixed hours. The evening meal followed vespers and then the students were allowed to relax until the final office. After only two weeks, Pamphile went to Paris, to prepare to take his final vows.

Fr Caprais was satisfied concerning Jef's dedication and felt that he had grasped the ethos of the Order from the very first day. The members of the Sacred Hearts Order were required to imitate the life of Christ in a fourfold way. Christ's childhood indicated their pedagogical role. Jef did indeed wish to become a teacher. Every day the monks and novices had to participate for half an hour in the perpetual adoration of the Holy Sacrament of the Altar, in remembrance of the hidden years of Jesus's life. The members of the Order had to commemorate Christ's apostolic life and the crucifixion by fasting and penance. Jef went to excess in this: he wanted to become 'a child of the Sacred Hearts', whatever the cost.

He took the first step in this direction on 2 February 1859, when he took an important, though not irrevocable, step by making the three provisional vows by which he was admitted to a probationary period in the Order of the Sacred Hearts of Jesus and Mary. He would wear a soutane and henceforth be known as Damien Joseph de Veuster.

The symbols were appropriate, since 2 February was Candlemas, the Feast of the Purification of the Blessed Virgin. He would purify himself of his secular life. We may imagine that Damien pondered at this time on his decision to leave behind his family life and the secular world, as well as the need to come to terms with solitude and isolation in his new life. The only letter to his parents which survives, however, is a businesslike request for his brother's birth and baptismal certificates, so that he can take his final vows.

Fr Caprais, a humourless man in his forties, was positive about Damien. He was the lecturer in ascetic theology and not popular with the students, because he was a perfectionist and demanded flawless work. The new superior of the Leuven monastery, Wenceslas Vincke, did not share Caprais's opinion, however. Vincke's way of inculcating modesty and concentration in his students was to repeat over and over, in a whining voice, for an hour at a time, the three words '*Silence, recueillement, prière*' ('Silence, meditation, prayer'). The students then had to close their eyes, in order not to be visually distracted. During one of these sessions, Damien was discovered carving the three words into his desk. Vincke was so angry that he threatened expulsion from the Order.

The incident was discussed in the half-yearly student evaluation. Another problem discussed at the time was that the headquarters of the Order in Paris had ordered the position of canon, which Damien held, to be discontinued, because there were so few of them. There were three possible solutions. Damien could leave the Order or he could become a laybrother. Both of these options were simple, but neither was fair to someone intelligent who had made so much effort. The third option was more of a problem: Damien could study Latin in his spare time. This was difficult but it was also a test of his stamina. If he could carry it through, then as a reward he would receive the opportunity to prepare for the priesthood.

Study in Paris (1859–1861)

Damien chose the most difficult path. He would study Latin, but he did receive help. Fr Germain, the economist, gave him extra lessons and, from August, he also received occasional help from his brother, who was now back from Paris. By May 1860, after about a year of study, Damien was able to translate at sight from the work of the Roman historian Cornelius Nepos. This was such an achievement that the superior sent Damien to Paris to begin his preparation for the priesthood.

He left by train for Paris on 7 June 1860, along with another novice, Chrétien Willemsen. It was quite an experience for both of them; until then, Damien had never been further than Braine-le-Comte. At the Gare du Nord, a French priest conducted them to a coach which took them to the Rue du Picpus, although their final destination was actually the village of Issy, just beyond the Bois de Boulogne, where the order had its novitiate in the Rue des Noyers.

The daily routine for the novices was strict: meditation, prayer, Divine Office, study and a short period of recreation. Three virtues were stressed: humility, obedience and silence. Silence, the lecturers explained, did not mean saying nothing, but controlling the flow of words: only those words that were wise and necessary should be spoken. The students ought also to obey their superiors, without grumbling, if their demands were justified, i.e., always. A subordinate ought not challenge the orders of the superiors, nor even give them a moment's reflection. Students had to recognise their own insignificance.

Humility, the virtue that was at the heart of the course, could be exercised in twelve ways. Humility was the fear of the Lord, the suppression of one's own will, and complete subjugation of oneself to the will of the superiors. Later, his bishop, Hermann Köckemann, was to accuse Damien of lack of humility, because De Veuster did not always obey him. In Issy, however, Damien had plenty of opportunity to practise humility, since he was teased by his fellow-students, just as he had been at Braine-le-Comte. The French novices regarded him as immature, thick, just a brainless Flemish peasant. Damien responded less violently to this teasing than he had at Braine-le-Comte, although sometimes he could not contain his anger.

The French students thought Damien ridiculous. One day when a group of them were standing together in the recreation ground, criticising the superiors and teachers, Damien charged up to them, red with rage. 'Your behaviour is unworthy of children of the Sacred Hearts,' he scolded, in his Flemish accent. This outburst was greeted by a chorus of disdainful laughter. In the classroom, if Damien found a topic difficult, or the lecturers were using complicated French, you could see him becoming red and puffed up with concentration and his classmates would start to giggle. Later, when Damien had become famous, his former classmates altered the story. Philibert Tauvel and Judicael Keringard denied that Damien had been teased. Their version was that the class would smile in a friendly way and wink mildly at the jolly 'fatso'. According to them, the lecturers used to help the Fleming, who found it so much more difficult, and encouraged him with a gentle '*Mon gros*', literally 'fat one', which is a friendly form of address in French, roughly equivalent to 'old fellow'. Nothing could have been further from the truth, however.

Monastic life was both physically and psychologically tough. Praying at a prie-dieu before the altar during the day was easy enough, but it was much more demanding to be asked to get up every week in the middle of the night to pray for an hour in a deserted chapel. Damien did this without any trouble and would even volunteer to take the two o'clock shift, the most demanding of all. Often, he would remain not one but two hours, praying to the sacred sacrament. The teachers supported Damien because he possessed an '*esprit de charité*', a generous nature: he never responded to teasing with teasing. He worked hard at subjects such as church history, theology, moral theology and the rule of St Benedict, in a language of which he was not fully master. However, the master of novices at Issy, Alexandre Sorieul, did fear that Damien was one of those who try to storm heaven and risk breaking their bones in the process. His old acquaintance from Leuven, Frézal Tardieu, was delighted that Damien was going to realise his dream of becoming a priest.

Damien's case for proceeding to his final vows was discussed in chapter, along with that of two other candidates, one of whom was Chrétien Willemsen. He and Willemsen were accepted. Damien prepared himself to take his final vows in the church of Notre Dame de la Paix in the Rue du Picpus on 7 October 1861.

Final Vows (1861)

Lying under a pall, to symbolise his death to the world, Damien took the monastic vows of poverty, chastity and obedience in a clear, firm voice. He was now a full member of the Order, with the possibility of one day becoming a priest. This required many more hours of instruction and examinations in such subjects as ontology, i.e. the nature of being or existence. He also studied Thomas à Kempis's *Imitation of Christ* and this late medieval devotional work appealed greatly to him. As a missionary, he was to miss this aspect of spiritual life.

The curriculum was demanding, but from those studying for the priesthood even more was required. In addition to their studies, they had to follow the full life of prayer and meditation of the religious, and that meant getting up at 4.30 every morning to meditate and pray. This was followed by mass and then prayer during the first hours of the Divine Office. After breakfast, which was taken in silence, there were classes until 11.30. Then they said a rosary and examined their conscience until the midday meal. From 1.30 the students had another three hours of classes until vespers. The evening meal was followed by a spiritual reading and the last hour of the Divine Office. Damien would extinguish the candle in his cell at 9.30 in the evening.

On Wednesday mornings, the students were allowed to take a walk. Damien was fascinated by the city. He visited the Tuileries, saw the Louvre and the Arc de Triomphe and prayed in Notre Dame and La Sainte-Chapelle. He preferred walks in the Bois, however, for he was not a city-dweller and he thought Paris 'rather melancholy'. In the winter, he was permitted to go skating on the lakes, but he found it difficult to cope with the teeming life of the city which spilled over into the Bois. The presence of so many women in fashionable clothes, including the streetwalkers, 'tormented' him and he gradually stopped going to the Bois.

He was happy in Paris, however. He found the Latin and Greek classes fascinating. His French was also improving, as could be seen from his yearly newsletter home, dated 16 January 1861. The style was grandiloquent: he was praying daily for God's blessing on his parents. He also expressed a sense that perhaps not all members of the family would survive the year. He should not grieve, however, he declared, for life was only a preparation for the blessings of the life to come. At Easter of the same year, he learned by chance of the death of his maternal grandmother and wrote reproachfully to his parents about their failure to inform him of her death. He was equally hurt that his brother, who does seem to have been told, had failed to write to him about it.

That Easter, the monastery received a visit from Monseigneur Etienne Jaussen of Tahiti. The latter officiated at a pontifical mass and also preached about the missionary work in Tahiti. Damien already knew something about this because Willemsen corresponded with a missionary there. Until now, Damien had always envisaged himself working as a teacher in Belgium but now he began to dream of missionary work in Tahiti and hoped that Monseigneur Jaussen would select him for this work.

In September 1861 his courses in Paris were complete and he was ready to enter university. Any gaps in his knowledge could be filled in during the propaedeutic year for the theological faculty at Leuven, the *Cursus Minor*. At the beginning of September, he travelled to Leuven with Jaussen and Euthyme Rouchouze, the general of the Order, where the two senior clerics were to consecrate a chapel. Damien took the opportunity to broach the question of missionary work with the bishop but the latter insisted that he should first go to university: Tahiti needed priests. Disappointed, Damien set to work on his studies. He shared a cell with his brother, who was amazed that Damien regularly slept on the floor. He took this as a sign of excessive penance but it is possible that Damien preferred sleeping on the floor because he suffered from back pain as a result of the childhood accident.

Liberal Catholic Studies in Leuven

From October 1861 to October 1862, Damien followed the *Cursus Minor*. The subjects were Bible study, general theology, a course on the sacraments and one on contracts and canon law. These were taught by 'liberal' professors, of whom the most prominent was 'dear' – as Pamphile called him – Ferdinand Moulaert. Leuven was, in fact, known for its liberal Catholic character and had come into conflict with the conservative

Pope Pius IX in 1861 over his encyclical *Jamdudum Cernimus*, which condemned liberal doctrinal renewal. In addition to his already heavy required programme, Damien also signed up for a course with Casimir Ubaghs, a proponent of the separation of church and state. However, in the summer of 1862, Ubaghs was forced by the Vatican to take early retirement.

After a summer holiday with his brother and Chrétien Willemsen, Damien began the *Schola Major*, the 'real' university course, in October 1862. He followed courses in moral theology with D'Hollander, with whom he had also had classes in the *Schola Minor*. Leuven followed the teaching of St Thomas Aquinas in this subject. Damien and Pamphile were particularly enthusiastic about Johannes Beelen, who taught Hebrew. His commentary on Paul's Epistle to the Romans was widely praised. Beelen was also one of the leading semi-traditionalists, as the Leuven progressives were called. The only conservative professor was Henri Feye, who taught canon law and who specialised in marriage law. He was firmly against mixed marriages of Catholic and non-Catholic.

All the lecturers valued Damien's pertinent questions and saw him as a future teacher. For the first time in his life, Damien was not perceived as a dunce. Nevertheless, he still regarded himself as incompetent. His superiors noted this and they increasingly admired his self-denial. On occasion at meals, those at the head of the table would take too much meat, so that there was not enough for everyone. Damien, who sat in the middle of the table, would just take vegetables, a penance for him.

Two months later, Pamphile completed his studies and was ordained priest. He celebrated his first mass in the monastery chapel on 1 March. The whole family, with friends and members of the village community, was present and afterwards the superior gave a small reception for family members. Pamphile and Damien were also allowed to make a visit home and their mother was allowed to ask for permission for Pamphile to celebrate mass in the church at Tremelo, which he did.

Plans for Pamphile to Go to Hawaii (1863)

It was intended that Pamphile should go to the Sandwich Islands with Chrétien Willemsen, who had made his final vows with Damien and who was already a priest. They were to be accompanied by two unordained brothers, Clément Evrard and Liévin van Heteren. Willemsen was to travel on to Tahiti. They knew next to nothing about the islands. The only document they had was the brochure by Fr Tardieu, which had spurred Pamphile, six years previously, to join the Order. Now he read the work again, but the picture it painted of the islands did not necessarily correspond with reality.

The volcanic islands had been discovered less than a century before by Captain Cook. Tardieu alleged that they were inhabited by cannibals. The Catholic Church had begun its mission there in 1818, when the chaplain of the French warship *Uranie* had baptised two chiefs. Tardieu showed that the Catholics had begun their missionary work two years before the successful Protestant mission had started. The Protestants had forced their puritanism on the innocent population, whilst poor whites had introduced prostitution and drunkenness. The Catholics were persecuted until the British consul gained permission for an Irish member of the Order of the Sacred Hearts to establish himself on the islands. Even so, Frs Bachelot and Maigret had been expelled in 1837 and Bachelot had died at sea.

In 1839 a French gunboat was able to enforce freedom of religion. Etienne Rouchouze, brother of the general of the Order of the Sacred Hearts, was appointed bishop. He visited his mission area and decided to return to France to make the case for a large-scale missionary programme. He succeeded in his aim, but on the return journey, the ship carrying the members of the Order sank. When all hope of survivors was lost, Maigret was consecrated Bishop of the Sandwich Islands.

The Catholics were no longer persecuted: King Kamehameha III had even granted land for a boys' school and the reigning king, Kamehameha IV, and his wife Queen Emma had attended a Te Deum sung for the arrival of the first group of Sacred Hearts nuns, who were to establish a girls' school in Honolulu.

Damien would really have liked to go too. After all, Evrard and Van Heteren were not ordained priests, either, although they were more advanced in their studies than he. Damien was gripped by religious fervour and missionary zeal, as his letters home and his regular private prayer to St Francis Xavier, the patron saint of missionaries, reveal.

Pamphile's final summer in Belgium was eventful. There were further tensions between liberal and ultramontane Catholics, in which Leuven took a lively interest.

On 19 September 1863, Damien received minor orders in the archiepiscopal palace in Mechelen, in preparation for the priesthood. He was made acolyte and tonsured. A few weeks later, he began the second year of the *Schola Major*, the third year of the university. Because Pamphile was to leave at the end of October, the two brothers spent as much time together as they could. A few days before he was due to leave, however, Pamphile became ill. He was feverish and had diarrhoea and sickness. Because these could be the symptoms of typhus, although there was no epidemic, the doctor declared him unfit to travel.

3

Sudden Departure for Hawaii
(1863–1864)

Leavetaking

Damien's thoughts were racing. If Pamphile could not travel, then there was a spare berth. It was true he still had two or three years of university to do, but he was a full member of the Order. The Sandwich Islands needed missionaries and he could take Pamphile's place.

He set out this line of reasoning to his superior, Wenceslas Vincke, who rejected it out of hand. Damien was not ready, he was still 'wet behind the ears'. In any case, he was to become a teacher, there was no question of trading places.

Damien was disappointed, but he did not give up. The rules of the Order required him to obey his superior, but his superior-general was higher in rank than his superior in Leuven and he was not forbidden to put his proposal before the superior-general Rouchouze.

It was a difficult letter. Damien had to convince the general that his own departure would be in the best interests of the Order. He found one argument. The cost of the voyage from Bremerhaven to Honolulu was FF1,000, an enormous sum. Could the Order accept such a loss, simply because Pamphile could not go? Already the Order had had to close schools in Belgium because of a shortage of money. The anti-clerical French government was seeking to stem the flow of money to religious houses. Moreover, the Order was involved in three legal cases, all of which hinged on money. The Hawaiian mission needed personnel and the loss of FF1,000 was simply unacceptable. The solution to the problem was simple, in Damien's view: he should be allowed to take Pamphile's place.

General Euthyme Rouchouze recalled the chubby Fleming from the journey he had taken in his company to Leuven two years earlier. In weighing up the situation, he felt that De Veuster had shown initiative and a sound sense of finances. On the other hand, Clément Evrard and Liévin van Heteren were not high-fliers and Damien himself still had everything to prove. Pamphile's withdrawal would mean that he would be sending three 'inferior quality' candidates to Honolulu, but it was better to send someone inferior than no one at all. The general wrote two letters. In that to Honolulu, which he sent by fast clipper, he informed Bishop Maigret that his expectations should not be too high. He was not sending high quality personnel; nevertheless there were five of them, including three future priests. In his second letter, he ordered Vincke to send Damien to Honolulu.

As the day of departure approached, Pamphile still lay sick in bed. Damien was sitting in the refectory, when the door flew open. The superior charged up to him, threw a letter on the table and yelled at Damien that he was mad. What idiot would leave before he was ordained? Damien said nothing, but grabbed the letter and ran to the cell he shared with Pamphile. 'I'm going in your place!' he shouted joyfully to his brother.

He had two days before his departure for Paris. He went to take his leave of his family, clear in his mind that he was leaving home for good. The parting was difficult. No one knew quite what to say and so they filled in the time with mundane activities, eating and paying visits, until the final moment of leave-taking came and Damien returned to Leuven the following day.

He found the parting from Pamphile painful, but he was convinced that the latter would soon follow him out – after all, his trunk was already packed. Pamphile asked Damien to bring him his copy of Alfonso de Liguori's *Theologia moralis*. He wrote in French 'We have always been together, now we are to part. How often shall I not see you before me in my thoughts? You will spend your life in Oceania, I, I know not where. We are joyful travellers on the earth. Self-sacrifice must be our supreme concern. After death, we shall meet again in heaven. Pamphile 22 October 1863.' Pamphile declared that the book would help Damien in the confessional, for the 'savages' would confess the most terrible sins and it was important to determine the correct penance.

Damien hastily gathered together his scanty possessions and went to the superior to deal with the final formalities. Vincke was still angry and made short work of the ceremonies. In their haste, both he and Damien forgot to draw up the required will, in which Damien left his future inheritances to the Order.

In Paris, there began five hectic days. Damien needed new soutanes and shoes and he had to have his photograph taken, a typically stiff and solemn nineteenth-century affair.

During a three-day retreat, Damien got to know Eutrope Blanc and Aymard Pradeyrols, two French brothers who would be travelling with him. They prayed for a safe voyage and a fruitful mission in Hawaii and Tahiti. The general warned them of the inevitable depression that would succeed their initial euphoria and of the sexual seduction to which they would certainly be exposed. Initially, their quest for souls would seem to be successful, but that would not last. The converts would quickly revert to their old customs. Such failures were always hard to accept and they would begin to have doubts about their calling. At the moment of deepest depression, however, salvation was at hand. They must always remember that the operation of grace took a long time. The rule required that they work in pairs: solitude was not good. Moreover, there was still a great threat from Protestantism on the Sandwich Islands and they would have to take up the struggle immediately.

The party left Paris at 9 a.m. on Thursday 28 October. They travelled via Namur and Cologne, where they stopped for several hours and visited the cathedral and looked at the Rhine. At midday on the following day, they arrived in Bremerhaven.

Departure

The party was to sail on the *R. W. Wood*, an Hawaiian three-master. The ship's master was friendly but spoke little French. They quickly learned, however, that they would have to learn English, since that was the medium of communication in Hawaii. The native language was *Kanaka*, a Polynesian language, extremely rich in vowels. As well as the five religious men, a party of nuns was also travelling as missionaries on the same ship. Both groups were to live according to their vows during the voyage, although, in fact, it was impossible to adhere to this strictly and the religious men and nuns did spend time together. They were under orders from the master to abstain from any attempts at proselytising among the crew, who were Protestant, if they were anything.

The departure was set for the following day and Damien wrote a farewell letter to his parents. He began with information about the journey. Then he continued,

> Dearest parents, We are on the point of leaving not only our fathers and mothers, brothers and sisters, not only our second family, our fellow religious brothers in Leuven and Paris, but also the beautiful continent of Europe, in order to take up our abode on a sometimes unquiet sea, ready to swallow us up, and all this to go and live among uncivilised people, who can be compared in many ways to brute beasts. This is a great sacrifice for a heart that fondly loves its parents, family, fellow religious brothers and fatherland.

Damien wanted to make this sacrifice: it was Christ's will and he was not afraid, for the Lord protected missionaries. He felt God's protection, for the missionaries were not frightened. 'We are in unbelievably good spirits. After half an hour together, we are exhausted from laughing and making jokes.' He asked his family to pray for him, so that he would have the courage to carry out God's will. Suddenly, parting was difficult and he wrote,

Farewell, dear parents, from now on we shall no longer have the joy of embracing one another, but we shall remain united in the tender feelings that we cherish for one another. Let us, above all, think of one another in our prayers and may we always be united with the Sacred Hearts of Jesus and Mary, in which I always remain as your loving son, J. de Veuster.

The sailing was delayed when the wind changed and Damien was able to add a few lines to his letter, arranging for family members to have his photograph and once again urging his parents to pray for him and to live God-fearing lives.

Suddenly, on Monday 1 November, there was a favourable wind and the master gave the order to sail. Unfortunately, the wind quickly turned again and the ship was not able to gain the open sea until 8 November.

The first stage of the voyage was difficult, with storms and then periods when the vessel was becalmed, until the ship reached the Tropic of Cancer. Almost all of the passengers, including Damien, suffered from seasickness. There were also tensions between the passengers and crew, when Damien tried to convert crew members, despite the master's express prohibition. Chrétien Willemsen, who was in charge of the party, also had differences with the master on the subject of Italian Unification.

Learning about the Kingdom of Hawaii

The master was a useful source of information about Hawaii, however, and conversations on this topic were a means of avoiding thorny issues. As the voyage became easier, the master spent more time with the passengers and told them about the country to which they were sailing.

Kanaka was the native name both for the Hawaiian people and for their language, and meant 'human'. Several people in the South Pacific called themselves this. When Captain Cook had discovered the archipelago in 1778, the population was divided into 'subject people' and *alii*, aristocrats. For example, if a *Kanaka* cast a shadow on a part of a royal body, he would be condemned to death. The *Kanaka* had to keep to codes of deep obeisances and total submission. These codes rested on taboos, *kapu*. So, for example, women were not permitted to eat bananas, nor to eat in the huts reserved for the men. The guardians of these often futile rules, which also might carry the death penalty, were *kahunas*, priests. They did not only have to punish those who broke the codes: there were also, on each island, several sanctuaries, temples where those who had broken a taboo could seek refuge. These sanctuaries were also run by *kahunas*. On the other hand there were also the *heiaus*, the temples of sacrifice, where until 1819 – and, it was rumoured, even now, in 1863 – human sacrifice was performed.

Cook had named the islands after John Montagu, Earl of Sandwich, then First Lord of the Admiralty. The French and Americans called the islands Hawaii, after the largest island in the archipelago. Damien misheard this as 'Awaia'. The native leader came from this island and was called Kamehameha. Cook had been murdered on the island of Hawaii by disillusioned *Kanaka* in 1779. Shortly thereafter Kamehameha, a young *alii* and son of a persecuted local potentate, began an uprising.

From 1796, Kamehameha conducted a war of conquest with the help of British sailors who had married high-born *alii* women. Many members of the royal family would descend from James Young, a British deserter. First, Kamehameha conquered his own island, using firearms. A decisive battle took place around the active volcano Mauna Loa, which Kamehameha won, despite inferior forces. The other islands followed and Kamehameha was supported by all the major powers, since the islands were strategically important. Great Britain, France, the United States and Russia all had their eyes on the Pearl Lochs near Honolulu, because this system of fjords was an ideal place to winter their fleet.

The question of who had converted the Hawaiians was a thorny one. It certainly was not Cook, for the Hawaiians were convinced that he was the incarnation of the white god Lono, who was supposed to return to the islands in a strange-looking vessel. When the *Discovery* and the *Resolution* sailed into a bay on the Big Island, as Hawaii was called, *Kanaka* women had swum out to the ship. Almost naked, they offered themselves, without scruple, to the white gods. Sadly, this act of devotion brought down the scourge of gonorrhoea and syphilis upon the island peoples.

Cook sailed north the following summer, in the hope of finding an ice-free passage from the Pacific to the Atlantic. He failed and when he returned in the autumn, he was killed in a skirmish by the islanders, who no longer regarded him as a god but as a conqueror, who had brought sickness in his train. There was now a danger of the Hawaiian population dying out.

From 1810, Kamehameha the Great ruled over the whole archipelago. The islands were vulnerable to external exploitation, however. Cook's expedition was followed by others, Captain Vancouver being his immediate successor. He sought to ingratiate himself with Kamehameha and gave him cattle. The islanders did not know what to do with them and the beasts were allowed to run wild on the green uplands of the Kohala Mountains, until they became a danger to the population.

Kamehameha commissioned a British deserter, John Parker, who had married a high-born Hawaiian, to round up the wild cattle and keep them. Parker requested to be given the land on which the beasts were running wild as pasture, and was granted this enormous area as an estate.

In towns like Honolulu on Oahu, Lahaina on Maui and Kailua or Hilo on Hawaii, poor white settlers established a trade for the ships that called in. They taught the Hawaiians to drink and smoke and introduced the concept of prostitution into the relaxed sexual world of the Polynesians.

The trade in sandalwood was a real industry. This perfumed wood was particularly sought after in China. In no time at all, the great forests on the island of Molokai were chopped down, but no new trees were planted and the trade came to a standstill.

Whales wintered in the waters round the islands and so, too, did the unsavoury whalers. This meant that they could continue whaling during the months when it was too cold to do so elsewhere. Whales brought wealth: the meat was dried, and the skeleton sold as whalebone for corsets. The most important part of the mammals, however, was the blubber which produced oil for lamps. The whalers strengthened the islanders' impression that modern western society survived on alcohol and paid sex.

The Directors of the Congregational Missionary Movement decided to send their group of missionaries to Hawaii in 1820. Kamehameha II had succeeded his father in the previous year, but the real ruler was Kaahumanu, the favourite wife of Kamehameha the Great. She recognised the importance of literacy and wanted the *alii* to master this art as soon as possible. The missionaries did more than just teach the children of the chiefs in their school in Honolulu, and later on other islands. They brought Puritan values with them. Sunday working was not allowed, alcohol and tobacco were forbidden and prostitution was a deadly sin. They crossed swords not only with the whalers but with the Hawaiians. However, they also brought doctors with them, who knew how to treat some of the new diseases, such as chicken pox and measles.

In the mid 1840s, the whaling industry began to decline. So many whales had been slaughtered that it was necessary to hunt further and further from the islands. The most enterprising whalers withdrew, because their market was also collapsing. In the 1850s, a method of preparing paraffin oil and petroleum jelly had been discovered. These two petroleum derivatives gave a more constant flame and smelt less than whale oil.

Fortunately, at that same moment, the sugar cane industry began to flourish. In 1845, King Kamehameha gave permission for the establishment of an industrial sugar plantation in Koloa on Kauai Island. The business went badly because the owner did not slip the local chief enough money to encourage the Hawaiian workers. R. W. Wood, the owner of the ship on which the missionaries were sailing, was at that time working as a ship's doctor in Honolulu. He invested increasing amounts in the moribund business, until he became the majority shareholder and took the business over. He cut out the local chief and paid the workers better, so that the business became more profitable, so profitable, in fact, that Wood established a second plantation on Maui Island, which he developed along the most modern lines. One of Wood's foremen developed a centrifuge for separating the sugar from the molasses. The ship had been bought from the profits of this venture and was carrying back tools and machinery for the further mechanisation of the business.

The outbreak of the American Civil War in 1861 brought increased demand for sugar from the Union States of America. The local workers could not satisfy the demand for plantation labour and so the white politicians who advised the king decided to bring labour from Portugal and Madeira, as well as China and later Japan.

In 1863 the king was Kamehameha IV. His consort was Queen Emma and they had a son, Albert, named after the late Prince Consort, who had stood godfather to him. If the missionaries on board the *R. W. Wood* thought they were sailing to a land of cannibals, they were mistaken. The king was assisted by a government. There was an Upper House, a body in which the *alii* sat, and a Lower House, with elected representatives, mostly whites. Hawaii had an army, a police force and a law court. The postal system was efficient. Each island was governed by a governor and a white sheriff headed the police force. When they arrived, they would find their belongings checked by customs and import duty would be charged. Hawaii had most of the trappings of civilisation, including a substantial debt.

Arrival in the Hawaiian Islands

The ship crossed the line on 21 December. The master was pleased. He had the doldrums safely to starboard and the winds were steady. As they sailed further south, towards the Horn, they had to endure storms. On 20 January, they saw Patagonia on the horizon. The master chose not to pass through the Straits of Magellan, but skirted the coast of Tierra del Fuego and passed through the Straits of Lemaire. Again the ship was battered by storms and was driven off course, southwards. Only on 2 February did it enter the Pacific.

The master reckoned that they would reach port on

19 March and on 17 March they had their first sight of land. 'Awaia', Damien noted in his diary. The next day they sailed past the islands of Maui, Molokai and Oahu, and that evening, too late to dock, they anchored off the reef before the harbour of Honolulu. The following day, Saturday 19 March, the day before Palm Sunday, the party disembarked, after a voyage of four and a half months.

4

Consecration as Priest in Honolulu (1864)

The First Days in Hawaii (19–28 March 1864)

After they had landed and passed customs, they were greeted by Modeste Favens, the provincial superior. Bishop Maigret was not there to welcome them, since they had arrived some two weeks earlier than expected and he was taking a rest on the other side of the island. Local people, however, waved and smiled in greeting and they were presented with fresh fish, fruit and vegetables, and garlanded with flowers as they passed through the streets.

The party made its way to the newly built cathedral, its low-built towers a sign of the frequent earthquakes to which the islands were subject. A Te Deum was sung and then the new arrivals parted, each group going to its respective institution.

As the party of brothers sat eating a meal of fresh fruit and vegetables in the refectory, the door opened and a spare man of sixty entered. They recognised his bishop's cross immediately and stood to receive his greeting. The bishop had set off for Honolulu as soon as he had heard of their arrival.

Maigret's greeting was friendly but in fact he was disappointed by the newcomers. There were currently only eighteen priests on the islands and many of them were old hands who were worn out. Of the newcomers, only Chrétien Willemsen was an ordained priest, and he was to travel on to Tahiti. The remainder of the party was of poor quality, inadequately educated and unordained. Only Damien, Clément Evrard and Liévin van Heteren could be considered for ordination and

Maigret determined that they should receive the sacrament as soon as possible.

He was astonished at Damien's enthusiasm. The young man wanted to start work that very day. The bishop explained that the work programme would begin on Monday, but in the meantime, Favens could show him round the town. They first visited the prosperous area around the law courts, where the cathedral was also situated. This was the area where the whites and the *alii* lived. He saw them riding in stately coaches drawn by thoroughbreds. For Damien, though, it was when they reached the poorer quarters that he felt he was seeing the real Honolulu, moving round from hut to hut. He was struck by the neatness of the thatched dwellings. There were mats on the ground and the cooking utensils were outside. He noted to his parents,

> A third of the archipelago is already Catholic, among whom there are many extremely God-fearing people, they are not concerned about what other people think of them – almost all of them wear their rosary round their neck. They do not set their hearts on silver and gold, indeed they give little thought for the morrow. It is enough for them that they have taro to eat that is not too dear. They do not spend a lot on clothes. The men generally have nothing more than trousers and a kind of shirt. The women wear a long garment that hangs straight, without any hemp in it.

Damien wanted to learn the language as quickly as possible and used a time-honoured method. He made word lists. Favens explained that Hawaiian had very few consonants and that his name would certainly end up as Kamiano.

Damien was happy. On Palm Sunday, he enjoyed the enthusiastic waving of palm branches and he estimated that about three hundred people received communion during the high mass. After every service, he had to go with the others to the west door, to shake hands, thousands of them. He noticed how keenly the congregation reacted to the bishop's sermon. For an instant, they were all elated, but for the most part, they sat with downcast eyes and looked sincerely penitent. Damien looked at their shabby clothes. They wore no jewellery, but had flowers in their hats. He concluded that the *Kanaka* were not seekers after worldly goods, but good people, not savages.

In the College at Aluimanu (Spring 1864)

At last, Monday came and he was to be given his programme. To his pleasure, things were moving quickly. On Easter Monday, he, Evrard and Van Heteren would travel to the other side of the island, where the Order had a college, the gift of a previous king. There, he would receive an intensive course in Hawaiian, as well as preparing for the priesthood, under the watchful eye of the bishop's Irish assistant, Arsene Walsh. Damien was to be ordained in May. He spent Holy Week in Honolulu and, on Holy Saturday, he and Van Heteren were ordained subdeacon.

On Easter Monday, the three young men, accompanied by Walsh, left Honolulu around daybreak, for the journey on horseback over the volcanic range could take a day. Neither Evrard nor Van Heteren was an experienced horseman and Walsh was old, and tired quickly. The ascent was indeed long and difficult and Damien found his fellow-travellers a burden. The descent was easier, despite the showers, and they reached the estates that surrounded the college by evening.

Damien tried to use his period at the college to best advantage. Walsh appointed the thirteen-year-old Albert Kuniakea, a natural son of King Kamehameha III, as Damien's tutor in Hawaiian. Because the king's marriage had been childless and the present king was also a childless bachelor, the boisterous lad was a candidate for the throne. Walsh taught the three newcomers the sacramental rituals and theology.

The college was a world in itself and self-sufficient in provisions. With its pastures, arable land and fishponds, it was splendid. Damien especially enjoyed the trips out. Unfortunately, these were curtailed shortly after his arrival because a group of students had climbed a cliff one day and the same evening that very spot had suffered a rock fall. If any of the children had been killed, the school might have had to close and so caution had to be employed.

Leprosy: The First Encounter

Damien had heard a good deal about Hawaii, but he had not been forewarned about the presence of leprosy on the islands. The disease was rampant among the population, so much so that Kamehameha V brought the subject before parliament a few weeks after Damien's arrival. Steps had to be taken to tackle the disease.

The situation in Hawaii at the time of Damien's arrival was a typical mid-nineteenth-century one of informal empire, with the added, but again not untypical, complication that a number of powers were jostling for influence. In this case, they were the old colonial rivals, Britain and France, and the emerging economic power on the doorstep, the United States.

British influence had clearly been dominant in the early stages and the islands had a constitutional monarchy, with a two-chamber parliament on the British model. In 1841, the British annexed the islands outright, but they were unable to make good their claims here, for the territory was too close to the US sphere of influence, and the latter joined with France in some gunboat diplomacy to restore the islands' 'independence'. Kamehameha sought to take advantage of his restoration to strengthen his position. He set up an executive of five departments: interior, foreign affairs, treasury, education and justice. He also introduced universal male suffrage.

Socio-economic policy in Hawaii continued to be dominated by the informal colonial powers, however. In 1834, the king had recognised the inalienable rights of people and of property. This step paved the way for the introduction of private property, a concept hitherto unknown to the *Kanaka*. *Papa*, mother earth, belonged to everyone. The king could not resist pressure from white settlers, however, including those who had profited in the California gold rush. They demanded the right to buy plantations and other property, and Kamehameha was forced to undertake the Great *Mahele*, the great reform. The majority of the *Kanaka* were dispossessed. A certain amount of land was set aside for the people, and the rest was given over as private estates to the *alii*.

In 1853, it was the turn of the United States to attempt to annex the islands. This time, the British and French joined forces to forestall US ambitions, but it was in fact a smallpox epidemic that caused the American warships to turn tail and leave the harbour.

The following year, Kamehameha III died and was succeeded by his nephew, Alexander Liholiho, as Kamehameha IV. The latter had been sent on a study trip to Washington, London and Paris in his formative years, and he sought to save the kingdom by a commercial treaty with the United States, but Congress refused to ratify it.

Kamehameha's only son, Albert, had died of a lung infection during the time that the *R. W. Wood* had been away, and the king himself had died shortly thereafter, aged only twenty-nine. His brother, Lot, now Kamehameha V, seemed to be strong-minded. On 3 March 1864 he had abolished universal suffrage. Only those who could read and write and had some property were now allowed to vote.

Disease was the great problem for the islands, as Damien quickly realised. Walsh told him that when the Europeans had arrived in 1778, the Polynesian population was estimated to have been around 300,000. In 1853, there were only some 70,000 remaining, the rest having been wiped out by various diseases. Dr Hillebrand, a German who headed the Queen's Hospital in Honolulu, had warned of the leprosy epidemic and it was for this reason that King Kamehameha V had brought the matter before parliament.

Ordination as Priest

For the time being, this was not Damien's concern. He was preparing himself for his ordination, which was to take place on 21 May 1864 in Honolulu Cathedral. That day he lay, robed in an alb, with Evrard and Van Heteren, on the marble floor before the altar. After the gospel and the sermon, they approached the bishop's throne, one by one, and Bishop Maigret questioned them for the final time about their reasons for entering the priesthood. Damien was more than firm in his replies. He knelt before the bishop, who laid his hands upon Damien's head. All the other priests who were present did likewise, in token of his acceptance into their fellowship. Damien then received the stole and chasuble and was invited to concelebrate the mass with other priests, following his ordination.

The following day, he celebrated his own first mass and could not help wistfully contrasting his situation with that of his brother, who had done so with family, friends and half the village present. He had no trouble with the Latin part of the service, but preaching in Hawaiian was a great trial, although the congregation was sympathetic. He wrote to Pamphile, 'If my heart were not so hard, I think it would have melted to wax, so strong was the impression I had when, for the first time, I offered the bread of life to hundreds of people who once knelt before the old gods and who now devoutly approached the Holy Table dressed in white.'

In June, Damien was to go to the Big Island, Hawaii, where he had been assigned to the Puna district, near the volcano. In the meantime, he was to continue learning the language and to fulfil his priestly duties under the watchful eye of the three priests and five brothers who lived in Honolulu. Fr Hermann Köckemann had administrative responsibility for the Order in Hawaii, which suited his character. He kept the records up to date, wrote reports and maintained contact with the generalate. He had never had a posting, but had always worked in the progressive town of Honolulu. There was a certain degree of tension between the progressive superiors and the conservative Köckemann. He was musically gifted and Damien noted to Pamphile, 'It's amazing how he gets the *Kanaka* to sing.' Damien had called the bishop and the provincial superior 'simple', but that was not a word he used of Köckemann. During the recreation periods, his two superiors were constantly surrounded by *Kanaka*. 'They are like fathers with their children,' Damien wrote. Maigret was an unusual man, a pragmatist with an open outlook. As bishop, he was responsible for ecclesiastical matters. The 53-year-old provincial superior, Modeste Favens, was responsible for matters to do with the Order. Favens had studied in the monastery in Leuven, under the liberal Catholic Victor Jaussens, and had been ordained there. He had gone to Hawaii in 1845 with Charles Pouzot, who worked in Hilo, close to Damien's district.

Damien and Evrard had both been assigned a district on the Big Island. Because Maigret had more confidence in the better-educated Evrard, he had been given responsibility for the immense district of Kohala-Hamakua, which covered the whole of the north of the island. The mission had booked three places for 7 June on the *Kilauea*, a wooden steamboat that provided the transport service among the islands. The newcomers were to be accompanied to their posts by the bishop.

Their first port of call en route was Kaunakakai, a small harbour on the island of Molokai. Rudolph Meyer, a German married to an *alii* chieftainess, was supervisor of public works there. He was later to play a special part in Damien's life.

The next day, they put in at Lahaina, a port on the island of Maui, where the three priests who worked on the island were waiting for them. They said a mass together and then the travellers set sail again. Damien regretted that he could not stay longer with his experienced colleagues and offered up a brief prayer that something might happen to detain him. In fact, they were quickly driven back to Lahaina by a fire in the boat's engine-room.

The three men were now stuck on Maui Island, because repairs to the *Kilauea* might take a month and there was only one boat plying between the islands. Damien did not mind, because it gave him time to stay with Fr Aubert Bouillon, Fr Grégoire Archambaux and Fr Léonor Fouesnel. They told him yet more about Hawaiian life and culture.

On Sunday 17 June Damien paid a visit to several outlying plantations. On the way he was shocked to see people at work. It might be true that irrigation work had to go on day and night, in order to waste as little water as possible, but the Sabbath was holy.

It was almost evening when he returned to Lahaina, where he found Bouillon in a state of high agitation. Maigret had been delighted when a barque put in to pick up the stranded priests, but there was a problem: Damien was off somewhere in the plantations and no one knew where. Maigret won time by having the sailing put off until he had sung high mass, which he was anxious to do, since a recently converted Tahitian princess was to be in the congregation. This much the captain was willing to do, but he would wait no longer. Maigret realised that he could win no more time when an American took up Damien's place on the vessel.

In Lahaina, there were no more trips to the plantations, for Damien wished to rejoin his bishop as soon as possible. He spent his time hanging around the harbour, in the hope of catching a boat, and every day he dropped in at the little office where you could buy tickets for the *Kilauea*. For a good week, there was no news and then an advertisement appeared in the *Pacific Commercial Advertiser*, announcing that the *Kilauea* would put in to Lahaina on the evening of 30 June, on its way to Kailua on Hawaii. Damien had his booking confirmed straight away.

Trek through Hawaii, the Big Island

Damien had expected to be greeted with some derisive laughter when he arrived at St Michael's Church in Kailua, but the sarcasm of the embittered and tubercular Fr Régis Moncany was too much for him. Moncany was a French chauvinist, who did not like Flemings, Leuven or liberal Catholicism, and certainly did not like the plaintive Evrard, who had by now been staying with him for over a week.

Damien was ready to set off immediately for Hilo, where he hoped to find the bishop, but Moncany rejected the suggestion. Damien was a fool if he thought he could travel directly across the central area of the island. This area was made up of active volcanoes. Of course, he could try to cross the unending desert of lava, if he so chose . . . Evrard supported Moncany. The *pahoehoe*, the hardened lava, had made a fearful impression on him. Damien could try to travel via the south of the island, but, once again, he would have to cross volcanic terrain. If he had any sense, which Moncany doubted after his exploits in Lahaina, then he would simply wait for Fr Stanislas Lebret, who was willing to act as guide. Damien had no choice.

Evrard's whining was stultifying. Nothing was any good, nothing pleased him. The women were whores. The people were filthy in thought, morals and body as well. The country was ugly and possessed by the devil. Bishop Maigret behaved like a savage: he had even proposed that Evrard should take his turn in puffing the pipe that was passed round among the Hawaiians. Maybe it was a token of friendship, but Evrard did not smoke and thought it a filthy habit. He went on about it for ten days. When finally the day of departure arrived, Moncany breathed a sigh of relief.

The three men rode out of the town along a narrow road through the fields of lava. It was a boiling hot day, at the end of which they arrived at a trading post owned by an Irishman in Kiholo, a beautiful lagoon. Lebret and Damien were worried about Evrard, who was a useless horseman, without any stamina. Lebret shared Damien's opinion that he and Evrard should exchange districts, but the decision rested with the bishop. He wanted to give Evrard another chance. Perhaps when he saw his flock, his sense of calling would revive.

The next day it was the same story. They rode and walked across sixty-year-old lava, through which prisoners had hewn out a pathway. On their right, the dormant volcano, Mauna Kea, towered above them, and in the distance, the shadowy outline of the Kohala Mountains grew ever more distinct. The massive contours of the Hale Akala on Maui Island loomed up across the sea.

But Evrard had no eye for the beauty of his surroundings. He was afraid of falling, and his legs, back and backside were hurting from the long journey. His throat was as dry as dust and drinking did not seem to help. He was sweating profusely and understood now why Lebret had stuffed his soutane into his saddle-bag. He refused to give way, however: he insisted on maintaining his dignity as a white man and priest. When they saw a dark structure on a hill, Lebret said the terrace of lava rock was Puukohala *heiau*. Less than a century before, human sacrifices were performed in this temple, which had been erected by Kamehameha the Great.

Once again they slept with an Irish family, this time in the shadow of the heathen temple and the Protestant church, in the cattle-port of Kawaihae-Uka. The parishioners were overjoyed to meet their priest, for they had been without one for four years, but Evrard continued to look miserable and frightened.

The next stage was Waimea, on the grassy uplands that linked the Mauna Kea with the Kohala Mountains. The ascent was difficult. Thorn bushes ripped their trousers and drew blood. It was boiling hot. Damien could not take his eyes off the splendid scenery: high mountains all around and blue sea. At this altitude, it was as if a magic line had been drawn between the desert and the humid area of Waimea where cattle grazed on the green pasture. Lebret's work as guide was finished and he left. Damien remained with Evrard for a few days, although he needed to get on, because the bishop was ready to leave. Nevertheless, he wanted to give Evrard riding lessons and to put some heart into him.

On 20 July a Mexican, who worked as a cowboy on the vast cattle ranch belonging to John Parker, was leaving for Hilo and he was willing to act as Damien's guide. The two men galloped wildly across the plateau until a thick forest slowed their journey.

The journey lasted three and a half days, because they were mostly obliged to go on foot. Damien discovered the Hawaii of wide fjords, bays like amphitheatres and primeval forests, which stood like walls barring their route. The Mexican warned him that paths were often swept away by earthquakes and flash floods. It was too dangerous to travel at night. When they finally reached the coastal area around Hilo, the Mexican showed Damien clumps of sugar cane, the stems of which could cut through a horse's or a man's legs. He had to take great care.

Damien followed the Mexican to St Joseph's Church. Bishop Maigret was still in Hilo, but would be leaving on 25 July. It was absolutely necessary for him to be in Honolulu because the king had promised to attend the Te Deum in honour of Napoleon III. They spent a pleasant couple of days, although Damien did have to put up with the obligatory jokes and digs. This was normal with Maigret. The Norman, Fr Nicaise Ruault, in particular, was the butt of endless jokes about thick Normans.

There were serious moments as well. During the final briefing, Maigret told Damien that he must not underestimate the difficulties. Hilo might have a lovely church, but its pews were empty. The charismatic pastor, Rev. Titus Coan, had begun a successful recruitment drive. Charles Pouzot, the priest in Hilo, was not tackling the situation well, and had set a group of bully boys loose on a Protestant procession, which had been counter-productive. Pouzot himself blamed the loss of the faithful on the plantations. The owners were Protestant and the workers chose their bosses' faith on pecuniary grounds.

The bishop agreed that the Protestants were a problem, but nature was not a help either. A few years previously a destructive flash flood had swept many people in Hilo away, and a few years before that a lava flow had stopped only on the outskirts of the town. These natural disasters were bad enough in themselves, but the problem was exacerbated by the fact that they strengthened the Hawaiians' belief in the volcano goddess Pele.

And that was not all. Puna, Damien's district, had not had a priest for years. The other missionaries had paid brief visits, but that was not sufficient. Most of the converts had returned to their old beliefs or become Protestant. The children could only go to Protestant schools, because there were no others. Damien would begin with only 350 Catholics, but the flame was not quenched. Maigret was certain that the Hawaiians would return to the true faith. It was important to build a church, however, because that would be a clear sign of their presence, although churches did not last long in this region. An earthquake could easily bring them down and the humid climate attacked the woodwork.

Damien could begin with one church. The faithful from the hamlet of Hale Puaa, not far from Hilo, had collected 100 piastres and Maigret had doubled that sum, so that they could employ a carpenter. Nevertheless, Damien must regard his district as virgin territory, even if an eternal flame was still burning. If this was to be fanned, then he must accept all the hospitality he was offered. 'Sleep in their hut,' said the bishop, 'eat with them, enjoy the native food and don't be finicky. Listen to tales and to their complaints and show your appreciation. Joy is primordial: share it, join in. The people of Puna are hardworking peasants. Remember that the devil is always lurking. Temptation will always surround you. Always.'

Damien was sorry when the bishop had left but at the same time he was looking forward to his first tour of his parish on 28 July. Nicaise Ruault, an energetic, affable man in his thirties, who got on well with the Hawaiians, was his guide.

The tropical forest on the slopes of the Mauna Loa, called Lua Pele, Pele's abyss, by the islanders, exerted a sombre sense of threat. In the forest of ferns, Nicaise said farewell. Damien was now on his own. His description of his mission to Pamphile reflected only a fraction of the reality.

I am on the island of Hawaii, which is at least the size of Belgium. In the centre, there are three volcanoes, two of which seem to be spent. One is still active. Providence has seen fit to place me in the vicinity of that one. Wherever I go, from one side of the district to the other, I am walking on lava. (Letter of 23 August 1864)

5

Working on an Active Volcano
(1864–1865)

Getting to Know the Puna Volcano District

The first parish that Damien visited alone was Kapoho. The church there was infested with vermin and the priest's hut was in ruins but Damien was glad to be among his parishioners, whom he numbered at about three hundred.

During the introductions, he attempted to unravel the tangle of family connections within the *ohana*, the clan. There were children who were adopted by aunts. This was called *hanai* and Damien recognised it as similar to family practice at home.

He asked the Hawaiians to speak slowly, so that he could follow them. Hawaiian words had many meanings, depending on the context, and this made learning the language difficult. Prince Albert had told him that there were two languages: *Kanaka*, the language of the ordinary people, and the language of the *alii*. Damien hoped that he would quickly be able to master *Kanaka*.

Damien also made acquaintance with the native practices of natural religion and herbal medicine. Their religion was based upon the principle of opposing forces within the universe: good versus bad, day versus night, birth versus death, etc.

Although there were health problems that the local herbal medicine men were able to tackle successfully, such as infected wounds, they were powerless against two new diseases that were claiming many victims among the population. Tuberculosis and *Mai Pake*, the Chinese disease, which Damien did not at first realise was leprosy, were serious problems.

During his short stay in Hilo, Damien found time to write to Favens. His letter opened grandly, 'Since the first task of a parent is to provide his children with the necessities, I, likewise, find myself required to provide for my children, who have recently been regenerated by the water of the Holy Spirit, that which is necessary for their spiritual life.' There followed a humble shopping list: Catholic manuals, a large quantity of small red catechisms, mysteries of the rosary. The people in Puna were very poor and so he needed to be able to distribute these articles free. This seemed to him only fair, since he himself hardly ever had to pay for anything. It was true that his district was not large, but there were many sick people, who were so happy when Damien spoke to them about baptism. He wanted a chalice, because the gilding on the one he was currently using was peeling off. The paten was in poor condition, he needed vestments, altar linen, two consecrated stones and small candles.

Damien also wrote a note to his parents and a long report to Pamphile, whom he sought to persuade to come to Hawaii as soon as possible. He had baptised twenty-nine people; he had not mentioned this to the provincial because Pouzot had already done so. There was no longer any prejudice against Catholicism, a point Damien made twice in the course of his letter. He asked Pamphile to pray for him, that he would have enough zeal for his mission. He had to snatch so many Protestants from the hands of the pastors. He also had a request: could Pamphile send him two bells for his churches.

In his note to his parents, he was boastful of his achieve-ments, perhaps to set their minds at rest. Parting had been painful but now everything was going well. He spoke *Kanaka* as well as their own priest spoke Flemish – this was quite possibly a sarcastic comment, since the Belgian hierarchy and priesthood was French-speaking in the nineteenth century. Although he was still describing the *Kanaka* as kind, friendly, generous and hospitable in his letter to Pamphile, he described them to his parents as depraved. 'I have found myself in a depraved country, full of heathens. How great my responsibilities! How great my efforts as a missionary will be!

What purity of morals and uprightness of judgment I must have!'

The Hell of the Volcano

In Hilo, problems were piling up. The Catholic schoolmaster had converted to Protestantism and so Pouzot now had to teach in his place. In order to assist him, Damien took over part of his district. In mid-September, he set out for the camps of the cotton-pickers on the slopes of the active volcano Mauna Loa. The camp lay hidden in the forest. A family invited him to stay with them and he ate their *poi* with them, directly from the pot, using his fingers. He listened to their tales and puffed at the pipe that was passed around.

That night, as he lay sleeping on his mat, he was approached by one of the women. He rejected her advances but was unnerved, and decided to break off his stay with the cotton-pickers. He wanted spiritual advice and support and decided that Nicaise Ruault was the most suitable person with whom to discuss the matter.

This involved a journey past the crater and he decided that he wanted to visit it. He made his way to Volcano House, a small hotel in the forest owned by a Mr Stackpole. The day of his arrival, he rode around the rim of the crater, Hale Mau Mau – the House of Ferns – a distance of some thirteen kilometres, which took about two hours. The following day he joined a party, led by the volcano guide Upa, to enter the crater itself.

A Hard School

On their return to the rim of the crater, Damien took leave of the party and rode on to Kau, the island's most southerly district.

He stayed with Ruault for three weeks and they discussed what had happened to him in the camp. Real missionary work was so different from what he had been taught in the monastery and university. In Belgium and France, he had lived in seclusion from the world, now he travelled all over the place. There, he had had to be silent all day long, now he spoke all sorts of languages. He was living the life of a businessman, a burgomaster and a preacher, whilst what he really wanted was to work with the sick. The most difficult thing was to find time in his busy day for prayer and meditation.

Damien liked Hawaii, however, and he was gradually learning to be more realistic. His second letter to Favens was much less grandiloquent. He had received many of the things he had requested. He needed to build chapels, but accepted the view of his superiors that conversions came before buildings. Even so, he pressed for the building of one chapel at Kaimu.

Meanwhile, his colleague Evrard was finding life as a missionary even more difficult. He complained to Favens of loneliness and Pouzot arranged for Damien to visit him. Damien travelled via the eastern part of Evrard's district. Things began badly. In the first village, the Protestant village chief refused Damien permission to spend the night in one of the huts. He was obliged to sleep outdoors and was hungry, cold and wet. Damien was only able to stay with Evrard a few days. The visit failed to cheer Evrard up, however, and he hoped Damien would return at Christmas. But Damien spent the festival with Pouzot in Hilo. He enjoyed the church festivities, which were repeated with equal success at New Year, and wrote to Pamphile, 'I wish you a happy New Year. I have overcome the major difficulties that confront a new missionary. I am used to the language and the people.'

Things were not going well with Evrard. Pouzot brought him along at the Feast of the Epiphany, the feast of missionaries. Damien was shocked at Evrard's appearance. He and Pouzot decided that they would now officially ask the bishop whether Damien and Evrard could not exchange districts. Damien was a good horseman, who could cope with the large and difficult district. While they were waiting for a response, Damien began a new round of his own district.

By the end of January, he had visited all his parishes, but Evrard was still in Hilo, in a depressed state. His large district had been without a priest for more than a month and so Damien decided to visit it. He was welcomed in all the villages and once again he followed Bishop Maigret's advice by mixing on friendly terms with the native population. As he travelled along the east coast, he had to cross more than a hundred streams. Each time he stood before a river, he would murmur a quick prayer, for a flash flood could sweep him away. If the conditions were really too dangerous, he would camp by the stream and employ the time in reading his breviary or making reports.

The problems on the wet side of the island were, obviously, the rain and mud, the consequent bad paths and having constantly to climb and descend. The dry, western side was a burning desert. Only the Waimea plateau was perfect, except for the days when the *na ki puu puu* – the chilling rain that caused gooseflesh – fell. It was easy to work on the high plateau, although Damien would have liked his own church. On this first trip, he was enthusiastic and energetic. He longed to visit the remote valleys about which Evrard had complained. He enjoyed a challenge.

When Damien returned to Hilo, there was still no news from the bishop. Communications among the islands were temporarily suspended, because the steamboat *Kilauea* had been stranded on the reef before Kuwaihae-Uka. The news of the bishop's permission for Damien and Evrard to exchange districts finally arrived on 2 February.

Two political developments with relevance for Damien's future mission occurred at this time. On 3 January 1865 the Hawaiian parliament passed an Act for the Combating of Leprosy. The Board of Health was required to establish an isolation area for lepers and a hospital for suspected cases and people in the first stages of the disease, some three kilometres from Honolulu.

Damien had now discovered that the terms *Mai alii*, the nobleman's disease, or *Mai Pake*, the Chinese disease, referred to leprosy. These names were linked to the first known victim, Naea, a chief who had lived in the sugar town of Wailuku, on Maui Island. He was the natural father of Queen Emma, the widow of Kamehameha IV. The first signs of his leprosy were noted around 1840 and it was said that he had contracted it from his Chinese cook. The German doctor, Wilhelm Hillebrand, diagnosed the disease and forbade all contact with the outside world. Naea's extensive home became his place of exile and he respected the doctor's prohibition. After his death, however, his servants dispersed throughout the island and with them went the germs of the disease. A royal bodyguard of Kamehameha also turned out to have the disease.

Another event of significance to Damien was Kamehameha's decision to replace the department of Public Education by an Education Committee. This consisted of five members: a Catholic, Abraham Fornander, a Nonconformist and three Anglicans. The Committee immediately decided to cease supporting the Nonconformist school system. Fornander, whose daughters attended the Sacred Hearts convent school, became inspector-general. He shortly afterwards asked Damien to send suitable girls to Honolulu, to be trained as teachers. He made almost exclusively Catholic appointments to the post of schoolteacher, to the great anger of the Nonconformists.

At this time, also, the text of the papal encyclical *Quanta Cura*, in which Pius IX condemned both socialism and liberalism, reached Hawaii. Damien discussed with his colleagues the effects this might have on their work.

6

Kohala-Hamakua (1865–1868)

Missionary-Explorer

February 2 was the sixth anniversary of Damien's entry into the monastery in Leuven. He wanted to lose no time in taking up a new parish, because he wanted to make his official entry into the capital of his district, Kohala, on another anniversary, that of his landing in Honolulu. He had a real presbytery in Kohala City, with a living room and two bedrooms, one of which was let out to the schoolmaster. His predecessor had built a good church with two towers and its three altars and the candelabra with wooden flowers were the pride of the island.

Damien received a better reception from the population in his new district than on his previous visit. The position of the American Nonconformist missionaries had been weakened by the decision of their headquarters in Boston to declare the mission independent of the mother church. This meant that the pastors were now obliged to sustain themselves from the money they could raise from their flock. Damien was now able to make converts and his first round through the district took him six weeks.

He made an impression on the indigenous population by his hardiness and his willingness to share some aspects of their way of life. He was always in the saddle, visiting the communities in his district. One day, a Hawaiian asked him where his house was. Damien pointed to his horse. Sometimes, these trips involved making his way through almost impenetrable rainforest, at others, climbing sheer cliffs or fording fast-flowing streams. On one occasion, when he attempted to reach a remote community by canoe, the vessel capsized and he and his companions had to swim back to the reef. In Kohala he experienced an earthquake for the first time. His life seemed as much that of an explorer as of a missionary.

Plea for Churches and Chapels

In the summer of 1865, Damien was certain that he needed a chapel in the cattle-port of Kawaihae-Uka. There were Catholic *paniolos*, Mexican cowboys, living there. Their work was dangerous: it was no easy task to drive half-wild cattle from the rough mountain slopes of Waimea to the coast and then to heave them aboard the boats. These people deserved a chapel. Besides which, Damien wanted to compete with the Protestant chapel that the American missionary, Elijah Bond, had erected there, not to mention the Puukohala *heiau*, a native temple, built on the orders of Kamehameha the Great.

Damien informed the provincial that he had found the perfect site, on a hill, with the possibility of raising fruit and vegetables, for sale in Honolulu, to help funds. All he needed was permission from the owners of the land, Princess Liliuokalani and her American husband John Dominis, to rent the land, and funding from the Order to build the chapel.

Damien returned from a month-long tour of the district to find his request rejected by the provincial. He immediately found a berth on a boat going to Honolulu, and travelled there to urge his case. Moreover, he added a second request: he wanted also to build a chapel in the remote community of Waipio, which was almost inaccessible behind high cliffs and beyond deep valleys.

The provincial superior was again negative about the plans, declaring that the Order did not have FF3,000 to spare. However, he agreed to discuss the matter with Bishop Maigret and the latter was more sympathetic. Damien received funding for both chapels and was assigned a brother who specialised in carpentry to help him.

Lepers Exiled to Molokai

During his stay in Honolulu, Damien heard that the Board of Health had bought a piece of land for $1,800 on a peninsula on the northern coast of Molokai Island. The then chairman of the Board had been circuit judge on the islands of Maui, Molokai and Lanai and had recalled the almost inaccessible peninsula. A wall of rock six hundred meters high divided it from the rest of the island and it was washed on the remaining three sides by heavy and dangerous seas. There were three regions on the peninsula: Kalawao, on the east coast, Makanalua in the centre and Kalaupapa in the west.

The Board of Health restricted itself to a partial purchase of the Kalawao area. Agents had been able to persuade some of the inhabitants, the *Kamaaina*, to sell their property and move. The remaining villages would continue to be reserved for healthy people for the time being. The intention was that the exiles should provide for their own needs, because the *Kamaaina* were leaving well-tilled taro fields. The Board would provide them with meat, chickens and fishing tackle. Water would be no problem, because three valleys which breached the escarpment carried streams. The first bounty-hunters began to seek out lepers.

The relief hospital in Kalihi was formally opened on 13 November 1865. Sixty-two potential patients were transferred from prison to the hospital for examination. Forty-three of them were confirmed as having the disease. They remained in the hospital until the medical director decided whether they could stay in Honolulu for treatment or should be exiled to Molokai. Finally, twelve people – nine men and three women – turned out to be advanced cases and they were exiled on 6 January 1866.

The Board had stipulated that they had to provide for themselves, but this system did not work. They were already severely deformed: their hands and feet were contracted in spasm. In any case, they did not see why they, who had had their freedom taken away, should be forced to work into the bargain. Then, a week after their arrival, the leper settlement was pounded by a heavy southerly storm. Most of the houses were flattened and when a second group of lepers was brought ashore from the schooner *Warwick* on 21 January, they had no roof over their heads. The local population, who had already taken the first twelve into their homes, took these eight men and four women in as well.

Rudolph Meyer, the German who lived on the top of the *pali* (see p. 43), had been given general supervision of the leper settlement. He reported this contact between the healthy and sick, which was promoting a spread of the epidemic. He also discussed the problems with food and indicated that he could not take charge of the daily administration of the colony. Since Meyer was also manager of the ranch and superintendent of public works for the whole of Molokai Island, a former brother of the Sacred Hearts Order was sent to the settlement as superintendent. He was clearly frightened of the rebellious patients, for it was notorious throughout the archipelago that he carried a weapon with him at all times. It was the general view that law did not prevail in Kalaupapa.

On 6 February 1866 a third group of patients was stowed into the cattle-pens on board the *Warwick*. As they left, the exiles could have seen the steamship bringing the first party of tourists to the islands. The government encouraged these links with the American continent and looked to tourism as a replacement for the ailing sugar industry.

The Slow Process of Church Building (1866)

Damien's mission had been successful, in that he had baptised 167 people in one year, which was a record. After eighteen months, however, he gave up the system of 'fast-track baptism', because too many of the converts reverted to their former religious practices. He needed to take more care with the preparation of candidates for baptism, but for that, to his regret, he had no time, because he was busy with the construction of three chapels. He was absolutely sure now that he needed a companion and begged them to send Pamphile as his colleague.

Article 329 of the Order's rule declared that a missionary was not allowed to man a post alone. Favens supported this proposal and put it to the general.

Princess Liliuokalani had given Damien permission to use the land in Kawaihae-Uka for a church, despite the fact that she had already rented it out to a company. The construction began in December 1865, but it was a slow process, because of the nature of the site. The Californian redwood that was imported for the work had to be manhandled up the rock face with the help of local parishioners.

The building was not yet finished when the bishop arrived on the island in May 1866 to consecrate several new churches. Damien joined with eight other priests and brothers in accompanying him on his visitation of the island. The bishop liked to take his time on these trips, so as to give priests and parishioners alike a chance to talk to him, and it was not until mid-June that Damien had a chance to return to Kawaihae-Uka to see how work was progressing.

The bishop was pleased with Damien's work, although he was not yet able to consecrate any of the chapels. He gave Damien permission to use them as soon as they were ready, without waiting for formal consecration.

Everything was going well and in his annual report to the general on 20 December 1866, Damien wrote, 'I am still healthy and have completely adapted to the active life of a missionary. Unfortunately, the inner life seems to evaporate under the constant influence of bad examples and the harassments to which we are exposed.' The chief subject of the letter was chapel-building.

In his letter to Pamphile, Damien was rather more explicit. He had so many battles to fight: against the Calvinists, the *kahunas*, unfaithfulness in marriage and, above all, the general immorality and slight inclination for prayer.

Damien needed help, for he was under attack. Elijah Bond, the Protestant missionary in Kohala, had published an article in a newspaper, alleging that Damien's schools had extremely low standards. Bond was angry that he was losing not only Portuguese and Mexican, but also Hawaiian members of his congregation to Damien. Damien's schools were also winning pupils now that the government had decided to give Protestant and Catholic teachers equal pay. Bond also seems to have spread rumours that Damien was not so chaste as people might care to think.

These clashes between the Christian denominations could only serve to confuse the native population, who, in any case, found certain aspects of Christian doctrine, and of the various churches' practices, rather odd. They could not grasp the Nonconformists' teetotalism and prohibition of tobacco, whilst Catholic priestly celibacy seemed equally peculiar. Certainly, some of the Catholic priests had abandoned celibacy, and so the stories about Damien were quite readily believed on the islands.

Catholic and Anglican ritual suited the Hawaiians better than the sober Nonconformist services, since it was easier to assimilate to their own religious practices. Only the constant presence of whites in the neighbourhood prevented them from returning to their own beliefs, however.

Damien complained about the persistence of *Kanaka* religion in a letter to his parents. 'If someone is ill, then the *Kanaka* sacrifice to their old gods.' They also continued to believe in curses and Damien saw several people pine away and die because they were convinced that they had been cursed. What Damien did not say in his letters was that he had fallen under the sway of Hawaiian culture. He adopted its gestures and was becoming estranged from his former life.

He received little news and he reproached both Pamphile and his parents for this. He was constantly in hope of a letter that in fact never came. He thought of Pamphile every day. One day he would receive a letter from him. He spurred his parents to write by asking specific questions about the family and their doings.

In a round robin from the Order, Damien learned that Pamphile had been on a retreat in Paris. He hit out at him in a letter. 'Instead of playing skittles, you would be better employed coming here to convert these poor people.' He felt himself abandoned, a little betrayed. His mother had promised him a bell, but it did not arrive, and yet he needed three. At present, he had to blow on the large conch to call the faithful, as the *kahunas* once did. He was looking for support. In the confessional, converts told him about sins he had never even imagined existed. They were constantly relapsing into old sins. His initial ardour was gone and gradually Damien began to feel a sense of despair. The general had warned him of this when he left Paris. Even so, it came as a shock.

He could not take a gloomy view of everything, however. On Christmas Day, he placed an offertory box in the church at Kohala for the first time. He needed FF250 to repair the roof and to rebuild the tower, which had collapsed two years before, during an earthquake. People gave some money and a carpenter offered to do the work for free and promised to make the tower strong enough to take the bell that Damien's mother had promised and that would be coming sometime. All was not lost, and he preached a sermon on God's goodness and mercy.

On Boxing Day, Damien was working in his garden. He picked the beans he had sown a few weeks before and tended his fifty-five sheep, horses and mules. This was usually the job of the Flemish tobacco-planter who had rented the second room, but for the moment Damien found it relaxing. The following morning he had a fever, sickness and diarrhoea. He recognised the symptoms of typhus and immediately took an antipyretic. The illness only lasted a few days and by New Year's Day, he was strong enough to look after other victims of the epidemic, which remained under control.

Social Problems in Damien's District

Damien had received special permission to celebrate mass in his new chapel at Kawaihae on the Feast of the Epiphany, 1867. Flemings and Hawaiians had one thing in common: any excuse for a party was welcome, and this was the perfect opportunity. People came from far and wide and camped out on the beach for the event.

During the mass, Damien drew strength from the beaming faces. He noted that there were many non-Catholics in the congregation, who had simply wanted to be present at the event. This gave him hope and he preached with even greater fervour. After the mass, Damien joined in the feasting and celebrations without standing on ceremony.

The conversation among the merrymakers was not all gossip. They also spoke about the situation in Molokai, where things were going badly. The exiles did not receive visits from a doctor, there was no hospital, no nursing home and the families were not allowed to visit or look after the sick. The horror stories about Molokai were so terrible that the Board of Health had decided that they would build a school and a hospital. The Walshes, an Irish couple who had been unsuccessful in New Zealand, were appointed teacher and nurse. Their arrival was a signal for the former Sacred Hearts priest to leave and so Donald Walsh was promoted to be superintendent of the settlement.

Meanwhile, there were problems nearer home. The United States was now buying its sugar from low-wage economies such as the Philippines and China. As a result, a company in San Francisco that had acted as broker for Hawaiian sugar had failed. In turn, this company had links with Walker, Allen & Co., a business which exploited plantations in Kohala and operated the *Kilauea* steamboat. The American company's collapse brought Walker, Allen & Co. down.

This collapse meant not only that the *Kilauea* was impounded and there was no service between the islands, but also that the land on which Damien's church was built, and which he was sub-letting from Walker, Allen & Co., was confiscated for the benefit of creditors.

Damien was unable to go to Honolulu and so rode over to Kailua to consult the island superior as to what he should do. He also asked by letter for advice from Favens. At Kiholo, he found a letter from home. Enclosed were photographs of Pamphile and Pauline: he hardly recognised them. As he rode to Kailua, he had time to digest the news from home. He learned that Pamphile had been promoted to director of novices at Issy, near Paris. There was no chance of his coming to Hawaii.

In April, Damien was busy repairing his churches in Waipio and Warapuka, which had been damaged by earthquakes and storms. He had also begun on a new church in Waimea. He had received the land for the church from the daughter of the rancher John Parker, who had been educated by the sisters of the Sacred Hearts.

The building of the hospital on Molokai Island was also proceeding quickly at this time. Meyer had chosen to site it at the former city of refuge, Polapola, near the village of Kalawao. Wards with wide verandahs were built for the patients who were bedridden, and there was also a bathhouse, washhouse, shop, dispensary and a hut where *poi* could be pounded.

The white population did not greatly criticise this project, since the Hawaiian population had declined by another 8,000 in the previous six years, and now stood at only 58,765. This continued decline could cause labour shortages on the plantations, for Washington and Honolulu had finally signed a tariff agreement. Locally, however, the plantation owners were less concerned. They preferred Chinese labour, which they found cost less and performed better.

Initially, the healthy native population of Molokai thought that the whole business of exiling the lepers was a whim of the white man. More and more groups arrived, however, and the pressure on them to sell their land increased. They were also forbidden to take in the sick. The building of the hospital was the last straw for them. In the summer of 1867, the local population decided to send a deputation to the king. He received them on 28 July, in the presence of the minister of the Interior, who was ex officio chairman of the Board of Health. The deputation was informed that they had been paid for their property, which now belonged to the state, and they returned home having achieved nothing. More and more of the indigenous Molokai people began to leave their homes.

Building Chapels

From June to August Damien, together with his fellow-priests, accompanied Bishop Maigret on his episcopal visitation of Hawaii Island. This culminated in the consecration of the church in Kawaihae, followed by a service of confirmation, during which a sudden, very powerful gust of wind (a *mamuku* wind) almost destroyed the church.

More and more new missionaries were arriving and Damien was anxious to secure one of the newcomers as an assistant, for his district was too large. Despite pleading his case in person in Honolulu, however, he was told he would have to wait. The newcomers would have to be given time to settle in and there was a shortage of personnel everywhere. This was particularly true of the leper settlement on Molokai Island.

Damien spent the first months of 1868 in Waipio, an area he liked. It was a land flowing with milk and honey, its rivers and sea full of fish and shellfish and, on land, coconuts, bananas and edible ferns, although it was regrettable that the taro fields were being allowed to run to seed.

By the end of January, the church at Waipio was almost finished, but Damien still had no presbytery and had to sleep with a Portuguese family.

At this time, Damien was having a struggle to maintain his congregation in the face of the preachings of a young Hawaiian Nonconformist prophet called Joseph Kaona, who called his followers to repentance and threatened them with a catastrophe if they did not mend their ways. However, when he and his followers began to attack the property of whites, accusing them of being the cause of all the island's disease and social problems, Kaona was arrested, taken to Honolulu, declared insane and locked up.

Damien had received news of the death of his sister Constance from typhus and he was anxious to get his latest church in Waimea built, so that he could celebrate a requiem for her there. In the meantime, he was busy with repairs to his existing buildings, which suffered the constant ravages of the climate.

7

Eruption of the Volcano (1868)

The Wrath of the Fire Goddess

On 27 March, the day before Palm Sunday, a plume of smoke more than a meter high arose from the volcano, which had been rumbling for several weeks.

The next day, the celebration of the mass was interrupted by three large tremors, one of which threw Damien to the ground, and that evening there were two more. Damien decided to sleep in the open, well away from walls and trees.

The tremors continued throughout the night and the following day. Only in the evening did they diminish in number and intensity. Damien organised a prayer vigil, and many people participated. Their prayers seemed to have been heard and Damien was able to prepare the faithful for Easter.

On Good Friday, the congregation had just left the church when a large tremor shook the building and Damien was once again thrown to the ground. The ground was shaking and Damien had to crawl out of the building, feeling seasick. There, he saw that many trees had been brought down, all the brick and stone buildings were flattened and most of the wooden ones severely damaged. A thick black cloud filled the sky and the sun was dimmed and finally disappeared from view.

In the afternoon of 2 April 1868 the floor of the crater of the Kilauea volcano collapsed. The sugar town of Punaluu and other places along the coast were destroyed by the tidal wave caused by the eruption. The whole southern district of Kau, which was immediately adjacent to the volcano, was the most severely affected.

Two days after the disaster, the *Kilauea* set sail for Hawaii to bring assistance. King Kamehameha V, Charles de Varigny, the Finance Minister and Bishop Maigret were aboard, but they got no further than Maui Island, because Hawaii was cut off by a storm. It was only on 6 April, four days after the eruption, that the captain was able to steam into Hilo Bay.

The eruption had caused enormous damage. Houses and churches were reduced to rubble and grass huts had simply disappeared. Candles and cooking fires had set off fires which could not be extinguished. People had been wounded or killed by flying masonry. Roads had collapsed or been washed away. The captain hoped to be able to sail to the worst affected area via Kau. When they heard of this plan, the people gave him what they could spare of their household goods to take to the stricken people. The attempted expedition failed, however, when the captain was forced to turn back, fearing the presence of an active submerged volcano. He could not risk sailing to Damien's district.

For two months a thick pall of smoke hung over the Big Island and there were storms every day. Everything was covered with a fine layer of ash and many people suffered from breathing difficulties. There was a general feeling of despair and many people left the island. Damien at last received the assistant he had been requesting for so long. Maigret chose Fr Gulstan Ropert, a Breton, who was roughly the same age as Damien. They had studied together in Paris and met several times in Honolulu. Ropert landed at Kailua on 19 June 1868 and rode to Kohala. Damien and he decided to work as a team for the immediate future, because there was so much to do to recover from the eruption. The persistent dust cloud was causing ongoing problems, quite apart from the need to rebuild dwellings and roads.

The problems of the Catholic missionaries were intensified by the fact that the self-proclaimed prophet Joseph Kaona had been released from gaol, under popular pressure, and was starting to make inroads into both the Protestant and Catholic congregations again. The indigenous population saw his prophecies realised in the volcano's eruption and they blamed the whites for their disregard of local temples and deities, which they believed had called down the wrath of the fire-goddess, Pele.

Once again, however, Kaona's influence on his followers caused unrest, and this led the authorities to intervene. The group became embroiled in an all-out battle with the local sheriff. They killed a policeman and then dragged the sheriff from his horse and beheaded him. As a result, the governor of Oahu Island, John O. Dominis, was given the order to put down the rising with troops. This was done. In order to prevent too much simmering discontent among the population, official reprisals were limited to Kaona alone, and he was imprisoned for ten years.

The Harsh Aftermath of the Natural Disaster

It was about a year before life got back to normal, but the spiritual, moral and psychological aftershocks of the disaster were felt much longer. Many converts had given up the faith. Because almost everyone had lost all they had, people became self-centred and the former co-operativeness disappeared. Whereas, in the past, Damien had always been able to borrow ox-carts, now he had to rent them at extortionate rates. Foreigners had formerly lent a hand, but now most had left and even Favens, the provincial, demanded payment. In his New Year's letter to his parents, Damien gave a succinct list of the major problems: natural disasters, a sect, leprosy.

Like his father, Damien dealt with his griefs in stubborn silence, which bordered on despondency, and worked himself to a standstill. Ropert could not follow Damien's moods and after ten months decided to strike out on his own, taking over the Hamakua district, whilst Damien continued to serve Kohala. Their contact point would be the lovely valley of Waipio.

Damien relied on his mentor, Bishop Maigret, but he, too, was about to leave. The bishop announced, in March 1869, that he planned to attend the Council at the Vatican. He had not yet received a formal summons, but it was generally known that Pius IX was planning such a gathering. Favens feared that the 64-year-old bishop would not be able to cope with the cold weather in Europe and would become ill. The Catholic congregation shared this view and sent a petition to keep Maigret in Hawaii, but Maigret rejected this.

In Hawaii, Damien wrestled with himself. He wrote to Favens on matters of business and, to his parents, he admitted that he was FF400 in debt, because the building of the church in Waiaka had gone over budget. Things were not going well with him. If there was ever a period in which he experienced moral problems, then this was it. He reported that he was disturbed by the nakedness of his parishioners, was depressed and asked forgiveness. At the end of 1869, he wrote to the provincial, 'At the end of the year in which I have caused you so much trouble and concern, I humbly beg your forgiveness for my insubordination and lack of submission.' This is probably a reference to his excessive expenditure on the new church. A few days later, he was feverish and felt weak. From then on, he always felt cold. During his period of recovery, which lasted a long time for him – it would be months before he could make long trips again – he received a letter from home, which put heart into him again. He felt less abandoned.

Damien was not the only one who was having problems. The Walshes, who ran the leprosy settlement, were also suffering. Mr Walsh had not succeeded in introducing military discipline and he could not cope any longer. He needed a holiday. The family sailed for Honolulu, but on the way Mr Walsh suffered a cerebral haemorrhage and died at sea. The shock completely unsettled their son, whose mind was already disturbed. Mrs Walsh continued to try to run the settlement for several months, but was finally forced to give it up.

Her successor was a patient, an ex-captain in the Hawaiian Royal Guards. He was a person of authority and remained in charge of the leprosy settlement until 1872, when his illness became too advanced for him to continue. At this period, the request of several Protestants to be allowed to build a church was granted and they were given money for a small modern building. This was consecrated on 28 October 1871 and given the hopeful name of Siloama. In the New Testament, Siloam is a healing spring. The establishment of a Protestant church caused the Catholics to demand one of their own and a collection was made throughout the islands to finance it.

There is little documentary evidence in Damien's hand for the first half of 1870. Damien informed Favens that the church in Waiapuka was finished. He was worried about his schools. The Anglican bishop and Charles de Varigny had resigned from the Education Committee and had been replaced by Harvey Rexford Hitchcock, the son of a pastor who worked in the healthy area of Molokai Island. Whilst Hitchcock might well know more about education than the former judge, the Catholics feared they would lose their favoured position.

There was friction between Damien and the friendly, meek but frugal Favens. Bishop Maigret had always taken all the decisions, but he was still in Europe. From the correspondence, it appears that many of the difficulties were cleared up during the summer retreat in August 1870. There was also news from Europe: the general of the Order, Euthyme Rouchouze, had died.

On 1 September 1870 Damien confessed to the new general, Sylvain Bousquet, that he had found life very difficult before the arrival of Ropert. 'My four years of missionary experience have taught me that, together with the inner workings of grace, a missionary needs the "constant" help of a fellow-priest in order to dispel the black thoughts that arise as a result of daily contact with a sinful world and that give rise to an intolerable kind of melancholy.' He got on well with Ropert and the few days each month that they spent together were pleasant breathing spaces. For the first time in months, Damien sounded positive. The Protestants were no longer his chief cause of concern, now that the American missionaries were, one by one, turning to business. They were replaced by Hawaiians, who demanded payment for everything.

Bishop Maigret arrived back in Honolulu on 14 October with German recruits. Damien was pleased to see the bishop, although he had hoped that his brother, or perhaps his eldest nephew, would have accompanied him.

New Disasters

In both the spring and summer of 1871, there were storms, the second of hurricane force, on Hawaii Island, which damaged many houses and, once again, Damien's churches.

Bishop Maigret arrived to inspect the situation and Damien was able to consult him about many problems concerning his ministry. On the final evening of the episcopal visitation, news arrived that four members of the Order of the Sacred Hearts, including Frézal Tardieu, had been executed by the Paris Commune. This caused great grief and consternation among the Catholic missionaries.

At this time, there were some rumours in the community that Damien was having a sexual relationship with a woman who was suffering from leprosy and who was hiding from the bounty-hunters in the forest. Certainly, although he was sometimes afraid, Damien did visit lepers in their huts and heard their confessions. However, no confirmation of those rumours has ever been made, notwithstanding a prolonged and in-depth enquiry.

The Catholic church in the leper settlement, for which money had been collected, was dedicated to St Philomena in 1872. In the same year there were again storms and earthquakes, that once again damaged his recently built churches and caused one of Damien's newly arrived bells to crack.

In the autumn, there was a typhus epidemic. One of its victims was the childless Kamehameha V, who died on 11 December 1872. Because he had no heirs, the choice of king was between the militaristic Hawaiian nationalist, David Kalakaua, and the popular alcoholic, William Lunalilo, known as 'Whisky Billy'. The whites supported Lunalilo and, because they had a majority of the votes following the electoral reform, he was chosen. The price for his election was that he send a secret mission to Washington to negotiate a reciprocity treaty with the United States. The US navy would be allowed to use Pearl Harbour as if it were their own territory, in exchange for tax-free importation of Hawaiian sugar to the United States. The plantations needed support, for, since the eruption of the

Mauna Loa five years before, the weather had not yet stabilised, and there was, in addition, a plague of insects attacking the sugarcane.

At the beginning of April, Walter Murray Gibson, an untrustworthy adventurer, who had gained a certain degree of authority as a journalist, published a report about a meeting in the Protestant chapel Kaumakapili in Honolulu. There had been anti-white unrest during the meeting, the issue being the attitude toward leprosy. The article ended with the lofty words, 'Were a noble Christian priest or pastor to find the inspiration to offer his life to comfort the poor wretches, that noble soul would shine forever on a throne constituted of human love.' These passionate words gave the exiles hope and they sent a petition to the king, in which they requested that the new king pay them a visit.

8

The Decision (May 1873)

Fouesnel's Celebration in Wailuku

About three weeks later, Damien told his congregation that he was going to Maui Island for a church consecration. He rode to the point where he had arranged to meet Fr Ropert, but arrived before him. As he waited, he looked around over the beautiful Waipoi valley. When he heard Ropert approaching, he remounted his horse. Suddenly, his eyes filled with tears. He was certain that he would never return, that this was a final leave-taking. His companion was amazed to hear him say this, for there had not apparently been any talk of Damien's taking up another posting.

When they reached the port of Kawaihae, they joined some of the congregation, who were also going to Maui, for a service. Damien tried to reassure the congregation, but again he burst out that he would never come back, and wept. As he stood on the deck of the departing boat, he again bade farewell to the island.

They were met on their arrival by Bishop Maigret and rode with him to Wailuku, where the new St Anthony's church of Fr Léonor Fouesnel was to be consecrated. The celebrations began on 4 May and involved ceremonies of baptism and confirmation as well as the consecration, followed by feasting.

Volunteer for Work with the Lepers

At one point during the celebrations, Maigret asked Boniface Schäffer, a German missionary, to give an account of his latest visit to Kalawao. He told of many believers who were without a priest. Fr Aubert Bouillon, who was the one who best understood the Hawaiian mentality, had been to Molokai several times. He described the change in personality that many exiles underwent. They were despairing and so they put all norms of behaviour aside. They lived licentiously, because transient physical or sadistic pleasure was all that kept them going. He called it the '*Aole hanawai makea wahi* – the place where no law exists', and said that the saying, '*Na kanaka kuu wale aku no i ka uhane* – that people who arrived there gave up the ghost and died', was true. Many did nevertheless still try to make something of their lives. Above all, they needed a priest.

They had all read Gibson's appeal for Christian heroism. Bouillon was prepared to be the candidate to make the sacrifice, but Maigret refused the suggestion, because Bouillon had health problems. Bouillon continued to press for a priest to be sent to Molokai, however, insisting that they were dying without support. At that point Maigret asked for four volunteers who would each spend three months at a time with the exiles. Their colleagues would have to organise matters among themselves in order to cover the extra work. He asked if there were any volunteers. Again, Bouillon put himself forward but was refused. Gulstan Ropert, Boniface Schäffer, the newcomer Rupert Lauter and Damien put up their hands. Maigret accepted them and decided to send Damien first. The practical measures were taken over the next few days. Berths were reserved for the French consul, an Irish priest, the bishop and Damien on the *Kilauea* for a sailing on 9 May. Everyone except Damien would then sail on to Honolulu, after a short visit to the leper settlement.

Damien had four days in which to settle things with the bishop. Ropert would look after Damien's district while he was away, and then he, in turn, would take over his colleague's area. It was not intended that Damien should confine his efforts to the leper settlement – he was supposed to serve the whole island of Molokai. Maigret judged that one visit per month on 'topside' – as the rest of the island was known – would be sufficient. Maigret warned Damien to be careful. Come what may, he was to avoid any form of contagion. If a pipe were passed round, he must refuse it. He must not join in meals and eat from the communal pot with his fingers. The saddle of a leper was taboo and he was not to sleep in the hut of an exile. Maigret found his decision difficult. Three months was sufficient to contract the disease, and he was possibly sacrificing four young men. The decision was taken, however, and he had to go ahead.

The news that a white priest was to go to the leper settlement quickly got abroad, and reached the exiles themselves. It was not only the Catholics who were delighted at the news. The Protestant pastor Neuku, who was himself a patient, and his deacons thought a priest would be an asset, at least if he fought for a 'normal life'. He asked his congregation to support the arrival of the white priest.

The exiles had often seen promises reneged on and so they organised a petition asking for the priest to stay. More than two hundred people signed. This petition was handed to Bishop Maigret when the party landed at Kalaupapa, but he was determined not to agree that Damien should stay permanently on Molokai Island.

The party made its way to the new Catholic chapel, surrounded by members of the settlement, and prepared to celebrate mass. The building was full and it was boiling hot. Damien was confronted with all the physical unpleasantness of leprosy. There were too many people with suppurating sores, so that there was a stench of rotting flesh. Moreover, one of the symptoms of leprosy is that the sufferer salivates excessively. The people were constantly coughing, clearing their throats and spitting on the ground. Damien had to turn away in order not to be sick. He went to the open window, but the building was surrounded by ill people who had not been able to get into the church.

The bishop kept his sermon short, because he had to catch the boat. He hastened through the mass and then Damien, the Irish priest and the bishop had to face administering communion. They had to place the consecrated wafer on the infected tongues. They did it with repugnance, although they tried not to show it. The congregation itself was delighted at the visit of the bishop and had decorated the church with flowers. They had also, for this special occasion, asked Zepherin, a young boy who had once been a choirboy for the musical Fr Fouesnel, to sing the solo once more. The visitors did not realise it, but everyone else present did: it would be the last time. The boy had maggots in his feet and when he stood up, he needed someone to support him. The bishop recognised the boy and nodded to him, for he had once studied at Ahuimanu College. 'Once' was two or three years ago. His voice had not broken, for leprosy halts hormonal development.

Zepherin stood and sang the 'Hosannah' from Mozart's 'Coronation' Mass. Everyone was silent. The boy's treble rang out in the cramped space. At one point, when he hit a high note, things went wrong. The boy got a lump in his throat, but it did not matter. The congregation waited patiently until he had spat on the floor and then urged him to continue. At the consecration service in Wailuku, a few days before, the crowd outside the church had sung their own songs so loudly that they had drowned out the singing of the mass in the church itself, despite the extensive rehearsals and substantial choir. Here there was silence and respect.

These events marked the origin of Fouesnel's enmity toward Damien. Fouesnel had been preparing the dedication of his church for a long time, yet the event passed virtually unnoticed in the press, whereas there was tremendous newspaper coverage of Damien's arrival in the leper settlement.

Outside the chapel after the service, the bishop spoke to the crowd, asking them whether they were adequately looked after and whether they had any needs. They were cautious in their replies, because he was a figure of authority. He promised them that the Catholic mission would be permanent and, as a symbolic gesture, said that Damien would sleep under the pandan tree until his presbytery was built. The pandan tree is not a suitable tree under which to sleep, but it was a symbol to the Hawaiians of a foreigner who came to settle in Hawaii.

Then it was time for the *Kilauea* to set sail and the bishop and the rest of the party left Damien behind in the settlement.

Getting to Know the Molokai Leper Settlement

After the bishop had left, a young man, who appeared to be healthy, introduced himself as Joseph Manu. He did not live in the settlement, but in Pelekunu, the next valley. His parents were taro farmers and that morning he had set out early to bring a load of *pai-ai* bundles, the ingredient for *poi*, to the settlement. If the priest ever wanted to visit his valley, he must just ask him, because the boat only stopped off once a week.

A white man also introduced himself as William Williamson, a Briton. He was a nurse, but also a patient, since he had contracted the disease when working in the Queen's Hospital in Honolulu. He was now superintendent of the hospital in the colony. He warned Damien straight away that ordinary human contact was sufficient to catch the disease.

Damien spent an uncomfortable night sleeping under the pandan tree and the next day Williamson took him on a tour of the village. First they walked the five hundred metres or so to the river, in order to wash. A pipeline brought water from the source to the hospital, but those who were not confined to the hospital had to wash and shave in the stream. Clothes also had to be washed there, but since the Board of Health only made one set of clothes available to the patients, they had to strip in order to wash their things in the stream. The Hawaiians were not bothered by this, but Damien was. He regarded an improved water supply as a necessity, because anyone who was too ill to get over the walls and crawl through the thorn bushes, but not yet ill enough to be admitted to the hospital, had to lie around in their own dirt.

The hospital was new and clean, the wards were large, airy and spacious. The breeze from the open windows could not entirely disperse the stench of suppurating, maggot-infested sores and diarrhoea. Williamson remarked lightly, 'We have no enemies here save scabies, vomit, fleas and lice.' He showed Damien the prison, two cells with a small window, where not only offenders but those who were mad were locked up. Most of them died after only a few days of incarceration. Then they went on to the *poi* hut, where women were pounding the roots to flour in large mortars.

There was one hut that Williamson was not keen to show Damien, but he could not avoid it when they saw a man with a bandana over his nose, pushing a wheelbarrow toward the tiny building. The wheelbarrow looked as though it contained a bundle of rags. The man pushed the door of the hut open with his foot and tipped up the wheelbarrow, depositing a groaning heap on to the floor of the hut. He pushed at the feet, so that he could get the door shut again, removed the bandana from his face, and made his way back to the wards. 'The "dying-shed",' Williamson noted. 'To be avoided.' For Damien, that meant 'to be visited frequently', but he could not immediately go and visit the dying, for Williamson had not yet completed his tour.

They went into the village and visited a number of huts. Whereas, the day before, the patients had had nothing but praise for the *Papa Ole*, the Board of Health, now they spoke of *Papa Make*, the Board of Death. They were contemptuous of the lack of concern of people who could send the sick into exile. Yes, they were fed, but prisoners were fed, too. Yes, they received clothing, but they had to make do with one set for a whole year. When you got weaker, you simply had to hope that inadequate nourishment would bring death more quickly, because it was a myth that leprosy was a painless disease. Every day, they saw from their fellow-sufferers what their own fate was to be. When your fingers started to contract, you could hope to live two or three years longer at best. When your vital organs started to pack up – lungs, stomach – then you knew it was almost over. It was all very well for priests to talk about heaven, but when you were living in hell, 'heaven' was quite a distant prospect. Damien must understand that in these circumstances they wanted to stick to their customary pleasures. They grew sweet potatoes, the *ava*, because you could distil a very good liquor from it. A *haole*, Humphreys, who had just died, had had a distillery, but they refused to say where it was. With *ki* roots, you could make *uui uui*, which was even stronger. One glass was enough to get you sloshed.

Damien's Wish Granted Under Pressure from the Haole: Extension

In Honolulu, Maigret was grappling with his conscience, as to whether it was right or fair to sacrifice a priest. He was sympathetic to Damien and realised that he had had mainly financial problems on the Big Island. He continued to ponder the matter, particularly after he had read an article in the *Pacific Commercial Advertiser*, in which the king gave his response to the exiles' petition. They received all his sympathy and love, but the exiles must understand that their segregation was for the good of the nation. He could not visit them. This article greatly reduced the king's popularity. It sounded hypocritical and was in flagrant contrast to Damien's heroic behaviour.

Walter Murray Gibson, who had launched the appeal for a Christian hero, wrote again about the leper settlement. Maigret was moved when he read the article, entitled, 'A Christian Hero'. It ended with the words, 'Father Damien took his decision and was left behind among the lepers, without a home or any extra clothing, apart from what the lepers themselves could give him. The theological principles of the man are not important. He is without doubt a Christian hero.'

One morning, a doctor stopped his coach in front of the mission. He gave Favens $25 for Damien. Shortly afterwards, John O. Dominis, the governor of Oahu Island, was presiding over a meeting. When the business was completed, Dominis asked those present for a contribution to Damien's work: everyone gave something and the result was that $50 were collected. Dominis sent the money to the mission and reported the event to his wife, Princess Liliuokalani. More small gifts and expressions of support arrived, to the point where his superiors realised that they could not withdraw Damien from the post.

Damien himself did not want to leave. He wrote powerfully, almost commandingly, to his provincial, 'I am sending this message by the schooner *Waniki*, to let you know that, from now on, there must be a resident priest in this post. There are shiploads of patients arriving and, in consequence, there are many here who are dying.' He had spent his second night under the pandan tree and was awaiting the arrival of the wood for his house with impatience.

He needed a crate of wine and other articles connected with his ministry. He did not yet know whether he would be allowed to stay and wrote, 'I beg you to write to the Rev. Gulstan [Ropert] to take over Kohala until my return', but added his own strong opinion, 'unless you can persuade one of the fathers at Kona to take over from me definitively. You know my position, I wish to sacrifice myself for the poor lepers. The harvest here seems ripe.'

The stench in the church on the first Sunday was unbearable, despite the fact that Damien had opened all the windows. He was able to get through that part of the mass he conducted with his back to the congregation, but the gospel and sermon were intolerable. He kept the sermon short and managed until he got to the communion. He tried not to touch people's tongues or intake their breath, but he could not stop himself heaving.

He kept going, however, and whenever he had the time he explored his new surroundings. Siloama Church was a little higher up the side of the small crater that had thrown up the peninsula. He followed the path to the mouth of the crater, where the wind from the sea was biting. In the crater, though, it was warmer. There was a large number of people living there in caves, taking refuge from the cold of Kalawao, which got little sun. Sick people needed to keep warm, but later, Damien learned that some were living in the crater in order to avoid the many inspections by the Board of Health. Illegal *kokuas* were living underground there.

After a few days, Damien had settled into a routine. He would get up and walk to the river to wash and shave. Then he meditated in the church, said mass, had breakfast and made his first round. He visited the sick and comforted the dying, but maintained the necessary distance.

Damien's first visitor was Rudolph Meyer, mentioned earlier, the German who was married to a Hawaiian *alii* called Dorcas, with whom he had eleven children. He lived at the top of the cliff and had various jobs in order to maintain his family. He was manager of the cattle ranch that belonged to the Princesses Ruth and Bernice, inspector of public works on Molokai Island and the manager of the leper settlement. He also raised sugar cane on his own land. He was an hydraulic engineer, but had left Hamburg to take part in the California gold rush, without success. Finally, he had ended up in Honolulu in 1850, at the age of twenty-four. He had travelled to Kaluaaha on Molokai Island at the invitation of the Protestant pastor, Hitchcock, and there had met his wife and married her in 1854.

Meyer came to inspect the leper settlement once or twice a month. His first visit after Damien's arrival was not primarily to meet the new priest. The Board of Health, under the chairmanship of Edwin O. Hall, was pursuing a much stricter policy. So many lepers were being rounded up that there was a shortage of space in Kalawao. There was now the harsh necessity of persuading the *Kamaaina* to sell their property in Kalaupapa as well. Meyer was required to give them an ultimatum: if they stayed, they would henceforth be forbidden to leave the area, just like the exiles. For the lepers, there was the good news that they were no longer forbidden to visit Kalaupapa. They could move at will over the whole peninsula.

The thorniest topic of Meyer's visit was his commission to remove all healthy individuals from the settlement, including the servants of the wealthier patients, the *kokuas* and the *kamaainas*. The assistants, or *kokuas*, were healthy family members who had accompanied their sick partner, parent or child to the leper settlement. Many *kokuas* returned to their home after the death of their loved one and, in consequence, might spread the disease. In May 1873, there were about 500 patients and 200 healthy people on the peninsula. Meyer was convinced that the superintendent, Jonathan Napela, a judge from Maui, who had accompanied his sick wife Kitty to Kalawao, connived at this, as a *kokua* himself, and that he even helped to organise the practice.

In principle, Damien was permitted to remain until 24 May. He continued to argue his case for staying. There were 210 Catholics in the settlement and twenty candidates for baptism.

In the next valley, there were at least 300 people who wanted the ministrations of a priest. He was going to visit them on the Friday after Ascension Day. 'I beg you to let me know your decision,' he wrote to Favens. 'Which priest will have the privilege to gather in Our Lord's harvest? It is ripe here. Without a harvester, it will be spoiled in a very short time.'

Favens replied, 'No decision has been made, except that you may remain on Molokai until further orders.' The reason for this extension was, according to Favens, 'The *haole* of Honolulu are full of admiration for your sacrifice and are ready to offer you help. You have probably heard something of this.' Favens was concerned, saying, 'Take care that you do not catch this dreadful disease. I hope that the good Lord will spare you.'

Now that he could remain, at least provisionally, Damien could start to make plans. There were two urgent matters: the water supply must also be made to serve those exiles who were not in the hospital and there was also a problem with the graves. Only the wealthier persons were buried in a coffin. The others came under the 'three knots system' of Kalawao. The grave-diggers who worked for the Board of Health wrapped the bodies in a cloth, usually the sheet that had been covering the patient at death, and tied it up with a rope: one knot at the head, one at the feet and one in the middle. Then they tied the body to a pole and carried it to the churchyard. Digging graves in the lava was hard work and so the diggers made a round hole and doubled the body up to place it in the grave. If the grave were not deep enough, then there was a risk that wild boar might come and dig up the bodies at night. Damien thought building a fence around the churchyard would be a simple solution to keep the boar out. Another possibility was to cover the bodies with cement, but this could only be a temporary solution, because there were so many victims that they would soon run out of space.

Damien also had to inform his parents that he had gone to the leper settlement, without worrying them. He tried to approach the subject calmly and scientifically.

Leprosy is almost incurable. The disease develops gradually

as a result of a deterioration of the blood. The first signs are patches on the skin, especially on the cheeks. There is a loss of sensation in those patches. After a while, the whole body is covered with such patches. Then sores appear and these become infected, especially on the hands and feet. Fingers and toes are eaten away and at that point, the sores give off a sickly stench. Their breath poisons the air.

9

Accepted
(May 1873–January 1874)

The Death of a Child

After two weeks in the leper settlement, Damien took up the offer from Joseph Manu and travelled with him in his canoe to the Pelekunu valley. As he watched the canoe arrive with supplies, he noted how the exiles gathered around, the strongest pushing their way to the front, the weakest hanging back, and wondered how the system of assigning provisions could be changed.

Damien lodged with Joseph Manu's parents in Pelekunu for two days. It was relaxing to be able to live on a normal footing with people again. He held a service for the people in the village and then set out with Joseph Manu to visit a small group of Catholics along the north shore up to Halawa, a wide, fertile valley on the eastern cape. His reception was not friendly, for most of the inhabitants were *kamaainas*, who had been forced to leave their land in Kalawao.

From Halawa, Damien proceeded on foot and visited the many tiny villages and harbours along the south coast. Finally, he began the long climb to the summit of the *pali*. There was little shade and the sun was burning down. It was a hard climb, although the gradient up to the pastures where Meyer's cattle grazed was not particularly steep. He met the large family for the first time.

Meyer gave him a horse and together they rode to the *pali*. From there, Damien had to make the steep, difficult descent before sunset.

By the time he returned, Zepherin, the youth who had studied in Ahuimanu, had been reduced to a quivering bundle beneath a dirty sheet, his pleading eyes staring out from his swollen face. Damien had tried to persuade Williamson to keep the boy on the ward, but the nurse thought it was too demoralising for the other patients.

The door of the so-called 'dying-shed' closed with a thud behind Damien and the youth. Zepherin lay on the ground moaning. He wanted his mother, he wanted to go home to Wailuku. Damien promised him a heavenly home. His voice breaking, because this was a child, a Catholic, a pupil from the Sacred Hearts College, Damien said the Last Rites. It was difficult to find an untainted spot on the boy's head, to anoint him. A spasm went through the body and a foot shot out from beneath the sheet. Damien could see the maggots crawling around in the sores. He wanted to run away, but he was held fast by the boy's pleading eyes. Then, although the bishop had forbidden him to touch the patients, Damien began to stroke the boy's neck, where the skin was still untainted, and so the boy died.

Stricter Segregation of the Lepers

Shocked and nauseated, Damien went to the church to put away the sacred oil.

At that moment, Jonathan Napela rode up to announce that the wood for Damien's house and the bell had just arrived. Napela made the Board of Health's ox-cart available to Damien. Several strong men and a band of children were willing to help and together they loaded the wood up in Kalaupapa and unloaded it again at Kalawao. They even helped to sort the planks into piles of equal length, so that they were neatly arranged on the grass. They also brought the wood that was left over from building the church. When Maria, the wife of a Portuguese, asked for one or two beams, so that she could build a shelter, Damien gave them to her willingly.

The bell was heavy and it was quite a job to hang it in the tiny tower. When it was done, Damien asked the children to spread out throughout the area, to see how far away it could be heard. The adults quickly joined them and soon everyone was spread out through the settlement, awaiting the joyful sound of a bell that would in future mostly be employed to announce a death.

In Honolulu, leprosy was the main item on the agenda of the annual meeting of the Hawaiian Evangelical Society on 10 June. The debate was lively, but the vote was unanimous. The final motion declared that, if measures were not swiftly taken to protect the vital elements of the nation, 'our Hawaiian nation will become a country of leprosy sufferers within a few years.' This would mean,

> the disruption and total destruction of our civilisation, the property and zeal of our churches, our contribution, our Hawaiian Board and the missionary work. It will mean shame, defeats and a dishonourable collapse of everything that holds so much promise in our country. We are on the edge of a fearful precipice, full of horror, down which our feet are fast slipping.

The Hawaiian Evangelical Society called on all Protestants to report anyone who might have leprosy. 'Teach every leper who wishes to remain with his own people and refuses to leave, that he is sinning against human life and God's law.' The pastors had a duty to make clear to their congregation that segregation of lepers was prescribed by the law of Moses in Leviticus 13. A day must be fixed for fasting and atonement for the sins that had caused such a horror, particularly those sins which were aiding the spread of the disease. This sharply worded text was printed in its entirety in the *Hawaiian Gazette*.

Rudolph Meyer visited the leper settlement on 13 June 1873, but not to look at the building plot for Damien's house. He was come to brand Jonathan Napela as 'two-faced', because he was permitting illegal residents in the colony, and even allowing them into his own home. Officially, he was required to expel all *kokuas*, all non-lepers, unless they had a residence permit, but there were more than a hundred people from Maui

Island alone in the settlement. Meyer dismissed the police commissioner, but could not remove Napela. The latter was given the unpleasant task of informing the patients that the taro harvest had failed. There was a shortage of *pai-ai* and so the patients would have to make do with rice. Napela feared that this would cause a riot – *poi* was the Hawaiians' bread – but Meyer could do nothing but inform him that this was the unavoidable situation.

Meyer then set off for Kalaupapa where he spent long hours trying to persuade the *kamaaina* to sell their property. They could receive money or a much larger plot of land in Halawa. No one jumped at the proposal, however, and Meyer was obliged to give them his ultimatum. From mid-June, 1873, the leper settlement was to be completely segregated: if the *kamaaina* refused to leave before that time, then they would be forbidden to leave thereafter.

This complete segregation of the settlement was no simple matter and so a member of the Board of Health, Samuel G. Wilder, visited the leper settlement. Wilder ran a shipping line and was agent for the *Kilauea*. He was energetic and something of an adventurer. After an eventful life in the United States, he had visited Honolulu in 1856 and there fell in love with the daughter of an American pastor. He stayed and became a respectable businessman.

Wilder was a tough but good-hearted man, who tried to be fair. He recognised the need for the segregation of the lepers and intended to impose it strictly. It was his intention to pick up a number of illegal residents himself and throw them out, but his attempt failed completely. As they were dropping anchor, the Hawaiian crew signalled to the 'rocks', the ever-present look-outs for the boat, that someone from *Papa Ole* was on board, a VIP. For once, not all the 'rocks' waited for the boat. Some of the men turned their horses and rode swiftly to the village to warn the *kokuas* that there was about to be an inspection. On this occasion, the landing procedures took longer than usual, it was as though the Hawaiian crew had suddenly been overcome by lethargy. They clearly did not support segregation.

Highly Placed Helpers

In Hilo, the flamboyant barrister William Ragsdale had also read the article about the Hawaiian Evangelical Society. Ragsdale was half-Hawaiian and he was highly thought of, because he worked as the official interpreter in the Hawaiian House of Lords. He had also led King Kamehameha's party to victory in the elections held over the constitutional crisis on the Big Island.

He was socially and politically successful, but he had leprosy. When he had first discovered his condition, it had brought on a deep depression, but thereafter he had learned to live with it, taking careful precautions to conceal the symptoms. By the time he read the article, his condition was already in quite an advanced stage, and was beginning to affect his face.

As an insider, Ragsdale knew that King Lunalilo was serious about segregating lepers. At the beginning of 1873, there were scarcely 400 exiles, by June, there were more than 600. He knew that Prince Peter Kaeo had been detained as a leper in Honolulu a few days previously and so he had little chance of escaping detection. He preferred to give himself up and maintain his dignity. Consequently, he presented himself at the local sheriff's office and declared that he wished to show lepers their duty and fulfil a useful role on Molokai.

In Honolulu, Ragsdale's advanced stage of leprosy was confirmed by Dr Trousseau and he was exiled to Molokai. He offered to act for the Board of Health as its official investigator into social conditions in the settlement. He wanted to spend his time in the leper settlement as usefully as possible and promised to report everything he thought might be of use to the Board.

Ragsdale travelled to Molokai at his own expense along with Prince Peter Kaeo and so they did not have to share the cattle pens in which the other passengers were required to spend the voyage. When they found that Upa, the volcano guide who had once shown Damien the lava lake in Kilauea, was also on board, they invited him to join them.

When the new exiles arrived at the settlement, they were met by Jonathan Napela and shown to their new quarters. The next day, Napela told the new arrivals of an article by Dr Trousseau in the *Pacific Commercial Advertiser*. Trousseau refused to accept the status of the *kokuas*. Any healthy person who settled in the leper settlement would be declaring himself an exile. Napela, who was not affected by leprosy, accepted this and was not upset by it. He wondered whether Damien would accept this rule also.

The next day William Ragsdale went round from hut to hut to question people about how they had contracted leprosy and what the first symptoms had been. He would send the results of this research to Dr Trousseau. In this way, Ragsdale got to know the people and listened to their problems, which included the total absence of any medical care. He promised to press for an early visit by the doctor.

We Lepers . . .

Damien knew that the exiles found it hurtful that he never touched anyone or smoked the communal pipe. If he really wanted to win hearts, then he would have to risk infection. On 10 July he could no longer stand the situation and boarded the boat for Honolulu. This was a relief to the Board of Health, for it was one *kokua* fewer. On arrival, he asked Favens for 300 sets of clothes for the lepers and these were immediately granted. He also wanted to discuss something with his bishop, but first he wanted to arrange for his entry visa. This was refused, unless he was prepared to agree that he would never leave the leper settlement again. Damien explained to Edwin O. Hall, the chairman of the Board, that as a priest he was required to make his confession once a month, and he was already one month over the stipulated time. Hall did not accept this argument, and reported the conversation to a meeting a few days later. Damien was placing himself above the law and that was unacceptable.

Dr Trousseau took Damien's side, for he wanted to do something for the lepers. In all civilised countries, doctors and priests were excluded from segregation regulations. The privileges enjoyed by the medical personnel and the members of the Board of Health must also be given to clergy. Hall grasped this point but believed it would create a precedent. If Damien went on travelling in and out of the settlement, then the *kamaaina* would not accept being segregated, a mother would want to follow a child, lovers would want to stay together. If Damien really was a Christian hero, then he would accept segregation.

Damien raised the issue of marriages. On average, an exile lived about three to four years. In that period, people fell in love and some wanted to marry. Damien wanted to be able to perform marriages, if people wished it, but this was a problem for the Board. It would first be necessary to discover whether either of the partners had left a spouse behind. If so, then there would first have to be a divorce. Was all of this fuss really worth it? Hall thought that a marriage licence had never been issued to a leper hitherto, but did not exclude it for the future.

Damien discussed the situation with his superiors. If he returned to Molokai, it might be that he would have to remain there for the rest of his life. If he continued to avoid physical contact with the patients, he would never win their hearts. What point was there spending one's whole life in the leper settlement, if one did not achieve one's goal? He wanted to return and he wanted to risk his life. The superiors had to make a difficult decision: either they must send a priest off to his death, or they must destroy their image of the Christian hero. Damien continued to argue strongly and clearly for allowing himself to risk infection and his superiors agreed. He was permitted from now on to live as an Hawaiian but he must be allowed to enter and leave the settlement. The superiors thought that they would be able to win over the Board of Health.

Back in the leper settlement, Damien began his sermon with the words, 'We lepers . . .' The congregation looked astonished, for the priest seemed perfectly healthy. He explained that he was not sick in body, but in his heart, and that he felt like one of the exiles. Throughout the sermon, he used the Hawaiian pronoun which means 'we, everyone of us without exception' and not that which means 'we, a small group'.

That afternoon, he sat down with a group of pipe-smokers and, when his turn came, he took it. He went from hut to hut and ate with his fingers from the pot of *poi*. He visited every resident, adjusting his tone to the circumstances. With some, he spoke gently and tried to give them comfort, with others, he was a little tart, in order to get them to recognise their wretched situation, with yet others he threatened fire and brimstone, if they were not converted.

There was also a return to the daily routine of business matters. Once again, there had been a case of a body, that had been buried in too shallow a grave, being eaten by a pig. Damien made his proposal to Napela that the churchyard should be fenced in, but the Protestant deacon was opposed to the idea.

Everyone was opposed to the proposal by the Board to forbid horses in the settlement. This proposal had arisen because Ragsdale had reported to the Board that the horse droppings were causing a problem in the hospital grounds. If the horses could not graze there, however, there was no room for them, for there was not enough grass in the cow pasture. The settlement was already up in arms against Ragsdale, because he had written an article in the *Pacific Commercial Advertiser* in which he had declared that the exiles had better conditions than the plantation workers around Hilo. Since this was at the time that the exiles were having to eat rice instead of *poi*, his remarks were not appreciated, particularly when even the rice supplies began to run low.

Programme of Work: Nursing

Damien was happy. Now that he was truly sharing the way of life of the exiles, he was accepted. His church was full on 28 July while the overflow had to watch through the windows. In the evening, he held services for the sick in a number of houses in Kalawao, and these too were full. Then he set off for three meetings in Kalaupapa.

After two and a half months in the settlement, Damien had

decided there were four matters on which he wanted to take action. The most important of these was medical care. There was no cure for leprosy, but the patients suffered from all kinds of secondary infections – lice and tick infestations, scabies, lung infections, ulcerated sores, diarrhoea, coughs and so on. Only male nurses or nursing sisters could deal with these conditions, but there were none. Damien wrote to his general superior, 'If I had a dozen nursing sisters, they would be of the greatest service.'

He wanted to build an orphanage, because those children who were not accompanied were prey to pimps or were used as house-slaves. St Philomena's Church needed extension and he wanted to build another in Kalaupapa. If he could have a helper, he was prepared to do the work himself, because he enjoyed carpentry. Finally, he wanted a colleague. 'If I want to confess, I have to go to Honolulu, which is difficult for me, since I have no sea-legs. Sea-sickness weakens me very greatly. Moreover, I cannot cope with all the work, so that a second priest is absolutely necessary.'

The general decided to send a second priest. André Burgerman, who had worked in Tahiti and possibly had leprosy, very much wanted to work on Molokai.

The Water Supply

Damien took the view that the segregation regulations did not apply to him. The Board of Health must simply understand that it was his duty to serve as priest for the whole of Molokai. At the beginning of August 1873, just after a visit from Rudolph Meyer, he travelled with Joseph Manu for a tour of the north coast as far as Halawa. From there, he continued on foot to the south coast. He concentrated his attention on Kaluaaha, a little port where the Irish McCorriston family had a plantation. He stayed with them while preparing twenty-five candidates for baptism.

He was back in the leper settlement in the middle of August. He was pleased with the second-hand clothes that the sisters of the Sacred Hearts had sent him. The ones in better condition could be worn, the others could be used as bandages for the patients' sores. The Mother Superior, Sister Maria-Josepha, helped Damien in any way she could. She had raised the issue of the extension of St Philomena's with Princess Liliuokalani, who had spoken to Bishop Maigret about it. The princess was an important source of support for Damien.

The three-day visit by the Board member Sam Wilder, Dr Trousseau and the American journalist Charles Nordhoff was a farce. Dr Trousseau insisted on examining every patient; those who did not have leprosy might go home. He used the recently opened shop, run by Upa, the former guide to the volcano, as his consulting room. A crowd gathered outside. Inside the shop, one patient would come in and undress. Whilst Trousseau was examining him or her, the next patient was undressing and, the examination over, a third patient was putting his or her clothes on again. It was like an assembly line. Trousseau would stare at the man or woman and roar, 'Name?' He noted it down, looked briefly at the trembling body and pointed to a particular bottle. 'One tablet a day,' he cried, and then, 'Next! Name?' The patients who came out reported to the crowd on the thoroughness of the examination and they decided that the medicine would be just as useless this time as on previous occasions. Ragsdale refused to play the game, neither removing his clothes nor accepting the tablets.

Meanwhile, Sam Wilder was trying to come to an agreement with the *kamaaina*. If they promised to leave the leper settlement, then they could remain for three more years in Kalaupapa. The journalist said little, looked around, took notes and wandered around. The patients disliked this and believed him an American spy.

On the final day of the visit, Damien invited the three visitors, together with Napela, Ragsdale, Kaeo and one or two other senior people, to an alfresco lunch. He placed the patients together, separated by some flowers, from those who were healthy. He had borrowed crockery from Ragsdale and Napela, but he still did not have enough glasses, so he and Ragsdale drank red wine from a bowl.

Ragsdale continued to argue the urgent necessity of a water supply to the village. The small pipe currently proposed would not be adequate. Wilder gave his approval, on condition that Ragsdale supervise the work and that the labour be free.

In the end, Nordhoff did not write anything about Molokai in his series of articles, he wrote only about the other islands. If he had stayed, he would have been able to witness and describe a scandal, because the night after his departure, the patients got drunk and smashed the sterile medications that Trousseau had given them against the rocks on the beach.

When the pipes arrived a few days later, Ragsdale summoned all the men who were able to work, including *kokuas*, to come and move them. Only a few volunteers turned up, so Ragsdale sent them away to tell their friends that a cargo of *pai-ai* had finally arrived and that only those who had worked would receive their ration. The workers thought this was unfair. Sam Wilder had promised them food and clothing and now they were required to work for it. Dragging pipes and digging a trench were not tasks for sick people.

Ragsdale ordered them to work and, in his anger, picked up a stone and was about to throw it, but he saw them all do the same and was obliged to walk away. The workers idled about by the stream, until Peter Kaeo rode up, accompanied by Damien, the Protestant preacher Holokahiki and Napela, who was a Mormon elder. Peter Kaeo ordered them to work, and they began because of the promise that those *kokuas* who worked would be given a permit to stay.

One reason for the unco-operative attitude among the patients was the shortage of food. There was not only a shortage of the staple *pai-ai*, but also a lack of fresh meat. The sea was too rough to bring in beasts by water and it was difficult to drive them over the cliffs. Within the settlement itself, the pressure on space, caused by the constant increase in the number of victims and, in consequence, the size of the graveyard, meant that there was less and less land available for pasture but more and more mouths to feed. At times, tinned salmon became the only source of protein.

Damien Segregated (September 1873)

In the midst of all this, Damien received a letter from the Board of Health that was like a bolt from the blue. The deputy sheriff of Molokai, E. H. Rogers, had lodged an official complaint against Damien with Edwin Hall. He did so because he, in turn, had received a complaint against the Catholic priest from the *kamaaina*, who had been required to sell their property in Kalaupapa. Rogers knew it was the second time that Damien had broken the segregation regulations.

Hall ordered his secretary to send Damien a firm, formal letter on Ministry of Interior notepaper. Damien was informed that it had been decided, at the last meeting of the Board of Health, that he must leave the settlement. 'The local population, whose houses were bought by the Board to house the patients in the leper settlement, had lodged a complaint because they were no longer permitted to visit their former home and friends, a privilege that others did seem to possess.' Damien had disobeyed the official announcements of the Board of Health, published on 10 February and 16 June, for only agents of the Board were permitted freely to enter and leave the settlement, in order to bring supplies or for administrative purposes. Damien should not consider himself the special target of these restrictions, for, 'All members of the clergy who have submitted a request to visit the settlement have been refused permission, and when they heard the reasons, they accepted completely and without resentment the Board's decision.'

When Damien had left the settlement without permission he had expected problems, but he had not thought the Board would go so far. Depressed and angry, he opened a second letter, this one from Pamphile. It did not contain cheering news. His sister, Pauline, had died of a lung infection on 14 July in the convent in Uden in the Netherlands.

What was left of the dreams of their youth? The three of them had been going to work together, but now Pauline was dead, he was imprisoned and Pamphile was teaching in Leuven. Damien wept.

Damien was depressed, but more serious was the rebellion

that had almost broken out at Upa's shop. The cargo of *pai-ai* that Joseph Manu had brought had gone in one day. There were no further supplies. He had no meat either, and could give people only salmon and rice. People had come to the end of their tether and an angry crowd gathered in front of the shop. A man threw a stone and Upa quickly shut the door and closed the shutters. The crowd tried to break the door down but was dispersed by the police using batons.

A few days later, the Hawaiian Royal Guard in Honolulu rebelled against its Hungarian sergeant-major. The soldiers barricaded themselves in their barracks. After a week of negotiations, the king disbanded the guard. The 'Barrack-room War' was over, but the country no longer had an army.

Aubert Bouillon took advantage of the fact that all eyes were on events in Honolulu to pay an illegal visit to Damien on 1 October. He had already requested official permission to visit his colleague and hear his confession, but he had been refused. Now he had a pretext. A French seaman, who had not been to church in forty years, was dying on the south shore of Molokai and asked for the last rites. Damien was not allowed to go and so Bouillon did. He sat with the man for a while, talking about their homeland, and at dusk he set off, no longer dressed as a priest, but as a *pianolo*. He wore a red bandana under the seaman's straw hat and also wore one of his shirts. He rode to Kalae, the village where Rudolph Meyer lived, and went to one of his Mexican foremen, who knew about the plan and had agreed to show him the way.

He crawled down the cliff-side and made his way to the presbytery, where he woke Damien and they spent the rest of the night talking. The next day, Damien went about his work as usual, but returned home from time to time and, contrary to his custom, kept the door shut during his mealtime. Bouillon told him that his successor in Kohala was a German called Fabien. The superiors had decided that Damien could remain in Kalawao if he wished, but he was not obliged to do so, as they did not want to force anyone to make sacrifices. Bouillon heard Damien's confession and then slipped away over the cliff by moonlight. He slept the night at the Mexican's house and his return journey went unnoticed.

Consequently, Bouillon was amazed when the sheriff of Lahaina, on the island of Maui, charged him with paying an illegal visit to the leper settlement. He wondered who had given him away. It was simple: there had been a hundred and one small pieces of evidence that had betrayed his presence. At first, Bouillon avoided giving an answer but then he snapped that he knew the law, but it was his duty to visit a fellow-priest. It was his sacred duty to place God's law above that of men. This charge was, once again, Catholic persecution. The sheriff had difficulty keeping his temper. He pointed out that a pastor had also been refused entry to the settlement and the law applied to everyone, but it made no difference. Bouillon's stunt was known throughout Molokai and it gave a bad impression.

Later the same month, Favens visited Bouillon in Lahaina and they discussed the situation. The provincial decided to take the *Kilauea* next time it was going to Kalaupapa. Once there, he asked the captain to let him go ashore for a short while – after all a brief confession was better than nothing. The captain flatly refused and Favens could do no more than stand on the deck staring at the island in the pouring rain.

The sailors put out a sloop to the shore and the lepers moored it. As they were at their work, the sailors told the exiles about Favens. They were sorry for him, for he looked exhausted, perplexed and sad. The lepers called to one of the *pianolos* who had come down the mountain, to go and fetch Damien, and it was not long before the latter galloped up. He sprang from his horse and ran to the sloop. He knew that what he was planning to do was dangerous. On the deck, roaring bulls were tethered, lowered into the sea and attached to a sloop: an equal number on each side for balance. The beasts were in a frenzy, they kicked and twisted. When they touched bottom, the sailors unfastened the tether, so that the *pianolos* could drive them ashore. Sometimes one of the beasts would break loose and drag the sloop out of control in its terror.

Damien knew this, but he still rowed out to the steamboat. He asked the captain to be allowed to come aboard, since he was not ill, but he was refused. Favens leaned over the railings and asked how he was. Damien shouted that he was all right. Favens was angry and distressed. Damien asked to be allowed to make his confession anyway. Favens thought of the bystanders, but if they spoke French, very few of them, perhaps no one, would understand. Favens listened to Damien's confession and gave him his blessing and then Damien rowed back to shore and sat watching until the *Kilauea* had sailed away.

Everyone on board had been moved by what had happened, including the captain, who had been forced to refuse to let Damien on board. Back in Honolulu, Favens protested strongly against Damien's treatment. It was not persecution of the priest, however, for a few days later, Princess Liliuokalani was likewise refused permission to land at the settlement.

Action Against Illegal Distilleries

From October onwards, the death rate continued to rise. Damien found himself rushing from one hut to another, and, especially, to the 'dying-shed'. It upset him that during this period of high mortality the clatter of the *uliuli*-gourds could be heard ever more frequently. Kalamaia, a dangerous *kahuna ana ana* who performed black magic, had been deported there and was breathing new life into the local beliefs and customs. When Damien heard the *hoela*-drums, he would take up a heavy stick that he often carried and make his way in the direction of the noise. The revellers always chose a hut with two doors. Damien knew that if he broke down the front door, they would be able to escape via the back. He did not wish to fight, just to destroy the drink, so he would stand blocking the doorway, waiting until the last staggering drunkard had disappeared. Then, he would destroy the bottles and gourds with his heavy stick. When he was finished, he would rush to the back door, shouting, '*Poe keiki kolohe!*' ('Naughty children!').

When he found a distillery, he acted more cautiously. He would study the system, which was always both ingenious and simple. Sometimes, he would burn a sample of the liquor, in order to be sure that it was the highly intoxicating *okelehao*.

Damien's raids ultimately had little effect, because the revellers set up look-outs, to warn of his approach, and when he arrived he would find the hut empty.

Food Shortages and Riots

In October, William Ragsdale took over from Jonathan Napela as superintendent of the leper settlement. He was not popular with the people, who considered him a pawn of the Board of Health. However, Napela had been removed by Sam Wilder because he was not prepared to administer the new system of paying the patients a benefit cheque, which they could then spend in the shop, rather than giving them payment in kind. Napela also disliked the fact that those who had been in the settlement longer than six months were to receive more than those who had recently arrived. The new system also meant that the patients would have to pay prices for the goods which included the transport costs to Molokai.

Damien was supposed to receive the cheques for those Catholic patients too sick to collect them themselves. On the first occasion, however, they went missing and this caused a certain amount of scandal, with accusation and counter-accusation. The Board of Health agreed to provide Damien with new cheques, however.

The cheques made no difference to the shortage of food, and morale was low, despite the festivities that Damien had organised around the consecration of a new chapel in Kalaupapa on 1 November.

That evening, alone in his presbytery, Damien had had enough. How long would his segregation continue? How could he confess? Why were the journalists allowed to visit the leper settlement but not a priest? Tired and depressed, he wrote to the newly appointed French consul, Théo Ballieu, to express his frustration.

Bishop Maigret shared his feelings. He ought to have consecrated the church and been with his priest. This was too much. He went to the Board and demanded an explanation as

to why Damien was not allowed an exit and entry permit.
Chairman Edwin O. Hall gave him a copy of the letter Damien
had received in September. There was no question of persecution. This was a health measure and no exceptions could be
permitted.

Ballieu found sufficient grounds in Damien's letter to lodge
a complaint with Charles Bishop, the minister of Foreign Affairs.
He used the strongest language permitted to a diplomat.

> Never, in any country – even were it only half-civilised –
> were clergy – whatever their faith – hindered in their activities
> on the battlefield, nor were doctors – whatever their
> nationality – interfered with. Molokai is a battlefield, where
> the champions of magnanimity are few. It is well known that
> certain persons are permitted to enter the leper settlement,
> whilst others visit it from time to time on official business.
> Father Damien has a task and he is right because his cause is
> a noble one. He is not asking for exclusive privileges which
> should not be granted to the Protestant missionaries, whether
> American or European, who had shown as much courage as
> he, but he ought not to be hindered in his communication
> with his congregation.

Charles Bishop was married to Princess Bernice. He was more
of a banker than a politician, but he was not inclined to cross
the French consul. He was an advocate of Hawaii's becoming
part of the United States, but he certainly had no wish to
antagonise the European powers. He approached the Board of
Health and asked them for an explanation of the consul's
complaints. He reminded Hall that many Hawaiians, including
his own wife and Princess Liliuokalani, supported Damien's
work. Hall recognised that there was a political difficulty and
called an emergency meeting of the Board, which agreed that
all priests, pastors and other religious leaders should be granted
free movement in and out of the leper settlement.

Hall's main worry was that this decision might arouse feeling
against him among the exiles. He had just heard from Rudolph
Meyer that there were severe problems with food supplies. The

Board was continuing to deliver the same amount of *poi*, even though there were many more patients. The law of supply and demand was not functioning.

It was raining in Kalawao and there was a chill wind. For two weeks, the exiles had had nothing but salmon and rice to eat. When two relatively healthy men died, their friends began to complain that they had been starved to death. They gathered in front of Ragsdale's house, demanding *poi*.

On 15 November, a schooner dropped anchor in Kalawao bay. Everyone was delighted because there was a cargo of *pai-ai* on board. That Saturday evening, only the post was brought ashore. The following morning, everyone was on the beach, waiting to land the cargo, but Ragsdale, who had just converted to Catholicism, decided that no work could be done on Sunday. Unfortunately, during the following night, the wind got up again to storm force and before morning, the schooner had upped anchor and sailed away.

This caused huge resentment and anger among the exiles against Ragsdale. Armed with staves, they made their way to the shop, where Ragsdale was, yelling, 'We want *poi*!'

'Eat rice!' Ragsdale thundered in reply, and shut the door.

This was the signal for a wave of anger to sweep through the crowd. 'Down with Ragsdale!' they shouted. 'Lynch him! Bill is starving us!'

The police tried to form a cordon, but the crowd was in a frenzy. Damien heard the uproar and came rushing up. He elbowed his way to the front of the crowd and started yelling, in his turn, 'Aren't you all ashamed of yourselves? No one could have foreseen this bad weather. We're stuck here, let's make the best of it. As soon as I get an exit permit, I'll go to Honolulu and argue our case in person.'

The crowd dispersed, since there was no point remaining. Nevertheless, despite the fact that the riot was over, Ragsdale had the leaders arrested. This caused a further uprising, when the friends of the prisoners tried to free them and were in turn themselves arrested. Ragsdale wanted to send them all to Honolulu for trial, but the Board refused permission. Lepers were not allowed to leave Molokai.

The matter did not end there, however. A week later there was yet another disturbance about food. This time, Peter Kaeo gave Ragsdale a talking to: he must be more diplomatic in his approach. Ragsdale did not know how he was to do that, since the Board was demanding that he force the exiles to eat rice, salmon and bread, which were cheaper than *poi* and beef. In one year, the number of exiles had doubled. Feeding 800 people was an expensive business. When the exiles learned about this, they immediately sent a petition to the Board. Because they knew that this would make little impression, they also sent a letter of complaint to King Lunalilo. Their only hope really lay with the minister of Foreign Affairs, Charles Bishop, and so they approached him also.

These efforts met with little success. The Board discussed the matter, but had no money. The problem was a nuisance to them and so they put the blame on Ragsdale, who, they indicated, was handling the situation badly. The superintendent was furious, since he was not responsible for formulating the policy. Equally, powerless to tackle the cause of the problem, he, in turn, picked on scapegoats within his reach and threatened the four men who had written to the Board with exclusion from the ration list. This was too much for them and, feeling they had nothing to lose, they wrote to the Board again, asking them to remove Ragsdale from his post.

Sam Wilder arranged an urgent trip to the settlement and Ragsdale succeeded in taking him on a day-long tour without coming across a single patient. On the way, he offered a feeble explanation of what had occurred. Napela was the root cause of the discontent. When he was superintendent, he had favoured the Mormons – they were given everything and lived like lords. Ragsdale treated everyone equally. Wilder should look carefully at the petition: all 200 signatories were Mormons. Dr Trousseau was meanwhile examining all the patients who had complained of inadequate nutrition, but he found little evidence of poor nutrition. In his view it was not a question of hunger, but of taste.

The next day, the wind finally dropped and a schooner was able to land a cargo of *pai-ai*. Each exile received a substantial portion and full bellies brought an end to the uprising.

The 'Liberation' Contested

Damien did not tell his parents about the food riots. He could see from their letters that they were worried and he wanted to set their minds at rest. He asked a lot of questions about the family and its activities. He himself was still in the leper settlement, but they were not to worry, he went horse-riding a great deal. It was true that he could not leave, for when he wrote on 25 November he had not yet received the news of his exit permit. He had two churches – one of which he had built himself – and he lived in a small wooden house. He had a man who cooked meat and rice for him, made bread and fetched milk and he had his freshly brewed cup of coffee every day. He was just the same as when he left, a little older, but neither fatter nor thinner, still wearing glasses. There were funerals every day and he made the coffins himself. The nuns sent him lots of clothes.

To Pamphile he sent a longer, more open letter, in French. In eight years, some two thousand lepers had been sent into exile, of whom around eight hundred were still alive. 'Since all communication was strictly forbidden unless I permitted myself to be shut up – I, who have already lain beneath a pall on the day I made my vows – I considered it my duty to offer myself to Monseigneur, who did not have the cruelty to demand such a sacrifice.' He told briefly about his arrival, the nights under the pandan tree, the benefactions of the whites in Honolulu, and then he described his attitude to the disease. 'Although I do not yet have leprosy and, with the miraculous aid of the good Lord and the Holy Virgin, will hopefully never get it, I am "become" a leper among the lepers. When I preach, I say, for my part, "We lepers . . .".' He described the disease, the patches, the sores, the stench, and admitted, 'I find it very difficult to get used to it. One day during high mass, I was on the point of leaving the altar, gasping for fresh air.' He was used to it now and hardly noticed it, only sometimes when he was hearing confessions he had to hold his nose. Applying the holy oil was a problem, as well, because sometimes he did not know where to anoint the dying, their bodies were one open sore. There was no doctor in residence for the 800 patients. That was not so bad, since medical science was powerless to help, anyway. There were four or five funerals a week; some had coffins, others were simply wrapped in a sheet.

The letter ended on a cheerful note, for he had just heard from the French consul of his 'liberation'. Fr Theodore Lauter, who worked on Maui Island, organised a visit straight away, so that Damien could make his confession properly. Damien applied to Meyer for an exit visa and was given it. However, the manager did insist on waiting until he had received official written confirmation of their decision from the Board, which arrived on 12 December.

Many people were pleased for Damien, because now he could go and plead their cause in Honolulu, but not everyone supported him. The Hawaiian pastor, S. N. Holokahiki, lodged an official complaint against Damien on Christmas Day because, three days before, the latter had approved a woman's decision to have her dying husband secretly baptised a Catholic. The whole affair was a nuisance, because the Protestants had already dug a grave in their churchyard and all the preparations had been made for the service, but the funeral cortège passed the chapel and made its way to the Catholic church. The pastor demanded that Damien be removed from the settlement, where he had no right of residence.

Your correspondent believes that the permanent residence of the Catholic teacher is unlawful and advises those to whom this is addressed to consider the question carefully, to recall that the law forbids contact between lepers and non-lepers and to conclude that the permanent residence of the Catholic teacher is unlawful. Your correspondent recommends that the Catholics replace the aforesaid Catholic teacher by a Catholic priest who is also a leper, and further recommends that it would be better if a native Hawaiian of that faith were ordained priest in order to support members of the Catholic faith in their religion.

The Board ignored the letter. Hall had expected such reactions after the politically motivated decision to release Damien. The letter was a shrewd move, however, for the Catholics did not have a priest who was suffering from leprosy and at that time there were no Hawaiians admitted to a seminary.

Holokahiki continued his campaign against Damien. On 3 January, he protested against the appointment of Hupai as schoolmaster. Hupai had been supported by the inspector-general, son of a pastor called Hitchcock, but also by Damien. Holokahiki also complained that whenever Meyer visited the settlement, he always stopped by at the presbytery to drink a cup of coffee or a glass of water, but that he never called on the pastor. A few weeks later, there was another complaint. This time Holokahiki alleged that Damien was helping a woman *kokua*, married to a Catholic leper, to hide. Ragsdale had ejected her from the settlement in November, but now she was back again and had taken sanctuary in St Philomena's Church and was refusing to leave. In fact, she had contracted leprosy and could not be removed from the settlement, but Holokahiki's complaint against Damien's violation of the rules was added to the pile of others with which the deacons bombarded the Board.

Two Priests Vie for the Leper Settlement (February 1874–August 1877)

A Troublesome Colleague

The year 1874 began with a succession struggle in Hawaii. King Lunalilo had died on 3 February, after a reign of only one year, without leaving a direct or a nominated heir. There were four possible candidates. The king's sister, Ruth, indicated that she was not interested in the throne. Princess Bernice also declined because she feared it would bring her into conflict with her husband, the American Charles Bishop, who was in favour of annexation to the United States.

David Kalakaua was once again a candidate for the succession. His campaign centred principally on the issue of Pearl Harbour, which he did not wish to fall into American hands. His strongest card with the white population was his sister, Princess Liliuokalani, who was married to the American governor of Oahu Island, John O. Dominis.

Finally, Queen Emma, widow of King Kamehameha IV, emerged as a candidate. She did not have any clearly defined programme, but called herself the 'mother of the nation' and had the full backing of the Anglican Church. She also received some unofficial support in Catholic quarters, being allowed to use the Catholic printing press for her publications.

Damien heard about the succession struggle during a tour of 'topside' on Molokai. On 3 February, the Dutch Sacred Hearts father, André Burgerman, had landed in Kaunakakai.

Burgerman had been appointed to serve the area of Molokai outside the leper settlement and, when necessary, to give assistance inside the settlement as well. Burgerman had protested strongly against this arrangement, with firm support from Léonor Fouesnel, because the Dutchman had studied medicine for several years. Emboldened by Fouesnel's support, Burgerman set terms. He wanted to have the leper settlement and thought that he should immediately be appointed superior, because he was eleven years older than Damien. At forty-five, he had more experience than Damien, but he had not been a missionary any longer. Until 1863, he had been a teacher in various colleges of the Sacred Hearts Order in France. Monseigneur Jaussen, the Bishop of Tahiti, had chosen him to work in the mission, but after eight years he had developed a form of elephantiasis but which was feared to be leprosy. He went first to Chile and then France, where his colleagues found his dominant personality difficult to deal with. Because Bishop Maigret was asking for people and Damien, in particular, wanted an assistant, the general had thought it a good idea to send out Burgerman. If he did have leprosy, then it would be best if he worked in the leper settlement, particularly since he had some medical knowledge and he and Damien were both Dutch speakers.

From the start, Damien found Burgerman difficult to get on with. He showed absolutely no interest in 'topside', and when he arrived in the leper settlement on 12 February, he showed no disposition to leave. He wrung all the information about the settlement he could from Damien and others.

On 20 February, Damien was summoned to Honolulu by the new King Kalakaua, who wanted him to be present at the high mass to be sung in Dutch on the following Sunday. Burgerman could take over the settlement during Damien's absence.

The election of the new monarch had taken place on 12 February, and had resulted in an overwhelming victory for Kalakaua over the Queen dowager Emma. However, the supporters of Queen Emma rioted when they heard the news, killing one man, injuring many others and breaking into and pillaging the law courts. Order was only finally restored with the aid of British and American troops, called in from their warships in Pearl Harbour.

Royal Audience

Once his succession was established, Kalakaua quickly took several fundamental decisions. He nominated his younger brother as his heir. The young man was an Anglican but he had been educated in the Catholic College of San Mateo in California. The members of his Cabinet tended to be liberal and some of them had a reputation as freethinkers. The king promised to do everything he could to prevent the Hawaiian people dying out.

On his first Sunday in office, the king attended a Congregational service, and then he sent word to Bishop Maigret that he would be present at high mass in the Catholic cathedral the following Sunday. He also wanted to meet Fr Damien.

When Damien arrived in Honolulu, Fr Hermann Köckemann congratulated him on the fact that the new minister of the Interior, Hermann Widemann, was a Catholic. This was indeed good news, for the minister automatically became chairman of the Board of Health. This would ease Damien's situation on Molokai, where, in any case, he was making large numbers of converts. Damien was concerned that colleagues might become jealous.

Damien preached the sermon at the high mass attended by the king and his entourage. Afterwards, Maigret accompanied the visitors to the Mission House for a short reception. The royal party could not stay long because they had other official engagements. However the king was anxious to speak to Damien at length about conditions in the leper settlement. This proved impossible, however, because Köckemann and his choir performed for the assembled company and took so long that there was no further time. As he left, the king asked Bishop Maigret, the provincial superior, Modeste Favens, and Damien to come and see him at the palace the following day.

The king had a request: he wanted Bishop Maigret to anoint him king. The bishop, however, was obliged to refuse, unless the king converted to Catholicism. The king said nothing, but was clearly disappointed. He then turned to Damien and again asked him for a detailed account of the leper settlement. Damien ran through all the problems: clothing, food supplies, housing, emotional problems connected with confinement, the tensions among the various religious sects, the rough seas. The king listened attentively and interrupted him rarely, and when he did so, it was to ask for a more detailed explanation concerning the amount of meat or the number of deaths. Finally, the king asked Damien if he had any particular wish. Damien's one wish at this point was to be able to solemnise marriages. The people were in principle permitted to lead a normal life, and marriage was part of that. The king agreed to give immediate orders for the priest to be granted these powers, and the minister of the Interior signed the order that very afternoon. The king also had a request: Damien must report to him anything that went wrong in the settlement and anything he needed. He wanted to keep in touch.

After the audience, Damien did some shopping in the town before taking the night boat. When he arrived in Kalaupapa, he bumped into Sam Wilder, who had just completed an inspection of the settlement. Wilder informed him briefly that he should not listen to Peter Kaeo and Jonathan Napela in future. They were supporters of Queen Emma and had stirred up a lot of ill-feeling among the exiles. Ragsdale was not doing so badly. At his request, the weekly ration had been increased to a pound of rice and a pound of meat. *Poi* was out of the question, as the stocks on the islands were still simply too low.

Damien was pleased. He could solemnise marriages and he would that day be able to give this news to couples wishing to marry, and everyone was going to get more to eat. When he arrived at the presbytery he told Burgerman the news, but the latter was not impressed. He had been thinking things over while Damien had been gone. Chapels were needed on 'topside' and Damien was good at carpentry, so he could busy himself with that and Burgerman would deal with the settlement while he was at it. Damien angrily declared that Burgerman should first learn Hawaiian and then would be time enough for discussion.

Burgerman, however, took up his case with the provincial superior in Honolulu. He wanted a church in Kaluaaha, and he had something fairly substantial in mind. Damien immediately realised that such plans would let him in for a long job and felt that he could not cope. Nervously, he wrote to Favens, 'He knows as well as I that I have hardly any time and may not even be capable of doing the work properly. I urge you, therefore, once again, to send him one or two of the brothers.' Of course, if Favens continued to insist, then he would obey and he admitted, 'It is not that I do not like the work. On the contrary, I enjoy building chapels, but I enjoy converting my poor lepers much more.'

Favens asked Léonor Fouesnel, who was now in Honolulu supervising the rebuilding of the cathedral and was supportive of Burgerman, whether he could spare one or two brothers for a month or two. Fouesnel declared that it was out of the question, however.

Damien a Church Builder

Burgerman left the leper settlement on this occasion with a light tread, since he felt confident that he would soon be able to take over there, once building work began in Kaluaaha. If he was demanding, then the building work would take a long time and he would be able to establish himself in the settlement. If necessary, he might be able to have several churches built. After two weeks, however, he became impatient. It could take another month for the wood to arrive. He devised another plan. He sent a message to Damien that sounded like a cry for help. He still could not understand the Hawaiians and he needed help preparing the congregation for Easter. Would Damien come and help him hear confessions?

No sooner had Damien arrived on 30 March 1874, than Burgerman thrust a letter from the provincial superior, with instructions concerning the construction of the church, into his hand, and rode off to the leper settlement.

After six weeks on Molokai, he now hoped to be able to establish himself definitively in the leper settlement. He had a plan for achieving this. He started producing home-made remedies and handing them out to the patients. He washed and attended to sores and gave medical advice, and when Sam Wilder asked him what he was doing in the settlement, he boasted that the death rate had dropped to one or two a week since his arrival, whereas when Damien was there, it had been many per day.

The Board of Health was impressed by the results, until Dr Trousseau began to analyse the figures. Damien had been working through a particularly cold winter, when there had been a food shortage. The death rate always declined significantly when the warmer, drier season arrived. In any case, it was not clear whether Burgerman's figures were correct.

The superiors did not have this information and they began to wonder whether Burgerman were not more suitable to work in the settlement. They made no haste to provide wood.

Damien visited all the communities on 'topside' and on 17 April he was in Kalae, where Meyer lived. He decided to ride to the *pali* and he came across a group of horsemen there, who turned out to be the king accompanied by other members of the royal family and members of the Board of Health, including the chairman, Widemann. The king was surprised, concerned even, that Damien was not in the settlement. Widemann explained Damien's temporary commission. Priests were vowed to obedience, after all. Trousseau added that he would prefer to have Damien at Kalaupapa. Burgerman was a quack and he did not approve of it. The king made clear that he wanted Damien to return to the settlement. He had visited it, seen the despair and promised the people help. He then rode on.

A few days later, the wood arrived and Damien could at least start work. He had personal problems as well, but he kept silent about them. He had received a long letter from Pamphile with family news. Their ageing father's health was failing and, among other matters, Pamphile wrote that it was necessary to deal with the family inheritance. When Pamphile had discussed the matter with the Leuven superior he had been shocked to find that Damien had not left the Order power of attorney, as was the custom, before his hasty departure. Damien would have to discuss the matter with Favens. It would be quite a lot of work. Pamphile also announced proudly that he had sent one of Damien's letters to a German missionary journal with 17,000 readers and they were going to publish it.

Damien had shown himself ill-disposed toward Burgerman by missing the first Corpus Christi procession to be held in the settlement. When he informed Favens of the problem concerning his inheritance, the news was badly received and the whole of the mission in Honolulu spoke negatively about the carpenter priest. Burgerman was so much better: he at least had organised a fine procession and he was baptising people by the dozen. Damien, on the other hand, spent his time writing self-important letters to Europe, as all the members of the congregation in Honolulu now knew, since the letter had been published in the Order's magazine, *Les Annales*, and had been read out during the midday meal. Fouesnel, in particular, who greatly disliked Damien, could not stand so much conceit. Damien went on as though he had done everything himself. The mission had made great sacrifices, but Damien did not say a word about that. Fouesnel reported to the general with satisfaction that the bishop was shocked and that Favens had given Damien a stiff talking-to, 'which will stem his enthusiasm for writing down everything that into his empty head' (sic). As far as he, Fouesnel, was concerned, Damien could build his churches by himself. He would be given no help – in any case, he seemed to be good at carpentry.

Damien defended himself. 'As far as my published letters are concerned, I am extremely surprised. I did not write them with that intention.' He even proposed not to write any more. The church in Kaluaaha was almost finished and he was hoping, after a short visit to Honolulu, to be able to take a few days off with Fr Bouillon, before returning to the settlement. The news that he was almost finished was a signal to make more demands, however, and he was still in Kaluaaha for Burgerman in the middle of July.

Good news arrived from the king, however. He had made a donation of $250 to the leper settlement. He had also attended a meeting of the Board of Health and demanded that a treatment for leprosy should be sought. If there were any doctors who had any drugs, then they should be invited to the islands. There seemed to be two possibilities: Sing Akana, a Chinese herbal practitioner, and William O. Powell, an Afro-American doctor, who, it was rumoured, had cured people in New York. Dr Trousseau accompanied them both to Kalawao on 21 June.

Damien heard about the visit in Kaluaaha, where he was still at work at the end of July. The bishop had ordered him to repair the old house there. His letter to Favens was a long shopping list of materials he required. He wrote no more about the settlement, about which he knew nothing, except what he heard from parishioners. His only remaining hope was that he would be allowed to return to his parish after the consecration of the new church, which was initially set for 15 August. In fact, the ceremony was put back until 19 August, because that was the first occasion on which Fouesnel was free. The bishop refused to go himself. He still could not stomach Damien's arrogance, thanks to Fouesnel's constant gibes, although the official reason given for his absence was infirmity. Damien was disappointed and one part of his mind had hoped that the bishop, whom he idolised, would reconsider. Maigret had not asked Fouesnel to consecrate the new church, at any rate – that honour went to Bouillon.

Burgerman hoped to engage Fouesnel in his cause in the war for the settlement, which had only just begun. On the evening of the consecration festivities, he took the pompous priest aside and briefed him about the real state of affairs in the settlement. According to him, Damien had not made anything like the impression on the exiles that everyone imagined. Fouesnel should keep his eyes open – not all the inmates even knew the Fleming.

Fouesnel followed Damien during the descent of the *pali*. The older, heavily built man had no trouble keeping going. Ragsdale was waiting for Damien at the end of the path. He greeted him enthusiastically, but was blind drunk. Drunkenness formed unstable friendships, in Fouesnel's view. The other man, William Charles Crowningburg, who was also drunk, did not know Damien at all. Of course, what Fouesnel did not know was that this half-Hawaiian had landed as an exile only that morning. In the presbytery, Fouesnel went over to his own former parishioners, but he only took aside those who had just arrived. Damien had not been in Kalawao for four months and so could not know these newcomers. Fouesnel sounded them out about Burgerman. They were all in favour of the doctor-priest, because he gave them pills. They did not know Damien. After a few hours, Fouesnel concluded that Damien was not at all popular. The man had created his own mythology.

Back in the Leper Settlement

The parishioners kept their distance from Damien for the first few days. He had introduced himself and used the expression 'We lepers . . .', but he had left them for four months. After a few days, one or two of the congregation started to turn up to perform the stations of the cross, possibly from their own religious conviction, rather than for Damien. He asked the bishop's permission to celebrate mass twice a day. Burgerman had been given this privilege and it could be transferred to him, but he received no reply. However, he did receive word from Burgerman to say that it was urgently necessary to build a church in Kaunakakai and that Damien must order materials.

Damien had no one to talk to except Meyer. It was true that Kaunakakai had no chapel, so ought he go away again? Was another week in his parish all that remained? Meyer recalled an empty barn that could easily be transformed into a chapel, and it was a building with symbolic significance, because Catholics had been chained up in it during the period of persecution. Meyer promised to broach the matter with the bishop. He was not motivated by sympathy for Damien but by concern that Burgerman was a troublemaker. He was constantly having to intervene in quarrels between Burgerman and Ragsdale, or Napela or Trousseau. Burgerman's 'quackery' was also getting to be a problem. Meyer advised Damien to stay and persevere, because he had an important ally in the king.

Damien and Meyer discussed the situation and other topics in the Order's Hawaiian Mission. It was clear that there was a power struggle in Honolulu. Favens was old and his mind was beginning to wander; Maigret, too, was no longer young. The new generation was waiting impatiently in the wings. All the candidates were gathered in the Mission House: choirmaster Hermann Köckemann, a timid, scholarly recluse; the pompous Fouesnel, a man of the world, who was said to be considering leaving the congregation, and finally, the embittered conservative Régis Moncany, who was rumoured to be suffering from tuberculosis. Burgerman got on well with these pretenders to office and had spent two months living with them.

Moncany seemed to be the favourite to succeed Favens and he was already beginning to act as vice-provincial. He was concerned because several missionaries had skin diseases that could be a sign of leprosy. Since leprosy was thought to be the fourth stage in the development of syphilis, this would cause a scandal. Grégoire Archambaux, who worked in Lahaina on Maui Island, certainly had leprosy. Officially, Burgerman was diagnosed as having elephantiasis, but it could possibly be leprosy. Damien seemed to be healthy, but he himself had his doubts. He did not tell his superiors that his feet often felt burning hot, so that he could not keep them under the blankets. It was an unpleasant sensation that made him irritable. Perhaps it was the first sign of leprosy.

There was no cure. Damien got to know the Chinese doctor Sing Akana. He had selected five patients, including Ragsdale and Peter Kaeo, on whom to test his remedy. They received a few drops of his expensive mixture at intervals and were required to follow a strict diet: no beef or chicken, no fish with large shells and no duck. Some aspects of the treatment were easy enough: chicken was not available, so you could avoid eating it. The treatment failed and the blame was placed on the failure of the patients who were trying it out to stick to their diet. Those who were not being given the mixture kept watch on the doctor and, by combining all the information they were able to gather, concluded that the medicament was made up of tortoiseshell, saffron powder, some kind of dried flower and one or two kinds of leaf plus bark.

When Ragsdale swore to it that he was feeling better and Peter Kaeo started to talk about being cured, people began to hunt for the ingredients with raised hopes. Ragsdale was certainly calmer and directed the works on the quay at Kalaupapa seriously and patiently. These works were important, because if the quay walls were strong enough, then food supplies could be unloaded, even in bad weather. Unfortunately, as soon as the cold season began, the five patients involved in the test began to deteriorate rapidly. It was clear that Akana had failed. Those who had not received the treatment now turned against him and alleged that it was centipedes, snake skins and cockroaches that he was grinding down in his mortar.

The first of the winter storms gusted its way over Molokai at the end of October. Showers of heavy rain alternated with sunny periods, but the wind was constant. There was general sympathy for the king and queen who had just boarded the USS *Bernicia* on their way, via San Francisco, to Washington where they would have discussions with the American government and Congress about a bilateral accord. They were in for a rough voyage.

On 17 November 1874, the settlement was hit by a very heavy storm. The wind tore pieces of wood from the buildings and uprooted trees, the rain bucketed down and the sea pounded the shore. On the first day of the storm, five houses were destroyed and the inhabitants took refuge in the school. During the evening, the wind turned from the south to the west and increased to hurricane force. Damien was called out to give the last rites to a man. He rode through the driving rain and when he had tied up his horse, put his oilskin over the saddle. When he came back out of the hut, however, both oilskin and saddle had disappeared. Horse and man struggled against the wind until they both arrived back, drenched, at the presbytery. The storm died down for a while on the afternoon of the third day, but then got up again and only finally blew itself out in the course of the night.

Only then was it possible to assess the extent of the damage. Twenty-five dwellings had been destroyed and fifty were so seriously damaged that they would have to be pulled down, the only thing left being some of the wood. Trees that had been planted as windbreaks were down and papaya trees had been uprooted. The first estimate was that the damage amounted to at least $5,000.

Damien had kept silence until 22 November, but the situation was too serious and he wrote to his superiors, begging assistance. He began with a list of Catholics who had died and added a list of the wood that he urgently needed. He also asked for hop shoots, so that he could brew beer for himself and William Crowningburg. This request did not go down well with Fouesnel, who remembered Crowningburg's drunken state when he himself arrived at the settlement.

The Board of Health declared the storm a disaster and sent a group of Chinese labourers to Kalawao to rebuild the houses. The greatest need had already been met thanks to the wooden roofing planks that Favens had sent to Damien. In order to speed up the rebuilding, the Board permitted the wealthier patients to build their own houses, which they would then own. Gradually, the situation began to return to normal.

Episcopal Peace Mission to Molokai

Peace had returned. On 8 December, they were able to watch Venus eclipsing the sun, through smoked glass. That same day, Damien wrote his annual letters home, but he also added a note to Favens, requesting that he censor the letters. He gave a brief synopsis of his letter to his mother, which was written in Dutch. It was difficult to write his condolences for the death of his father, but he expressed his certainty that he was with his four daughters in heaven. He also reassured his mother about himself.

I'm all alone in my little cottage. The patients never come in here. In the morning, after mass, one of the women who is not ill comes to cook me some food, rice, meat, coffee, the odd pancake. In the evenings the leftovers with a cup of tea, that I boil over my lamp. I rarely eat at midday. Fifty or sixty hens lay me more eggs than I can eat. You can tell that Jef is still alive and kicking.

Pamphile received a long letter: one or two items of practical information followed by a piece of pure propaganda for the mission and the Hawaiian government. If his brother were to publish this letter as well, it would not get Damien into trouble.

In the end, 1874 had not been such a bad year. He had built a church and baptised 116 people, thirty members of the congregation had died and he had solemnised ten marriages.

The king and queen returned safely from the United States. They had been received in Congress and an accord had been reached, which was ratified in the Senate on 18 April. The only concession the Hawaiians had had to make was that they were not allowed to grant any part of their territory to any foreign power other than the United States. As soon as the accord was ratified, the price of a pound of sugar rose by two cents and the price of land by 25 per cent.

The economy was booming and so there would be more money available for health care – at least, that was what Damien's visitors were hoping. He had had a heavy fall and was confined to bed for several weeks. While he was convalescing, he learned that one of the marriages he had conducted, involving a man from Wailuku, had taken place while the man was still married back home. Although Fouesnel tried to use this against him, Bishop Maigret did not blame him. 'You have been the victim of deceit, just like everyone else,' he wrote. 'We should not have been more careful.' It was also a good sign that the bishop was going to pay a visit before the start of the rainy season in October.

The mission was riven by dissension, now that the succession struggle had come into the open. 'The devil of discord seeks to inspire our mission with his hellish breath,' Favens wrote. Between Damien and André Burgerman there already existed a state of open warfare, as Favens knew all too well. The purpose of Maigret's episcopal visitation to Molokai was in fact to gauge the ferocity of the feud between the two men. For this reason, he invited Clément Evrard, who had sailed to Hawaii with Damien, and Aubert Bouillon, Damien's friend, to go with him. He also wanted to find out whether Burgerman did, in fact, need more chapels and whether Damien really was doing good work in the settlement.

The visitation began on 'topside', where Burgerman proudly showed off his church. Kaluaaha had also been badly damaged by the storm, but the church was still standing. Damien was a good carpenter.

The next morning, the three priests were rowed to the settlement. Burgerman was not allowed to accompany them. Damien and Ragsdale were waiting for them on the shore and helped to beach the boats. Ragsdale immediately began to sing the praises of Damien, who had converted him. He was no longer a wastrel but a good Catholic. The bishop wanted to believe him, but perhaps Damien had coached him in what to say. The evening was convivial. Damien and Evrard recalled memories of their student days, while Bouillon and the bishop talked about the early days of the mission. The high mass that Maigret celebrated the following day was splendid. Louis, a boy who had once been in the Cathedral choir, sang the Agnus Dei from the 'Coronation' Mass perfectly. Maigret was moved to tears, particularly when the boy was obliged to stop for a moment to spit out phlegm. Maigret noticed now that there were holes in the floor, with leaves beside each one, to serve as funnels, so that the patients could spit out their phlegm without fouling the church.

The bishop stayed for over a week and confirmed about a hundred people. On the last evening, the visitors were sitting with Damien on the lawn, smoking, when people arrived from all directions and took their places on the grass in front of the presbytery. Maigret turned his chair around so as not to miss anything. Twenty youths waved banners to the rhythm of a brass band, which was playing Dixie music. Damien explained that the Royal Band in Honolulu sent its old instruments to the settlement. There were a lot of drums as well and Damien asked one boy to show the whistle he was playing. Damien had made it himself from an oil can.

Maigret had heard and seen a great deal. The standard reply from the patients was that the Board looked after them well. They had a roof over their heads and were given food and clothing. Damien looked after them well. He was their father. He gave them biscuits and tea and sugar, if they were ill. He did not discriminate between Protestants, Catholics or others. He had heard the same things said so often that it sounded as though they were rattling off a lesson but the eyes of these people spoke of sorrow.

The bishop was now ready for a confrontation between Burgerman and Damien and invited the latter to accompany him on the visit to 'topside'. Their departure was impressive. Two hundred people waved them goodbye, the majority of them kneeling when the bishop gave them his blessing. He blessed them again from the rowing boat.

The return journey was more difficult. There was only one sloop this time and Evrard proposed that he should travel overland. Even with only three passengers, the rowers had great difficulty in covering the distance against the current. Damien wanted to help, but he was seasick. They reached Haano, a small promontory. The rowers were exhausted and they put in to shore. Damien was delighted because it gave him a chance to recover. The settlement looked as though it had died out. Maigret suggested to the rowers that they should round the point on foot, as this would make the boat lighter. The track was difficult, they had to climb over rocks and Damien was full of admiration for the bishop. Evrard had told him that people wanted Maigret to resign but Damien could not understand this. At nightfall, they reached the three huts that made up the settlement of Puahaunui. A woman invited them to spend the night there. She vaguely remembered that there had once been *Palani* in the hamlet, but they had fled during the persecution. Then they came back, and then they had died.

Maigret sighed and suddenly he started talking about himself: his exile, the death of his friend Bachelot on board the *Waverly*. Maigret had buried him in Micronesia, at a place called Punipe. He remained alone on that island for seven months, surviving on fish and breadfruit. His hostess was moved and cried out, 'God protected you. He has given you a good and healthy old age. Thank you for giving Damien to us. He has visited us three times already in the last three years.' These were important words. Damien was obviously popular on 'topside'.

The boat was waiting for them at sunrise, but now it was rough going. There were high waves and Damien was very sick. He hoped they would put in at Halawa, so that they could complete the rest of the journey on foot, but the rowers went on. In Kaluaaha, they found Evrard and Burgerman waiting for them somewhat anxiously.

Now it was Burgerman's turn to argue his case. He showed Maigret the barn in Kaunakakai where he had to celebrate mass. Maigret recognised the place and thought it an honour to say mass in a place where *Palani* had once been chained up. The bishop spoke firmly, for the boat to Maui was ready to leave. During the crossing, Maigret and Bouillon discussed the situation. Bouillon thought there had been a lot of progress in the settlement since his previous visits and he was certain that Damien had had a hand in it, although he had not been responsible for everything. The whole business with Burgerman's churches did not seem to Maigret to be urgent and they decided to leave the priests where they were.

In Lahaina, Bouillon wrote a long letter to the general in which he told him that a lot of witchcraft was still practised on Molokai. It was also a bulwark of Protestantism. For this reason, it was quite justifiable to maintain a priest on 'topside', even though not many people lived there.

Patches on Arms and Back

Damien set to work building in Kalaupapa, but he did not follow the bishop's instructions. The wood for the church in Pelekunu had been delivered to Kalaupapa by mistake. When Damien saw it, he decided that he had far more believers in the western village of the settlement than the thirty Catholics who lived in the isolated valley. So he built the church that was intended for

Pelekunu in Kalaupapa. Then he took down the small chapel and sent the wood to Pelekunu, where he reconstructed it.

When the bishop found out about this, he was furious. The outburst had certain repercussions because the letter from Damien that had occasioned the crisis was translated into English and an American newspaper had published the text. When he read the letter, Louis-Lambert Conrardy, a French-speaking Belgian priest who was working among the Umatilla Indians in Washington State, wrote, offering to come and work with Damien. He was not the only one, but all these volunteers were rejected, unless they were prepared to join the Sacred Hearts Order, which meant going through the novitiate. Hermann Köckemann kept a close eye on all the correspondence that came in as a result of Damien's arrogant letter.

The atmosphere was not conducive to winning favours. Damien hoped that Burgerman would not raise the issue of the church in Kamalo again, but that is precisely what occurred. Despairingly, Damien asked Favens if there were not a brother available to work on these chapels, but after a year, Fouesnel still could not spare any of his workmen, despite Damien's statement of his case, in which he listed all his various tasks, which now included keeping an eye on the situation in the hospital. William Williamson, the British nurse who had shown him round when he arrived, had died and had been succeeded as supervisor by John Ostrum, a British sailor. The latter was willing enough for the task, but was hardly a shining example of morality.

This was the frame of mind in which Damien celebrated the New Year with Burgerman. The latter came down to the settlement once a month, so that the two priests could hear one another's confession. Damien felt that Burgerman did not belong in the Order, and wrote to the general to tell him so. He did not belong on Molokai, nor even in Hawaii.

Pamphile wrote to him in English, in order to practise the language. He gave family news and Damien wrote a relaxed letter in reply, although he once again asked Pamphile to stop publishing his letters. He had not been beyond Kalaupapa for six months. In his spare time he cultivated a small plot of ground to provide food for his chickens, which in turn provided him with food. 'I am still in good health,' he wrote to his mother. 'I feel stronger and better than ever.'

In fact, he was not so sure about this, for he feared he had leprosy. He had discovered patches on his back and arms. When he treated them with an abrasive lotion, they went away, but they always reappeared. The strange thing was that no sweat appeared on these patches any more, although he did still have feeling in them. He let his beard grow as a form of protest against his condition. To Pamphile, he wrote, 'Ah, come to my aid with your devout prayers!'

Damien would become just one more 'leper' in the frightening statistics. The number of patients continued to rise and the needs of the patient community increased. In order to keep costs within bounds, whilst not neglecting the patients, the Hawaiian parliament decided, in June 1876, to send a commission of enquiry to Kalaupapa. An American specialist, Dr George Woods, joined the Commission of Thirteen as an advisor. He was a ship's doctor aboard the USS *Lackawanna*, a warship patrolling the Pacific. If there was a leper colony at the ship's port of call, then Woods would visit it and he had built up his reputation in this way. He had visited the settlement on Molokai at its inception in 1866. Now, therefore, he would be able to determine how matters were progressing.

The political visitation was weak. The MPs withdrew on to the verandah of the house that the doctors occupied during their visits. The exiles sat on the grass. The gentlemen in their top hats and tails posed polite questions, the patients gave non-committal replies, because they hoped that if they were on their best behaviour, they would be released. One MP tried to induce conversation by asking about the weather. Was it too cold or too hot? Was the food suffiently varied? Was it adequate? Was it of good quality? These questions received no more reply than any other. When another MP asked if there were anyone present who thought he was not a leper and if any such person would step forward, the crowd surged towards the verandah and the visitors beat a hasty retreat.

Dr Woods did wish to examine the patients individually.

The faces of some of them were so marked that it was not necessary for them to undress. Forty individuals seemed to be marginal cases and, after examination, it appeared that two people might possibly have been wrongly exiled. Prince Peter Kaeo was furious, since he was once again declared to have leprosy.

After this procedure – Woods thought it was worse to recondemn the people, because they already knew the consequences – there was a second general meeting. This time the angry crowd did not restrain itself. The patients had nothing but complaints. It was too cold and windy, especially in Kalawao. They were given rotting taro and the food was downright bad. One of the politicians simply put a stop to the flood of complaints by declaring that they were unfounded. The group then packed its bags and left.

A week later, Dr Trousseau's successor, Dr McKibben, made his first visit to the settlement. Against his own wishes, he gave Prince Peter Kaeo an exit visa. Kaeo was allowed to return to Honolulu, where he was placed under house arrest. However, he took up his place in the House of Lords again, although he did not achieve anything of note. Rumours continued to circulate that he was ill.

Visit of the Leper Specialist Dr Woods

Woods's seven-day visit at the beginning of July 1876 did not produce any results from a medical point of view. The article that he published in an American journal simply summed up the existing knowledge about leprosy, but it had enormous consequences for Damien. The doctor was tremendously impressed by the improvements in comfort and administration in the settlement over the previous eight years and he ascribed all of this to Damien, a man for whom he had the greatest admiration and sympathy. He did not mention the fact that important investments, such as the building of the hospital, had been made before Damien's arrival, nor that King Kalakaua supported the settlement and stimulated further investment. He did repeat the typical nineteenth-century missionary rhetoric. All of the orders urged their missionaries to present themselves as jacks-of-all-trades. It was even fashionable to produce a list of jobs – priest, doctor, nurse, administrator, carpenter, gardener, gravedigger – that the lonely man carried out in hostile conditions. Damien certainly did this and the doctor, who was a Catholic, but who had no idea of how missionary propaganda was conducted, simply swallowed it.

Woods's visit certainly did not begin positively. The sea was rough and he had to jump from the rope-ladder into a bobbing rowing boat full of lepers. They caught him and in the bay more patients had formed a line to help him ashore. He was caught by one hand after another and this he disliked. Two men were awaiting him: William Ragsdale, whom the doctor could see at a glance to have advanced leprosy, and an apparently healthy Damien, who seemed both youthful and energetic. A healthy person among all these deformed ones was reassuring and the doctor chose Damien as his confidant.

On the way to Kalawao, Damien said nothing, while Ragsdale was constantly singing the praises of the man who had converted him. Damien was responsible for everything and so Woods concluded that the new white houses, that the Chinese coolies had built, were also Damien's work. He must have been the one who had arranged for the Hawaiian hibiscus and other bushes to be planted. Everyone adored the priest and they were constantly being stopped by people who hung aromatic leis around their necks. The Boston-born doctor did not realise that he was being welcomed because they hoped he had brought them a cure. Woods had to stay with Ragsdale in a room reserved for healthy people, but he felt uncomfortable, even though the lawyer kept his distance.

As they sat on the terrace after dinner, they suddenly heard music, including the *Star-Spangled Banner*. Damien then appeared on the terrace and introduced the boys who played in the band. Dr Woods was to take the serenade as a token of thanks for his trouble in coming to visit them.

When the concert was over and Ragsdale had gone to bed, Damien and Woods stayed on the terrace talking until late into the night. They became friends and Woods followed Damien around. He went to mass and admired the people's devotion, but the heat and stench in the tiny church made him sick. He accompanied Damien on visits to patients and was shocked to see Damien puffing on a pipe that came from the mouth of a leper. He ate from the family gourd. The doctor warned Damien that he seemed to be courting infection, but the priest explained that it was only in this way that he could win the people's trust. Deeply impressed, Woods noted this, too, in his diary, which he was later to publish.

A high point was 4 July 1876. Woods started awake at sunrise and heard the American national anthem being played outside. He went to the *lanai* and Damien was there with the brass band. He congratulated him on the US Centennial and invited him to attend the mass he was to celebrate in honour of the occasion. Woods had not expected this attention and he had pleasure in attending the mass in dress uniform. The sick congregation arrived, dressed in their best, with garlands of flowers around their necks and flowers in their hats. Damien celebrated mass in a chasuble of festal white and the congregation sang for the United States.

Ragsdale had also prepared a surprise. He served a *luau* at the Board of Health's expense on the grass in front of the church. Woods received his own food, cooked by a healthy woman as usual, but such an event was so unheard of to him that he could not believe his eyes. He watched people constantly coming up to Damien and saw that he was popular with them. All of this, too, was to be written about.

Damien was happy that day. 'This is my worldly task,' he said. 'I shall get leprosy one day, and when I do, I shall carry on working for my children as long as I can. I shall give them moral and material support. I want to help to heal their mental and their physical wounds. The government really helps us and we can count on the support of charitable individuals as well. Ragsdale does a lot, too.' Damien's English was not particularly good and when he could not find a word, he used French or Hawaiian. No matter – a priest who brewed his own beer in a leper settlement was allowed to make linguistic errors.

Woods spent a lot of time in the hospital. Already, in 1870, a Norwegian doctor, Hansen, had discovered the bacillus, *Mycobacterium leprae*, that was the cause of the disease, so Woods's conclusion that syphilis and leprosy were not the same disease, but that syphilis, by weakening the body, did make it more susceptible to leprosy, was not really breaking new ground. The plague was severely depleting the Hawaiian population and he thought that the race was predestined to suffer the disease. In his report he noted that leprosy was a form of chronic neuritis, as a result of which a granular tissue developed around or even within the nerves and the ganglia. This degeneration explained the loss of sensation, the contraction of the fingers and toes and the loss of vitality in the affected areas. This was why parts of the body died off. During autopsies in other parts of the world, he had established that the organs could also be affected.

There was no cure. Arsenic and tonics could slow the progress of the disease; good hygiene and care of the sores slowed its inexorable progress. He had done tests on so-called treatments, such as *Gurjun* oil and Dr Akana's ointment, but they did not work.

The doctor described the first symptoms. Damien was alarmed, but he did not show it. Fatigue and a tendency to depression were initial signs, followed by loss of sensation in certain parts of the body and premature ageing. Lepers with growths lived on average eight years from the onset of the disease, while those with patches could go on for around eighteen years.

The doctor and priest parted as friends. The publication of the long scientific article of praise made Damien internationally famous in medical circles by the end of 1876.

Tug-of-War with Burgerman

The Commission of Thirteen had recommended the building of new wards and of a crematorium. They thought it inhuman to require the dying to live surrounded by churchyards. The first idea was a success, but the Hawaiians refused to allow their dead to be cremated. For them, immortal life resided in the bones. The costly building was turned into storage space.

Grégoire Archambaux, who lived with Bouillon in Lahaina, came to preach a mission. He was touched by the sight of the lepers and simply could not cope with the idea of sick children. When Damien accompanied him to the top of the *pali*, he was over-emotional. He kept on about the friendship between the French and the Flemings. Damien suspected that he had problems.

St Philomena's had once again become too small and Christmas was celebrated in a building site. A few days later a splendid white yacht, called the *Sunbeam*, appeared in the bay. An expensively dressed man and woman were rowed ashore by their crew and introduced themselves as Thomas and Annie Brassey. They were the son and daughter-in-law of a British industrialist, who had railway companies in India. Damien joined Ragsdale in showing the couple round the settlement. When they returned to England, they spoke about him in London society and Annie Brassey wrote about Damien in her account of her travels, *A Voyage in the Sunbeam, Our Home on the Ocean for Eleven Months*, published in 1879. This was a further contribution to Damien's growing fame. The well-known Scottish authoress, Isabella Bird, also mentioned Damien, whom she had never met, in a lengthy appendix to her account of her journey through Hawaii. Moreover, the controversial letter that Pamphile had published had by now been translated into English and German.

In the months during which these books and articles were in preparation, Damien promised Burgerman that he would build some chapels for him, but he would only come when the wood arrived. Damien did travel to Honolulu for the funeral of the crown prince, William Pitt Leleiohoku. After the service, he had a long conversation with the king and queen and with Princess Liliuokalani, who thought it unnecessary for him to build churches for Burgerman. She wanted him to stay with the exiles.

On his arrival in Honolulu, Damien received a letter from his brother, Gérard, who informed him that Constance's son was demanding his share of the inheritance and even wanted to turn his grandmother out of her home. Damien quickly wrote to Pamphile, urging him to see that this did not happen.

He spoke to Bishop Maigret about the situation. The bishop was under fire himself from Köckemann, who thought that the elderly superiors should resign. Favens now walked with the aid of a stick and Maigret had been taken ill at the altar on one occasion. Köckemann wrote lengthy letters to the general considering the potential candidates and indirectly pushing his own claims. Damien was concerned at this prospect. He got on well with the bishop and past quarrels were now forgotten. He was not sure he could rely on Köckemann's support.

Damien's Own Daily Rule

Damien stayed with Dan and Ann McCorriston while he was building the church in Kamalo. The family were having a hard time, because their sugar plantation had burned down and they had little money to start up a cattle ranch. Damien built a simple church, which he finished in August.

The bishop insisted that he attend a retreat around this time and Damien noted in pencil his own daily rule, to which he would henceforth conform.

5 a.m. get up without hesitation, choose subjects for meditation, wash and dress properly

5.15 a.m. in church morning prayer, read about subject of meditation, avoid all possibility of distraction

6 a.m. preparation of the mass, wait for congregation

6–6.30 mass, on Sundays meditation until 7

7 a.m. after the service, normal instruction about subject of meditation, change, tidy up. Everything must be neatly in its place, permit no disorder in the sacristy. A half hour of prayer

8 a.m. light breakfast, no meat or fish, coffee with bread and

eggs, smoke a pipe, discuss business, household worries, feed the chickens with the children etc.

9 a.m. prayers of the Holy Office, permit no interruption except for urgent matters. Say you are busy. Breviary, study of theological subjects and the holy books until midday.

12 a.m. lunch, no familiar conversation with the cook and his wife, afterwards visit the sick. On horseback only if it is distant, otherwise on foot. Every time before leaving short visit to the Holy Sacrament, no useless conversation. Always be friendly without being familiar. Waste no time talking. Be home at 5 p.m. at the latest

5 p.m. vespers and if there are converts in the church catechism

6 p.m. evening meal, early in the winter so that the servants are not in the house after sunset. (Be strict with all girls or women who are still in the mission after sunset)

7 p.m. paternoster, then breviary, matins and lauds, spiritual reading

10 p.m. if not sleepy, then read a chapter of the New Testament and then to bed

Damien also wrote down his resolutions, as the preacher on the retreat had commanded him:

My resolution is:

— to concern myself as little as possible with the material needs of the lepers and to become involved as little as possible with government matters, unless absolutely necessary and at the special request of the superintendent;

— keep everything tidy in the sacristy, in my house and with my clothes;

— combine poverty and tidiness;

— behave simply and in a friendly manner to everyone,

whilst maintaining the necessary reserve in conversation;

– not to gossip and stop everyone who does;

– not to waste my time in useless conversation.

That the remembrance of past errors may make you behave more humbly now, accompanied by remorse, whilst you renew your good intentions for the future.

Be strict with yourself and forgiving toward others. Honour the Lord scrupulously in your prayers, meditation, the holy service and the offering of the sacraments. Be joined to God in your heart and remember constantly in temptation that you would rather rot at that moment than commit the slightest sin. Passion ought always to make you sigh. The words 'dissolvi et esse cum Christo', mean that you long to die and be with Christ.

Keep before you the invisible judgment of God, who watches over you and knows all the free actions of your will, for in this way you will withstand sin. He is calling you at that moment before his judgment seat. Be on your guard.

Remember your three vows, by which you are dead to the world. Nothing that you possess is your own and it must not be used for personal satisfaction. The pleasures of the flesh: chastity makes you the equal of angels, but sex makes a devil of a priest. No sensuality and no searching out of the sources.

Let your superiors do with you as they think fit. Jesus allowed himself to be buried in an isolated spot, but his body remained united with God. Let us follow Jesus Christ, his inner and outer life, his soul and body, from his conception to his grave. Then we can have confidence that we shall arise again in his glory. Remember God's unchanging nature and imitate it with constant perseverance. Think of God's eternal essence and work courageously for that eternity.

Damien wanted to keep strictly to this rule, which was suitable only for a contemplative monk. By this time, he had eight yellow patches on his body and they were spreading. He took sarsaparilla to purify his blood and kept rubbing the patches with an abrasive lotion. He had to preserve his strength, for Burgerman was preparing a major attack.

II

War with Burgerman over the
Leper Settlement
(October 1877–August 1880)

Damien and Burgerman Both Superintendent

The conflict broke out as Ragsdale was dying. In October, Damien confided in Meyer that Ragsdale could not live much longer. The Board would have to look for a successor. On All Saints' Day (1 November), Burgerman paid a visit to Meyer, who explained the problems of finding a successor to Ragsdale. The only candidate was Captain Sumner, the son of the captain of the *Waverly*, the ship on which Maigret had been taken into exile. Sumner had charisma and an air of naval authority, but he also had an eccentric lifestyle. It was an advantage that he was half-Hawaiian and so would be able to be on good terms with both groups of the population. Then, to Meyer's astonishment, Burgerman offered himself as a candidate for the post. His position was not illogical: he had come to Molokai to work in the leper settlement. He felt he had been taken in, because no one in Paris had told him about Damien. Meyer did not really believe this, but continued to listen, particularly when Burgerman offered to work for board and lodging only, receiving no salary.

This gave Meyer the idea of appointing Sumner as titular superintendent, while Burgerman did the work. Burgerman could also act as medical supervisor in the absence of the doctor. Meyer did not expect Damien to object to this; on the contrary, he thought he would be doing him a favour by providing him with a fellow-priest – and thus a friend – on a permanent basis. Burgerman asked Meyer to keep their conversation strictly confidential until he had spoken to his superiors.

Burgerman told Damien that he had large patches on his body and no longer had any feeling in his right hand. He was certain he had leprosy and demanded to be given the settlement as his parish. If this demand were not met, he would leave the Order. Damien advised Burgerman to have his condition examined by a doctor, but Burgerman responded to this suggestion with an angry outburst. Damien did not know what to do about what he had been told and so he booked a passage to Honolulu for 15 November, so that he could discuss the situation with his superiors. Sam Wilder, who was now chairman of the Board of Health, was also on board. He was distressed because he had just taken leave of the dying Ragsdale. During the crossing, the two men discussed the succession. Wilder asked Damien to deal with ongoing business until a suitable successor could be found, something he had already been doing during Ragsdale's final illness. Damien thought of the personal rule he had drawn up during the retreat, but regarded this request as force majeure. He asked Wilder to keep their conversation confidential until he had spoken to his superiors. Maigret advised him to allow things to run their own course for the time being, but he did receive permission to run the settlement on a temporary basis.

Ragsdale was still alive when Damien returned, but it was only a matter of days. Even before the death of the flamboyant *luna*, a letter arrived from Burgerman in which he announced that the Board of Health had appointed him superintendent. Sumner would deal with administrative matters. Because he had arranged everything without Maigret's permission, he asked Damien, his confessor, to raise the matter with the bishop. He wondered if he would still be able to say mass. The response would determine whether he made his entry into the leper settlement in his soutane or in civilian clothes. Burgerman had no intention of continuing his work as priest on 'topside' and he asked Damien to request the bishop to send one of the new priests to Kaluaaha. Damien should not consider the position for himself, because he had apparently offended the community in Palaau by several sharp things he had said when he was building a chapel in Kumimi. What was certain was that Burgerman wanted a dispensation from his vows. He would say mass for the last time the following Sunday.

When Meyer knew that Burgerman had written to Damien, he wrote officially to say he was planning to put Burgerman in effective charge of the settlement, whilst Sumner would be given the formal title of superintendent. He asked Damien to take care of ongoing business until the new managers were ready to take over. He constantly repeated that Damien must allow business to take its course. He must not make any innovations. Because Ragsdale was still conscious, Meyer asked Damien to give him his final *aloha*, but in the meantime he was nevertheless arranging for Burgerman to have Ragsdale's house. He said nothing about what was to happen to the future widow.

Damien could not reply, because Meyer had left for Honolulu. He himself also had to leave, because he had been summoned as a witness in a court case in Lahaina. By 6 December, he was back in Kalawao to celebrate the requiem for Ragsdale. The same day, he wrote an official letter of thanks to the Board of Health for the confidence it had shown in him. Meyer's plan to appoint Burgerman and Sumner as a team had apparently not been approved by the Board, because Damien had been asked to continue taking responsibility for the settlement until a suitable successor had been found, not Sumner, and not Burgerman either. Damien had asked an American patient to help him with his letter to the Board, in order to ensure his English was correct. 'You are aware that I have sacrificed my health and all I have in this world, and in consequence you may trust me.' If the Board wished to call upon Damien's services for a longer period, they must, however, first consult Maigret.

This letter had only just been dispatched when he learned that Burgerman was indeed to become superintendent. That evening, he wrote a sharply worded note to Meyer, who had also returned to Molokai. He refused all future co-operation with the Board, because it, in the person of Meyer, had been responsible for suborning a priest from his parish duties. Meyer replied that the Board had been unaware that Burgerman was acting without his bishop's permission. Burgerman was, after all, an adult and he knew what his responsibilities were.

Meyer, who had a feverish cold, was extremely embarrassed by the situation. He wrote to Damien three times on 7 December. One letter was conciliatory: he insisted that Damien should reconsider his decision. Another of his letters was purely concerned with matters of business: an official announcement about the purchase of *poi* and the delivery of salmon and rice. Damien had made a number of administrative errors, for example by failing to sign a number of pages. In the third letter, Meyer proposed a meeting of the two priests and himself at his home. In his opinion the best solution would be to discuss the whole matter thoroughly.

The dispute had spread, however. Burgerman had moved into Ragsdale's house. He spent much time on a long letter to Europe, in which he puffed up the results of his mission on page after page. In the end, the feud between the priests benefited the settlement, because each one sought to outdo the other in proving to the exiles that he, and not the other, would best serve the exiles.

Burgerman, who had in fact requested a dispensation from his vows, was completely the missionary. Damien paid the *pianolos* a premium because they had landed the cattle safely, despite a heavy sea. He had tried to discharge from the hospital a number of patients who were too healthy to be there and had those who refused put into the prison. He signed a permit for the healthy husband of a blind woman to enter the leper settlement and did the settlement's bookkeeping. He tried to ignore the complaints that Burgerman's friends piled up against him. He was completely the superintendent and had little time for his priestly tasks.

Meyer meanwhile was looking for another candidate to fill the post. The Rev. Mr Kahuila was not in the running, even though he had been MP for Kau, and his wife Williama was a good teacher. He had once been a follower of the Big Island prophet Kaona during the latter's rebellion and was still regarded as a 'rebel and disturber of the peace'. It was possible that Tom Birch, who was also an MP, had leprosy. He was half Irish and half Hawaiian and was used to assuming responsibility. If that were confirmed, he would be the ideal candidate if the Sumner-Burgerman management went wrong. If not, there was always Damien, at least if he were given permission by the bishop. Meyer clearly did not know what to do.

All kinds of moves, of varying degrees of propriety, were made by various interested parties, including the patients, in favour of one or other candidate. Damien himself also took certain steps. He wanted to secure the food supply and ordered ointments based on tar and sulphur to treat sores, cough medicine and gargle syrup. He asked for a supply of Corbett's Sarsaparilla, a blood purifier, which he took himself. This supply was aimed at Burgerman, who had once again stepped up his pill production.

No incidents took place in January, but given that there had already been two months of conflict, Meyer put pressure on the Board, on 16 January 1878, to come quickly to a decision. The supply of *poi* was not going smoothly. Burgerman had returned to 'topside' at this point and so Damien felt able to leave the settlement for a few days with an easy mind. He was hoping to find fresh taro in Pelekunu and borrowed a patient's canoe in order to row to the valley. The sea was calm, so he did not need to call on extra help. He said mass and heard confessions in the tiny church that had once stood in Kalaupapa. Then he went into a hut to haggle with the farmers about the price of *pai-ai*. While they were negotiating, he could hear the wind getting up. Alarmed, he went to the beach to see what was happening and found the canoe had been shattered against the rocks. He could sit out the storm in Pelekunu – but that could take days – or he could take the dangerous path from the valley.

He really had no choice, for, since the arrival of the rebellious Kahuila, there had been unrest in the settlement. Kahuila incited everyone to disobedience and because his wife Williama supported him, it was proposed to revoke her *kokua's* permit.

Damien learned from Meyer that an angry riot had broken out, and, despite the fact that it was the middle of the night, he went down the mountain. When Williama received her expulsion order, she and her husband rushed to Sumner and Burgerman, who had returned to the settlement. They gave Damien the blame. Furious, Kahuila assembled his followers to resist this unjust expulsion with armed force. Damien made his way to the pastor's house. When the latter saw him, he made as if to attack, but the new sheriff, William Crowningburg, mounted a charge with his officers, and the two sides came to blows. One of Kahuila's followers fought with a bloody head wound, until he was beaten unconscious. When the police attacked them with clubs, the rebels retreated. The police charged for a third time and arrested Kahuila, who became hysterical and disturbed the patients in the hospital with his cries and screams. In the end, it was all a waste of time, since Williama could not leave anyway, because the *Warwick* was not able to put in because of the heavy seas. When the storm abated. Damien decided to send Kahuila to Honolulu in chains.

The couple continued to protest and, in Honolulu, it was decided that the only thing to be done with Kahuila was to return him to Molokai. The Protestant church refused to accept the way Kahuila had been treated. A man named Castle, who was a substantial tradesman in the city, lodged an official complaint against Damien on the grounds of abuse of authority. If Damien were found guilty, he would be dismissed as *luna*.

That evening, Damien wrote to his superiors that he was in very low spirits, because he had had to arrest an ordained man, a pastor. This incident had made it clear to him that it was difficult to combine his mission with an administrative role. The Board must know that his appointment, for which Maigret had still not given his permission, was temporary.

Around this time, Maigret was shown a petition sent to the king. The signatories were exiles who indicated that they would be happy to see Damien disappear to 'topside'. Burgerman provided them with the necessary medical care. Doctors rarely visited the sick bay and there were no nurses.

Shocked, Maigret sent Bouillon to Molokai to inspect. Burgerman admitted that he was behind the petition. The Board had accepted his offer to work as medical agent for board and lodging. When Bouillon objected, Burgerman again threatened to leave the Order.

For his part, Damien wanted to step down as *luna*. He was exhausted and confided to Bouillon that he had received death threats from Sumner's men. Bouillon had to make a decision: he appointed Burgerman as priest in Kalaupapa and gave him permission to act as medical agent. Damien would also officially resign as *luna* and thereafter serve Kalawao and 'topside'. Sumner, who was known as a vulgar, miserly fellow, became super-intendent, with, as his deputy, the American Clayton Strawn, who had been 'a black birdee', a slave trader in the Pacific before he contracted leprosy.

This did not resolve all the conflicts – quite the reverse. Strawn encouraged misconduct. His motto was 'Let the lepers enjoy themselves for as long as they can.' He frightened off all those who came to Damien for material help and thought that Damien and his sermons could go hang. He packed the bundles of *pai-ai* in smaller packages and sold the remainder at extortionate prices. He was hated. One day, a group of angry horsemen surrounded him, but, unperturbed, he barked at them that they might kill him, if they would, he would be free of leprosy the sooner. The gang hesitated and Strawn burst into derisive laughter. Crowningburg, who was always tipsy, encouraged drinking binges. Right-thinking citizens were angered by these 'parties' and accused all the officials of alcoholism. Damien himself was mentioned in one petition.

King Urges Resident Doctor (May 1878)

The *luna* question had focused attention on Molokai and the king himself, therefore, brought the leprosy problem before parliament. Walter Murray Gibson, the journalist who had called Damien a Christian hero, was an MP and he supported the king. Gibson had risen to prominence very quickly, for he was already a member of the Committee on Health Care and was chairman of the Finance Committee. He was a member of the parliamentary delegation that visited the leper settlement and concluded that there was a particular need for a resident doctor. Parliament accepted his proposal to increase the budget for Kalaupapa to $160,000, double the amount for the previous year. Work on the construction of seven dormitories in Kalawao and four in Kalaupapa was immediately put out to tender.

Now that a resident doctor was coming, Burgerman's popularity declined dramatically. Whereas in January he had seemed to be the only hope, now he was called a quack. Now that the Board no longer supported Burgerman, the mission sent him back to 'topside'. Damien was once again the only priest for the lepers. He also received permission to spend $75 on adding an extra storey to the presbytery.

The *kokuas* felt that they should receive more money for their work, if the leper settlement was having its budget increased. The Board refused their request and they went on strike. Damien wanted to go to Honolulu to argue their case with the Board, but Meyer advised him against this, pointing out that it was impossible to please everyone.

This was evident, as the documentary evidence shows that Damien had various disagreements, great and small, with inhabitants of the settlement. He upset a pastor, for example, by riding on horseback through a Protestant churchyard and he quarrelled with Sumner, because the latter wanted *kokuas* who might have contracted leprosy to be sent to Honolulu for examination. Damien lost his temper and was rude to Sumner, who made a complaint to the Board.

The major problem remained Burgerman, however. In August, he demanded the whole of the settlement for himself and again threatened that, if he did not get his way, he would leave the Order and cause a scandal. Damien left immediately for Honolulu, to discuss matters with his superiors. He was shocked when Maigret informed him that, during the *luna* crisis, he had offered Burgerman $200 to leave Hawaii and that the offer still stood. Damien did not want to be responsible for

Burgerman's leaving the Order. Moncany, however, remarked sarcastically that it was too late for that, since Burgerman had disappeared.

Placebo Experiment and the Controversial Burgerman

In mid-September, rumours began to circulate that Burgerman would not participate in the celebrations for Maigret's golden jubilee as a priest, because he had left the islands.

There were major festivities, including a splendid pontifical mass. After the mass, the bishop greeted the crowd from the steps of the cathedral. A tall, well-built man caught the eye: Burgerman. Damien, who was standing behind Maigret, stiffened. He hoped Burgerman would not make a scene and spoil the celebrations. In civilian clothes, Burgerman stepped forward to kiss Maigret's ring and give him the good news. He had officially been appointed agent of the Board of Health.

The patients were furious. They demanded a real doctor, but Burgerman stubbornly persisted, ordering a long list of medicines from the Board. He also made his peace with the Order and demanded his parish in Kalaupapa back. Damien would have to take care of 'topside'. Burgerman had gained every point.

Damien also had something up his sleeve, however. On 14 June the crew of the *Warwick* unloaded a large chest from China, addressed to 'Father Damien, Catholic Mission'. The crate was crammed with phials containing ochre-coloured, rectangular Hoang Nan pills. It had cost Damien a good deal of effort to acquire this reputed treatment for leprosy. A Dominican who worked in a leper colony in Trinidad had used Hoang Nan successfully. The headquarters of the Sacred Hearts Order in Paris had acquired the address for Damien, who ordered the medicine, via Trinidad and Paris, from Cochin, China. The instruction leaflet described Hoang Nan as a powder that stuck to the underside of leaves at certain times. Collectors scraped the powder off with a bamboo spatula and stored it in earthenware pots. It healed snake bites, dropsy and leprosy.

Damien had great hopes for the treatment, but also doubts. He had to be sure and so he worked out his own research method. He noted carefully the names of all those who had put themselves forward. In his office, he divided those who had been selected into two groups, each made up of an equal number of people with tubercular lumps and of those with leprosy causing loss of sensation, of men and of women, of early and of advanced cases. He opened some of the pills and replaced the medicine with a substitute. The next day, he gave the test group the real medicine, while the second, control, group received the placebo. All of the volunteers had to promise to abstain from alcohol and uncooked food. Each week, he questioned the patients and noted every new symptom, positive or negative, and so was able to follow the progress of the treatment accurately. Without ever claiming the honour, Damien had discovered the now famous placebo experimental method.

Dr Emerson, Resident Doctor

The experiment took time and so did Burgerman's accommodation. Officially, he was to take up residence in Prince Peter Kaeo's house, but that was at some distance from Kalaupapa. The house belonged to the Board. Burgerman demanded that Damien immediately take down the house and rebuild it next to his own church. Damien was willing to do this, but insisted that he must first have permission of the Board and of his superiors. Burgerman was furious that he was making such a fuss and would have gone to live with Henriette Speyver, if she had not shown him the door. Burgerman had a relationship with this former pupil of the Sisters of the Sacred Hearts. Aggrieved by this rejection, and knowing that a certain Dr Nathaniel Emerson was to be the resident doctor, Burgerman sent Damien a note full of insults. Once again, he threatened to leave the Order. Although night had already fallen, Damien set out on a peace mission to Kalaupapa and promised to start straight away on the building work.

Damien tried to remain calm. He had no choice but to learn to live with Burgerman. On Boxing Day, 26 December, he wrote, 'We have to take account of his Dutch character and go easy on him a little, because he could do much good here.'

Emerson, the new doctor, was an American, but had grown up on Oahu Island, the son of a missionary. He spoke fluent Hawaiian and was perfectly at home with *Kanaka* customs. On account of his services in the Union Army during the Civil War, he had received a veteran's student scholarship to Harvard to study medicine. After that he had specialised at the College of Physicians and Surgeons in New York. He was thirty by the time he had completed his training and had subsequently worked in the United States for nine years. When he saw the advertisement for the post of Inspector General for lepers and leper stations in Hawaii, he was seized with the ambition to discover a cure for leprosy.

His arrival in the leper settlement on 3 January 1878 was triumphantly received. He immediately set to work to gather as much information as possible about the functioning of the settlement and about the disease. Basic needs were being met, but the quality of life left much to be desired. He had the ration of *poi* doubled and ordered soap for each patient.

Ambrose Hutchison was a young half-American who had arrived on the same sailing as Emerson. He, however, had made the journey in the cattle pens of the transport ship *Mokolii*. No one was waiting to greet him and so he had to ask a passer-by to direct him to the hospital, to which he had to report. Damien was just coming out of the hospital when he arrived. He introduced himself and noted Hutchison's name in his notebook. He invited Hutchison to come and see him whenever he liked but he had to hurry off, because he had an appointment with Emerson and Sam Wilder. They wanted him to tell them about his experiment with Hoang Nan. Emerson advised Damien to go on with his experiment although he did not place much faith in its outcome.

Sam Wilder was a friend of Damien's, and Emerson too. Burgerman, however, regarded Emerson as a threat, and he did his best to set the patients against the doctor. Emerson was given a salary of FF25,000 a year for care that Burgerman gave for nothing. Emerson refused to touch them, examined them from the top of the steps and put their medicines on a pole. He, Burgerman, tended their suppurating sores and handed them their medicines. On Sundays, Emerson went hunting – he had a gun because he was nervous, so Burgerman stated – as recreation.

In fact, Emerson was doing a good deal, although he had underestimated the scale of the work. During his first visit, Ambrose Hutchison asked him to intervene in a case of robbery. The deputy superintendent Clayton Strawn and his companions had robbed a dying man. Emerson regarded the affair not simply as one of theft but also of corruption. He could see to it that the stolen goods were returned to the rightful heirs, but he could not do more than that. Now that he had seen how things were in reality, he feared he could not survive in a society where the *luna*-captain Sumner lived with concubines.

Damien understood these problems all too well. His life was so different from that of Pamphile, for whom the most alarming incident was falling into a brook. He had returned to the monastery soaking wet. This tale took many pages of one of Pamphile's incredibly long letters, mostly filled with trivial news. Damien's reply to this one was brief and written in English. 'Not wishing to make myself prominent in public print, that is the te [sic] reason why I have delayed to answer yours and the rev [sic] Superior's last year's letter.' His work was routine; he had nothing to report.

Damien's intention was to prevent anything being published about him, because Burgerman, supported by Fouesnel, would use anything he could lay his hands on against him. In his letter to his mother, his tone was optimistic. He was living in a nice house and was well. His Hoang Nan pills were effective and he had baptised 120 people. He reserved the truth for the general. Almost jubilantly, he reported that all symptoms had disappeared. He had been mistaken. 'I have not fruitlessly placed my health under the protection of the Sacred Hearts.' Burgerman was doing good work as doctor and many of the patients had more confidence in him than in the well-paid government doctor.

This sentence seems to show that Damien harboured no jealousy, although it was unfair to Emerson, who had only been in post a month. The truth, however, was in the postscript. 'It is vital that a new missionary should fill the post that Fr André [Burgerman] has left vacant . . . Do not rely on him as your child. He wishes to be independent, and that causes me grief. I have no other colleague on this island. Send me a good child of the Order, not a stubborn gentleman.'

Damien was in debt and needed money. Despite the fact that the budget for Molokai had been doubled, there was still no help for children unaccompanied by their parents. Damien wanted Emerson's support in setting up an orphanage. Emerson was shocked by the extent of paedophilia in the leper settlement and raised the matter. Maigret hesitated at first, because he wanted to put as much money as possible into the new St Louis College that was being built in Honolulu. Finally, under pressure, he sent wood sufficient to build a dormitory for twelve boys.

During those days, Emerson was a true and reliable friend. When Damien had to pay tax on the imported Hoang Nan pills in May, he got the import duty lifted. Sam Wilder wanted to ship the pills free in future, because the first results seemed to be positive. The test group was doing better than the control and Damien even had hopes that half of them would be cured. Strawn was receiving the medicine, but complained that if he got drunk he had tremendous pain in all those parts of his body that were affected by leprosy.

Emerson was less confident but kept all options open for the time being, because leprosy was a strange disease. Sometimes, substantial progress was registered before the disease reached a more advanced stage. One thing he was clear about was that both Burgerman and Damien gave out far too many pills. Even a harmless cough-mixture could have side effects. In order to keep a check on things, he decided that he alone would prescribe medication.

Measles Epidemic

In July, Emerson arrived late because his boat had capsized. This was a blow, because he wanted to close the path on the *pali* as soon as possible, in order to keep the measles epidemic, which was causing deaths on 'topside', out of the settlement. Initially, it appeared that he had succeeded in his aim, but at the end of August the first cases started to appear.

Moncany broke the quarantine, because he came on a peace mission to Molokai. During the retreat in Honolulu, Burgerman had made such a strong attack on Damien that their differences seemed irreconcilable. Burgerman repeated that Damien must go, because he himself had leprosy. For his part, Moncany knew that Damien possibly also had leprosy and so they both had to stay. During his visit, Moncany ascertained that both priests had their supporters, but that the general preference of the exiles was for Burgerman. In Moncany's opinion, this was because Damien was a man *sine concilio et sine judicio*, a hothead who talked through his hat.

He thought it important to explain to Damien the basic ideas of the retreat he had missed and, on this occasion, Damien wrote out a personal rule that was realistic in his usual sloping hand:

> 5 a.m. get up, as quickly as possible to church, morning prayer, worship and meditation until 6 a.m. Mass, instruction and absolution until 7.45. After that organise something for the Christians. 8 a.m. breakfast, followed by a little talk and household chores. 9 a.m. spiritual reading, followed by study and correspondence until midday. 12 a.m. lunch. After lunch, visiting the sick and visiting Christians so that every week I should see everything that is going on in every household in our district. If I can be back around 5 p.m. vespers and household chores. 6 p.m. evening meal at nightfall, rosary, breviary, evening prayer, between 9 p.m. and 10 p.m. to bed.

Moncany took a stern line with Damien. Henceforth he was not to permit Mormons into his home, nor allow horses to graze in the churchyards, even though it was the only place where grass grew, and he was to give no extras to the needy. The state was doing enough.

Hoang Nan was Damien's only card, but it seemed to work. Clayton Strawn's contracted hand was relaxing and the patches disappeared, except for those on his belly. Emerson studied the results and decided that Hoang Nan was a tonic, but he feared that it was not a cure. However, he proposed that the Board should take over Damien's supply of pills in exchange for an old cart, a horse and tack. Damien wanted to convert the vehicle into a hearse.

At this period, the death rate was very high. First there was the measles epidemic and then it was followed by a particularly cold winter. As if this were not enough, two new epidemics, typhus and mumps, broke out on the islands in December. Liévin van Heteren and Aymard Pradeyrol who had travelled with Damien to Molokai were two of the victims.

Damien himself feared once again that he had leprosy. His belly was covered with itchy patches. He wanted to show them to Dr Emerson, but the doctor was being employed in Honolulu. His replacement was the young Dr Wiener, who was clearly a different type. In the first place, he did not want to sleep in the doctor's house, but stayed with Damien, in order to have company in the evening. He also touched the patients, but Damien did not agree with his reasons for doing this. Wiener was not afraid of infection, because he believed leprosy to be the fourth phase of syphilis. When Damien showed Wiener his patches, the latter burst out laughing. Damien had scabies. He prescribed carbolic soap and a lotion to kill the mites that had lodged themselves under his skin.

Relieved, Damien began the preparations for Christmas, but the celebrations were miserable. The church was empty because too many people were sick or had died. There were no burning torches thrown down the mountainside by Meyer's men on New Year's Eve. Instead, Damien spent the evening quietly chatting with his twelve orphan boys.

January was no better. On the last day of the month, he was called to the side of a three-year-old girl who was dying. She was too young for the Last Rites but he was able to give her a *lomi lomi*, a gentle massage to help her soul escape to God. The child was frightened of the solitude, the unknown and the dark and Damien promised her that when his turn came, he would come and lie beside her. He made her a coffin and he dug her grave and buried her with tears in his eyes. He needed spiritual support and began to read his breviary on his terrace. Gravediggers wandered past with a spade. They sought a spot and began to open the pit he had just closed. That was his spot, next to the cross. He wanted to rest there and went over to them angrily. They did not care where they dug and wandered off to seek another place.

There were too many deaths and that evening after the third burial, Damien broke his silence. He wrote Pamphile a propaganda letter in French, straight from the heart. 'I have been living among the lepers for almost seven years. In that time, I have had occasion to witness close at hand and, as it were, to touch human misery in its most repulsive form. Half of my patients are no more than living corpses, which are already eaten by worms.' The reality was repulsive.

> Since the churchyard, the church and the presbytery form a park and I am the only nightwatchman in this beautiful kingdom of the dead, in which so many of my children in the spirit are buried, I take pleasure in saying my rosary there, or meditating on that eternal felicity which many of them already enjoy, on the misfortune of those few who would not obey me and who now suffer in purgatory. I admit that the churchyard and the death hut are my most beautiful books of meditation, both as nourishment for my own heart and as preparation for my instructions.

He broke his silence at the moment when Bishop Maigret was losing control of the mission. In Paris, the general and the other superiors had closely questioned Régis Moncany, who had gone there, because Köckemann's letters gave the impression that there was a power vacuum. Moncany said that it was Favens, in particular, who was becoming senile, who could not cope. The superior therefore decided to set up a Provincial council to assist the enfeebled provincial. Régis Moncany, Hermann Köckemann, Gulstan Ropert and Aubert Bouillon were appointed to it. This was promotion for Köckemann, but it did not satisfy his ambitions. The appointment of the 38-year-old Ropert, the priest from Britanny who had worked with Damien on the Big Island in particular, rankled, especially when it was rumoured that this relative newcomer was to represent the Hawaiian Islands at the General Chapter in Paris. Köckemann had hoped for that task.

Léonor Fouesnel approached Köckemann and insinuated that Ropert had fathered a child by a widow. Köckemann did not write about such matters. He was more subtle. He complained that he was often insulted because he was constantly having to find solutions for problems that Maigret had caused. Nevertheless, he remained obedient to his superiors; more than that, he always praised them in public.

Departure of Dr Emerson and Burgerman

There were problems enough in the mission. Damien, Burgerman and Archambaux had leprosy and Boniface Schäffer feared he had contracted the disease. Pouzot was on the verge of a nervous collapse and Albert Montiton, the newcomer from the Puamotou Islands, who had already quarrelled with a lot of people, especially Köckemann, was suffering from a most irritating skin disease. Burgerman, Bouillon, Schäffer and Fouesnel were all threatening to leave the Order.

One scandal after another broke in the mission. Damien's successor on the Big Island, Fabien Schausten, had fathered a child and the matter came to court. It cost the mission much effort to have the case dismissed by the Waimea court. Schausten took the place of Liévin van Heteren, who had just died, in the Ahuimanu College, but was dismissed from the Order shortly thereafter. There were the rumours about Ropert, and Damien, too, was supposed to be leading a profligate life.

Burgerman was living with Henriette Speyver. Damien once again wrote to Moncany about the relationship and this time the vice-provincial believed him, not least because Dr Emerson confirmed it. The superiors decided that Burgerman must leave. They offered him a pension that he could retain if he left the Order. The superiors had decided he was no good because he refused to hear Damien's confession.

Perhaps even more serious for Burgerman was that the Board also wanted him removed from the settlement. He seems not to have grasped the precariousness of his situation, because he demanded rations and his own cook in return for his medical services, just at the point when Emerson was furious with him because he refused to dole out fewer medicines. He told the patients that Emerson's medicines were poisonous and that the patients would be wise to stop taking them. Emerson considered that Burgerman was undermining his authority. Moncany thought the situation critical once again and asked the general for the third time to remove Burgerman from Hawaii. In the interim, Burgerman was ordered to remove to Lahaina on Maui Island. Damien would remain in the settlement alone.

Burgerman did everything he could to remain. He put a formal end to his relationship with Henriette, heard Damien's confession and promised the Board to give up medicine. He did this at the moment when his services were welcome, because Emerson could no longer cope with his own work. The blow that Burgerman gave him was the last straw. Burgerman had stormed into the doctor's house and accused him of leaking the fact of his relationship with Henriette Speyver. Emerson had no time to deny this before he received a severe blow. Emerson now considered the matter completely settled and demanded that Burgerman be expelled from the leper settlement.

He himself also wanted to leave. He needed company, healthy people. For clerics like Damien, the leper settlement was a penance, but even Damien sometimes needed to spend time away to get a 'breath of fresh air'. Emerson could not cope with being in the settlement on a full-time basis. He promised to stay until a replacement was found.

Now that Burgerman and Emerson were both leaving, the patients feared that they would be left without medical help. For a short time it seemed that a solution was being worked on, but when, in July, Burgerman started living with Henriette Speyver again and also giving out pills, Sam Wilder had an expulsion order made out. Damien was shocked when he heard this news and rode to Kalaupapa to find out if it were true. He rushed into the living room. Burgerman lost all self-control and shouted, 'Je te brûlerai la cervelle!' – 'I'll blow your brains out!' He ran into the back room and opened the drawer where he kept his revolver. Damien saw something glint and rode to Emerson for help. Later Burgerman said he had gone to fetch his pipe.

Emerson took the situation seriously, because it was well known that he had a revolver. He asked Clayton Strawn and William Crowningburg for police protection around his house and began immediately to write a letter to the Board, in which he said that he, Emerson, knew from personal experience that Burgerman was a 'violent and uncontrolled man', in short, a 'bad' fellow. He was shacking up with a leper woman. In itself, that was a matter of taste, but given that he was continuing to work as a priest, he was a 'hypocrite'. This 'charlatan' attacked Emerson's method of work, something which ought not to be done by one real doctor to another, let alone by a quack to a medically qualified practitioner. 'I feel obliged to warn,' Emerson wrote, 'that if he retains his permission to stay in the settlement, the peace of this community will soon be rudely disturbed.'

Damien was careful in his letter to the Board. 'I have God alone as my witness and I do not wish this to have any legal repercussions. I wish only to explain why I am requesting you to remove this dangerous man from the settlement.'

Burgerman was required to appear before the French consul on the grounds of unlawful practice of medicine. The complaint had been made by the minister of the Interior, Samuel Wilder. The mission wanted Burgerman to move to Lahaina, but he remained in Kalaupapa, a fact which drove Emerson to distraction. When his successor Dr Charles Nielson was designated, he left. Nielson was a good-looking, well-dressed man with a charming manner. He hoped to find a cure for leprosy and wanted to carry out autopsies in Kalaupapa. Emerson warned him that the Hawaiians would not accept this, and so Nielson had several bodies put in metal coffins and transferred to Honolulu. He also experimented with a treatment from Norway that he hoped would be effective.

The patients and Damien signed a petition to keep Emerson, who understood the Hawaiians and spoke their language, but he refused, with tears in his eyes. He was so exhausted that he had to be carried onto the sloop. Burgerman watched him from his presbytery.

In August, Damien took part in the annual retreat. He needed spiritual nourishment and needed to consult his superiors. In his absence, Moncany sent Burgerman detailed instructions about travelling to Lahaina. No one would be waiting to pick him up. Burgerman remained where he was. He finally left the settlement on 14 August. He was no longer required to appear before the French consul, as the mission had been able to get this case filed as well. Burgerman was never to return to Molokai. He worked for many years in Lahaina, although he continued to be a difficult man, who was often in conflict with his superiors. He mostly did medical work and was popular with the people. He never buried the hatchet with Damien, but died as a member of the Order in 1908, aged seventy-nine.

12

A Royal Honour
(August 1880–October 1881)

Visit by Princesses Liliuokalani and Likelike

In September, the king appointed Walter Murray Gibson
chairman of the Board of Health, hoping that a politician would
be a better leader of the Board than a businessman. In the settlement the news was received positively, because Gibson had
achieved a doubling of the budget, but the appointment ended
in scandal, and Gibson resigned.

In Kalaupapa, very little changed. On 3 January 1881,
Damien had an audience in Honolulu with Queen Kapiolani,
who was about to leave on an international tour. He explained
that it was above all the medical care in the leper settlement
that stood in need of improvement. He attended the winter
retreat and had a long conversation with Köckemann, who
seemed to be sympathetic to him. Köckemann wrote to the
general that it was improper to leave Damien alone.

Damien had just returned to Kalaupapa when Dr Nielson
came to vaccinate the patients against cowpox. There was an
epidemic in Honolulu. He used a scalpel which he wiped each
time on the same piece of rag, for reasons of hygiene. Damien
reacted violently to the vaccination, developing a large
open sore.

The cowpox epidemic spread rapidly and so the inhabitants
of Molokai asked for quarantine regulations to be imposed.
The 319 patients also signed the request. It was granted and no
ships were allowed to put in until a boat 'with a white flag on
the foremast and an Hawaiian flag on the mainmast' should sail

past, to announce that the epidemic was over. The quarantine was partially lifted on 24 May and the settlement received its first post. Damien learned to his horror that the mission was once again saddled with a legal case. The prestigious college in Honolulu had collapsed the day after the opening and a child had been killed. Maigret had immediately dismissed the Irish priest, Larkin, who was responsible for the building. It was decided that in future no one should be taken on who was not a member of the Sacred Hearts Order, because they were 'wolves in sheep's clothing'. The Belgian missionary, Louis-Lambert Conrardy, who had once again offered to work with Damien, was fobbed off.

When passenger transport was re-established, there were several deportations, including two white children: Henry Wright, a former pupil of Ahuimanu College, and a young man called Cullen, whose father had put him forward, in order to save the rest of his family.

There were also some distinguished visitors. Princess Liliuokalani and her sister, Princess Likelike, stepped ashore, almost unexpectedly, for a day-long visit to the settlement. The inhabitants scarcely had time to put up triumphal arches and sweep the paths. Liliuokalani had been following the situation on Molokai since 1875. Her motto was '*Hooulu lahui*', 'Increase the race', and restricting epidemics was a way to save the Hawaiian people.

The princess asked Damien to explain things to her on the drive to Kalawao, because she wanted to learn as much as she could in her short visit to the leper settlement. She also questioned Clayton Strawn and Captain Sumner. Despite the fact that it was an unofficial visit, Sumner wished to make a speech of thanks and he asked the princesses to take their places on the verandah of one of the hospital wards. The exiles sat on the grass. It was a lengthy speech and the princesses occasionally looked bored. Then the princess stood and addressed the crowd briefly, telling them that she did not forget them and wished to do her best to help them. She told them to speak freely and conceal nothing, because she wished to be aware of their problems. She then listened to their tales of woe for an hour, sometimes shedding tears and putting her head in her hands. She learned that the settlement badly needed a girls' orphanage, that house repairs urgently needed to be done before the cold season and that there was a housing shortage. Above all, she learned that medical care was inadequate and that they needed a 'real' doctor – not a gallant man like Nielson, who lacked the necessary energy – and, particularly, nurses. At the end, the princess sang a song she had composed herself, in farewell: '*Aloha Oe*' ('Fare thee well, till we meet again'). She was moved and troubled as she spoke briefly to Damien before her departure.

Elevation of Bishop Köckemann

It is not clear whether the debacle of the college in Honolulu was the reason for Bishop Maigret's removal from office. Hermann Köckemann and Léonor Fouesnel had, after all, been bombarding the general for years with tales of mismanagement by their elderly superiors. Whatever the case, at the end of June, Köckemann received news from Paris that he had been appointed suffragan. Maigret, like Favens, would remain superior for life, but Köckemann would henceforth do the work. Köckemann asked Fouesnel to accompany him to San Francisco for his enthronement. Damien congratulated Köckemann during the August retreat and was among those who waved him off at the quayside, but Bishop Maigret found his enforced retirement hard to accept and called Köckemann a usurper.

Father Albert Montiton, a Tense Companion

Immediately prior to his departure, Köckemann had made two important decisions: he had dismissed Fabien Schausten – Damien's successor on the Big Island – from the Order, on the grounds of immoral behaviour, and appointed Albert Montiton as Damien's companion. There were those who had their suspicions about the latter decision. Montiton was immediately segregated as a leper, without any medical examination. It was already widely known within the mission that Montiton and Köckemann were hostile to one another. This would relieve the bishop of the excitable Frenchman for good.

Damien knew that Montiton suffered from a skin disease which caused constant irritation and which, according to the tales he told, he had acquired as a missionary on the Puamotu Islands. Damien had heard that Montiton was talkative, musical and a good sailor, but he got worked up over the least thing. Nevertheless, he did not want to make a fuss, because he had been given a companion.

Meanwhile, he was giving his full attention to the retreat in Honolulu. He examined his conscience thoroughly and found that he had committed many sins. He was too demanding, he needed to behave more calmly, and he wrote in his notebook '*Festina lente* – make haste slowly'. He must be stricter with himself. Was he really generous? Didn't he interfere too much in other people's business? He was also too familiar with the orphan boys and treated them as though they were his own children. He needed to summon up greater reserves, must stop gossiping and not judge others too quickly. He had not always shown the appropriate respect for God, had been distracted during prayers and read his breviary in a routine manner. Sometimes he had absolutely no desire to pray and did not prepare the mass. He had eaten before communion and had not prepared his sermons. He had not shown adequate respect for ecclesiastical matters and for the Holy Oil. He had removed his soutane in order to work better. His preparation for confession is extant. 'I was too often angry and have triply sinned against the furies (impure thoughts, nakedness, contact). I have spoken evil and have hurt the feelings of the Mormons.'

Within a few days, however, when Montiton arrived in Kalaupapa, things immediately looked bad. Montiton wanted to know straight away whether what he had been told on the Big Island was true. Did Damien have a mistress? Damien snapped back that he must see for himself that he kept his vow of chastity, but Montiton would not stop going on about 'fornication'.

Montiton knew how to tell a tale, however. He had met Pamphile in Leuven and gave splendid accounts of the convent and his conversations there. He had travelled through the whole of Europe, when he went there for medical treatment, visiting one doctor after another, but he had also awakened the enthusiasm of younger men for missionary work. He had prayed at Lourdes and had an audience with the pope. He talked nineteen to the dozen about that. He won the Hawaiians' hearts with his tales, for he was fluent in their language.

Montiton thought that he should be the superior, since he was fifteen years older, but Moncany did not agree. He called Montiton an *énergumène*, a rowdy character, and a *brouillon*, a troublemaker, in his reports to the general, adding that nothing was ever right for Montiton. Everything had to be done again. He treated rudely anyone who did not dance to his tune. Damien had trouble with Montiton from the very start, but he did not let this appear. He wrote to Köckemann that they got on well.

Royal Honour (October 1881)

When he returned from San Francisco, Köckemann followed protocol by requesting to be allowed to wait on Princess Liliuokalani. The date was set for 20 September. Köckemann decided not to ask Maigret to accompany him, because the latter still had not come to terms with his deposition. The French consul, in full court dress, did accompany him, along with six priests. The bishop was greeted with full court ceremonial and during the reception the princess announced that she wished to honour two members of the clergy. The first, and highest, honour was for the former bishop, but because he was not present, she presented the order in council and the decoration of Knight of the Royal Order of Kalakaua to the French consul. This could have been seen as insulting to the new bishop. Köckemann, who was constantly criticising Maigret in private because he had not resigned himself to his dismissal, declared in public that Maigret had 'contributed to the well-being and independence of the country'.

The second honour was for Damien and this, too, the princess presented to the French consul, although Köckemann wrote to Paris that the princess had asked him to give Damien the decoration in person. However, first a letter was sent by post.

The captain of the *Kilauea* hardly ever went ashore at the settlement, but on this occasion, he wanted to hand the royal document to Damien in person. A crowd thronged round the priest and urged him to read out the letter, which he did.

Kalakau, king of the Hawaiian Islands,

To all who read these presents, greeting. Know that we have designated and commissioned, and by these presents do designate and commission

The Reverend Father in God Damien de Veuster

as

Knight Commander

in the Royal Order of Kalakaua, to exercise and enjoy all rights, perquisites and privileges thereto appertaining and to bear the insignia as provided in the decree. In evidence hereof we have patented this letter and affixed to it the seal of the kingdom, given by our hand in the palace of Honolulu this twentieth day of September in the year eighteen hundred and eighty one.

Signed

Liliuokalani, Regent for the king, chancellor of the Royal Order of Kalakaua.

The regent had added the following text herself:

It is my wish to express to you my great appreciation for your heroic and unselfish work among the least fortunate of the subjects of this kingdom and to bear public witness to the faithful, patient and loving care with which you are working for the bodily and spiritual well-being of those who are, of necessity, cut off from the tender care of family and friends. I am aware that your work and sacrifices arise exclusively from your desire to help your unfortunate fellow human beings and that you seek your reward and inspiration in the Holy Father and Lord of us all. Nevertheless, it is my wish to ask you, Reverend Father, to receive the order of Knight Commander of the Royal Order of Kalakaua, as a token of my sincere appreciation for your efforts in many ways to remove the misery and relieve the distress of the unfortunate lepers in Kalawao. This I saw with my own eyes during my recent visit to your mission. Your friend. Regent Liliuokalani.

The letter was greeted with jubilation. The two pastors Kaawa and Kahuila withdrew and returned shortly afterwards to take round a petition, thanking the princess for the honour. They asked everyone, of whatever denomination, to sign, apart from Damien.

Meyer came down to the settlement the same day with more good news. Liliuokalani had got the Board to agree to set up a girls' orphanage. It was to be a large house, surrounded by a verandah. Damien could choose the site himself. For reasons of propriety, he chose a piece of land at some distance from his presbytery, but not too far, so that both the boys' and girls' orphanages could be served by a single cookhouse. Meyer drafted a scheme that very day.

All the newspapers carried the news of the honour on the front page, but with different emphases. The *Hawaiian Gazette* stressed the fact that Liliuokalani had risen above 'petty-minded cliques'. This broad-minded woman placed service above religious beliefs. The *Pacific Commercial Advertiser* spoke of Damien, who 'had revived the saintly heroism of the bloody arenas of Antiquity'. 'Was it not a greater boon to be thrown before the wild beasts, than to be condemned to life in the poisonous atmosphere of a leper settlement?'

Damien knew that all these honours would arouse yet more jealousy. So he wrote to Köckemann that there was a good deal of fuss and bother concerning the priest from Kalawao and he hoped it would not arouse any envy.

It was also necessary to write a letter of thanks to the princess. He used the reverse of a letter for the draft, but the letter was only copied and sent a month later. He probably received help with it from a native speaker.

Your Royal Highness, having received your kind letter, in which you ask me to accept the honour which Your Royal Highness wishes to award me, in recognition of my humble services to the lepers, I shall do so willingly, despite the fact that I am unworthy to submit to the request that I receive the honourable title of the rank of Knight Commander of the Royal Order of Kalakaua from your royal hands. This is a lasting and public recognition of the present unity and good understanding between the royal family and the Catholic Church. As far as my mission in Kalawao is concerned, I do solemnly promise Your Royal Highness and the Honourable Board of Health, as Knight Commander of the Royal Order of Kalakaua, that I shall do my utmost for the spiritual and worldly well-being of the unfortunate lepers.

Episcopal Visitation (October 1881)

Damien was delighted at the news that Köckemann would confer the honour on him in person on 8 October. He began to prepare the candidates for confirmation straight away and the day before the bishop's arrival he visited the parishes on 'topside' to inform people there of the visit. At dawn, he stood waiting on the quayside at Kaunakakai, a harbour on the south coast. He was kept waiting for twenty-four hours, because the boat was late.

When the bishop had recovered from the voyage, the two men set out for the leper settlement. Köckemann had brought a large amount of baggage, including mattresses, crockery and so on, in order to avoid the risk of infection. The descent of the *pali* was difficult, because the bishop suffered from vertigo and Damien had almost to carry him down. At the foot of the *pali*, there was a welcoming committee, including Strawn and Sumner, and a pastor, whom Damien introduced as a 'brother in Christ', and Köckemann found himself obliged to mount into a saddle that had possibly been used by a leper.

As they entered the settlement, riding beneath a triumphal arch, they were greeted by a choir, led by Montiton. The bishop was nauseated by the stench in the church during the service and was hardly relaxed at the idea of staying in the presbytery with Damien, because of the rumours that the latter had leprosy. He was anxious to get away as soon as he could, and preoccupied by the fact that Damien had called the Protestants 'brothers in Christ'.

After a pause for rest, Köckemann joined Damien outside, where a crowd had gathered for the award ceremony. There was a large number of speeches, all in praise of Damien. The bishop himself said, 'In the absence of her brother, Princess Liliuokalani has found it appropriate to honour publicly Father Damien's noble work by appointing him a Knight of the Order of Kalakaua.' He took the fine medal and pinned it carefully to Damien's soutane, to general applause. Damien made to take the medal off, but Köckemann told him to keep it on for the remainder of the bishop's visit. Damien responded, with a broad smile, by saying that it outshone the bishop's cross.

Köckemann then completed his duties by hearing confessions, administering communion, confirming candidates and baptising catechumens, in both Kalawao and Kalaupapa. In the latter village, Köckemann granted a petition from the parishioners to extend their church by making it cruciform.

Then he made haste to leave. At the foot of the *pali*, he was given an official farewell and the Rev. Kahuila spoke a few words, explaining that he and Damien agreed that there should be peace and toleration in the settlement, because, in the face of death, Protestant and Catholic were equal. He asked Köckemann, in the name of all those who sought to do good, to give them his blessing. The bishop was alarmed. He replied that they must accept their 'segregation', because it was for the good of the country, but unity and co-operation were extremely important. He then gave his blessing to all present, Protestant, Mormon, heathen and Catholic, and then rushed off up the path and hastened to the boat.

Back in Honolulu, Köckemann had the shock of his life. His finger nails began to fall out and he feared he had contracted leprosy. The doctor advised him to wear rubber gloves, a safety measure he would continue to take until the end of his life.

Patients Dumped in the Sea (Autumn 1881)

Following Köckemann's departure, Damien visited the parishes on 'topside'. When it was time to return to the settlement, however, it was pouring with rain and so he stayed with Meyer until the weather should clear up. The next day the weather was even worse and he was contemplating another restful day until someone came with a message that there had been a serious accident in the settlement. Despite the storm and the fact that it was night, he managed to get down the mountain.

Everyone was in a great state, spoke of cold-blooded murder and showed him the corpse of a drowned exile. The schooner *Warwick* had been lying at anchor in Kalawao bay for some time, but it had been too dangerous to put out the boats. For years, it had been the captain's practice to take the exiles back with him if the weather was too bad to put them ashore, but on this occasion, he forced them to jump into the surf. Meyer later suggested that there had been a problem on board. Whatever the case, those in the settlement were witness to a crime. The strongest among the exiles and the *kokuas* jumped into the sea to save those who were drowning. Twenty people either swam or were helped ashore, but two did not make it. Damien arrived in time to give assistance. He also comforted one of the dying.

After the funeral, the atmosphere in the leper settlement was revolutionary and the affair caused outrage throughout the islands. Princess Liliuokalani declared that 'leprosy was a disease, not a crime'. All over the islands, anonymous posters began to appear on walls and trees, calling for terrorist acts, in the most provocative language, for the sick had been 'thrown into the sea like dogs'. Those who supported segregation must expect violence. Plantations would burn.

Damien was depressed and upset. He was in open conflict with Montiton. The latter was convinced that Damien slept with women in the settlement and that Elikapeka Punana, the wife of the cook Barnabé, was hushing everything up. At this time the two priests had switched parishes, so that Damien could work on the enlargement of the church in Kalaupapa. Montiton went on and on about Damien's 'affairs', until Barnabé became so incensed that he threatened to leave his job and also threatened Damien and Montiton with violence. Köckemann did not attach any credence to Montiton's tales of love affairs, because he had twice stirred up similar trouble on the Big Island. The problem was that Damien was getting to the end of his tether. 'Everything would be fine here,' Damien wrote, 'if Albert [Montiton] learned to control himself and wasn't so demanding. Please excuse this outburst, but Elikapeka's husband, who looks after thirty-four orphans, is threatening to resign. Régis's [Moncany] irritating orders test my patience to the utmost and then I have to deal with my colleague's excesses.' Köckemann's decision was typical of him and left everyone confused. Damien was responsible for the whole of the settlement, but had the power of decision only in Kalawao, while Montiton was subordinate to Damien in everything, but was to work completely independently in Kalaupapa.

There were other problems as well. Dr Charles Nielson had managed to do next to nothing in the past eighteen months. He drew his salary as government doctor and spent it gambling on horses in Honolulu. In October 1881, he suffered a heavy loss. He borrowed some jewels, as he said, to show his wife, and disappeared in strange circumstances to New Zealand.

Once again, the patients were without medical care and so the Board appointed Damien assistant-physician. After eight years in Kalawao, he was able to deal with small problems. His tone was sarcastic when he wrote to order Epsom salts: 'Thus

far, we are managing quite well without a medical officer of
the kind we had recently.' The real problems quickly arose.
'Assistant–physician' was a vague position and the British sailor
John Ostrum did not want Damien involved in the hospital's
affairs. His chief concern was hygiene. He wanted a 'clean'
hospital and Damien was now urging that patients be given
more freedom. The dispute was quickly over, because in
December the Californian doctor George Fitch was appointed
and he took over all responsibility.

Dr Fitch was prepared to work hard. He had left his young
wife behind in San Francisco and wanted to save enough money
to set up a practice there. He had the full support of the
Protestants, which immediately made him suspect to Köckemann. Damien's relations with Fitch were good. Their first
point of discussion was that Fitch was totally convinced that
leprosy was the fourth stage of syphilis. His reasoning was
logical: there had been neither syphilis nor leprosy before the
arrival of Captain Cook. The first cases of leprosy appeared
after the venereal disease had become well established in the
population and Fitch believed that there were no lepers who
did not have syphilis. Damien disagreed, because he suspected
that he was a countervailing example. By this time, he had
hardly any sensation in his foot. In order to give force to
his theory, Fitch hoped to be allowed to inoculate a healthy
person who had been condemned to death. The prisoner would
serve his sentence in complete isolation so that the doctor
could determine whether he got leprosy without getting
syphilis first.

In the midst of all this, it was pleasant to receive news from
home, even if Pamphile's lengthy missives contained little news.
Damien's mother added, with an unsteady hand, 'Dearly beloved
son, my motherly blessing and pray for me. I shall pray for you.
C. Wauters'

13

Nursing Sisters Invited to the Settlement (January 1882–November 1883)

A Leprosy Hospital Near Honolulu

Dr Fitch had not been appointed to work on Molokai Island, but in the new hospital for lepers in Honolulu. Princess Liliuokalani had carried out this project after her visit to the leper settlement. She received support from the planters, who watched their Chinese coolies becoming ill and feared that their plantations would be razed. One of the demands of the resistance movement was a hospital in Honolulu.

A windswept salt marsh near Honolulu was chosen for the hospital. Kakaako was sufficiently far away from the city to avoid infection, but close enough to permit visits. The site was tightly enclosed and the wards were built on piles. The land between the buildings was barren. The intention was that those who were suspected of having leprosy would be transferred to Kakaako after their arrest, where they would be examined by Fitch. If leprosy was confirmed, those cases which were mild and could possibly be cured would be allowed to stay for treatment, whilst the hopeless cases would have to go to Molokai. Kakaako quickly became the hospital of hope and Kalaupapa the dump for the hopeless.

Kakaako offered treatment. King Kalakaua had visited the hospital of Dr Shobun Goto in Tokyo, where lepers received a treatment that consisted of herbal baths and medicines. A white person from Honolulu believed he had been cured of leprosy by this method and, in gratitude, offered to meet the costs of a Goto-bath system in Kakaako.

Damien's parishioner Henry van Giesen was appointed director. He had followed his half-Hawaiian wife, Carolina Sweetsman, who was related to Queen Kapiolani, as a white *kokua* to Molokai.

From the very start, the plan to keep only mild and 'unconfirmed' cases in Kakaako went wrong. Captain Sumner, for example, whose condition was far advanced, was allowed to move to Oahu, because he was half white and an *alii*, and there were similar cases. Nevertheless, Damien's impression of the hospital, when he visited it in January 1882, was positive. He hoped to be able to introduce the system of herbal baths to Molokai if the trials in the hospital proved effective.

Damien was in Honolulu for the winter retreat. During his stay, he was summoned by Bishop Köckemann, who wanted to discuss Damien's medical activities. Montiton, whom Köckemann admitted to be difficult, was demanding that Damien should stop these. Damien objected to this, on the grounds that these activities gave him greater weight in the hospital and also allowed him to combat debauchery more effectively. In any case, it was only a temporary solution. He had said nearly nine years ago that nursing sisters were badly needed in the settlement. Léonor Fouesnel was going to Europe to recruit teaching brothers for the new college. Perhaps he could also find some sisters. Köckemann did not respond to this suggestion, but did permit Damien to continue his medical work.

Damien also discussed the policy on marriage with the Board. Before his arrival on Molokai, an act had been passed forbidding lepers to marry. However, this legislation had effectively been set aside by Kalakaua in 1874, when he had permitted Damien to solemnise marriages. Now, the Board wished to reimpose the legal restrictions: since Kakaako was intended for mild cases and only those whose condition was hopeless went to Molokai, it would be irresponsible to allow *kokuas* to marry lepers and risk infection. Once again, the Board wished to remove all healthy individuals from the settlement and the first step was to remove Damien's licence to solemnise marriages. Damien argued that those patients who had the support of a *kokua* were much better able to cope with their illness, but he was overruled.

Damien had an altercation with Montiton concerning a marriage in mid-April 1882. A dying man wished to marry the woman with whom he had long been cohabiting. Montiton said that this should not be done until proof could arrive from his former parish that his first marriage did not count for the Catholic Church; he refused to hear the man's confession. Damien viewed things differently. His maxims were that in case of doubt there is freedom, but there must always be charity and that one should always be constructive, not destructive. Damien not only heard the man's confession but performed the marriage, since the man had only hours to live. Köckemann supported Damien's decision to hear the man's confession, but not his decision to perform the marriage ceremony. Nevertheless, he showed no hostility to Damien, writing on this occasion, 'I am deeply fond of you. I appreciate your dedicated work for the good of the souls.'

An Oecumenical Festival Avant la Lettre (Corpus Christi 1882)

The settlement was, in many ways quite intentionally, a world apart, and not surprisingly it developed its own mores over time, which differed in certain respects from those of the outside world and which were a closely guarded secret from the outside world.

One of the ways in which social practice in the leper settlement differed from the world beyond was in the degree of co-operation and harmony among the different religious groups. The Corpus Christi procession of 1882 was an example of this. The religious leaders of the non-Catholic religious groups asked to be allowed to participate. For once, Damien and Montiton were in agreement that they should be allowed to do so.

Members of all the different creeds took part in preparing the festival and the feasting, and likewise participated in the processions and religious ceremonies. The procession was somewhat chaotic, with the various religious groups that participated joining in one another's hymns and music, not always successfully. Damien and Montiton took it in turns to carry the holy sacrament, and they were careful to adjust the pace of the procession to take account of the invalids who found it difficult to walk. The whole event was a festival of respect for one another and Montiton expressed this when he said, in Hawaiian,

> This celebration is unique. We Christians who are present here wish to demonstrate our belief in God, who is three in one. Today we worship Jesus Christ, our Eucharistic king, the Lord and Saviour who is present in the Holy Sacrament. We worship his love for mankind and the Holy Sacrament that he instituted on the day before his death.

Nevertheless, Montiton seems to have been happier to have non-Catholics participate in Catholic celebrations than to countenance Catholic attendance at non-Catholic worship. When Damien attended the Protestant wedding ceremony of one of Meyer's children, a few weeks later, Montiton protested loudly.

Montiton's Grumbling Intolerable

The summer of 1882 made plain the disastrous state of medical care in Kalaupapa. Dr Fitch was ill and was unable to visit the settlement until 5 December. Consequently, there were no deportations, because since the drowning incident a doctor always had to be present. The need became so dire that Damien amputated a foot with a saw, much to Montiton's anger. 'This business with the doctors is a mess,' Meyer wrote.

When you need them, they aren't there and even the simplest

remedies aren't available. The more I see of this doctoring business, the less faith I have in the system. It seems as if the Board just wants to have a doctor in name. I don't want to criticise Dr Fitch, because the man has done more than the other doctors but the system the Board has set up is wrong: either you have a doctor who is there all the time, or you don't.

Montiton complained about Damien's medical work to the superiors and Moncany thereupon forbade him to continue with it. Köckemann also advised him not to continue, because it could cause a scandal. Fitch advised Damien to ask for an official permit and he sent a formal request to Walter Gibson, the new chairman of the Board of Health. 'Having things in black and wight [sic],' he wrote, 'I would be able to act for the welfare of all concerned without being molested by anprincipled [sic] men whom's [sic] jealousy is very painful for me.' He was, of course, referring to Montiton.

The two men also quarrelled over Damien's request to the Board that he be granted guardianship of the orphans in the settlement, with special responsibility for their welfare. Montiton did not think this was Damien's task.

Damien lost his patience. He wrote to Köckemann,

I have several children under my guardianship. It was not easy to get permission for this. I have always sensed the opposition of a jealous administration. If you do not approve of my actions – Albert [Montiton] is strongly opposed – then I shall leave Molokai.

If you do not curb Albert's insufferable disposition you will find me on your doorstep without having summoned me. I can no longer live at war with the colleagues whom the Order sends me.

This is the only document in which Damien threatens to leave Molokai. Köckemann did not succeed in restraining Montiton.

Promise of Nursing Sisters

Damien did not then know that preparations were in hand for the realisation of his dream. During Köckemann's courtesy visit to the king on his birthday, 1 November 1882, Kalakaua asked the bishop to find nursing sisters for Molokai and teaching sisters for Hawaiian girls. Their travel and expenses would be paid. Köckemann was alarmed. Inviting nuns to come, so he thought, would strengthen the prejudice against Catholics among the socially prominent. Irritated, Kalakaua advised the bishop to be patient.

Köckemann did nothing, because he doubted the king's word and Gibson to him was a scoundrel. In any case, he had no idea where to find nursing sisters. American and Irish orders would, in any case, be better than French nuns, who followed a strict conventual rule, which was impossible in Hawaii.

Meanwhile, the Board was considering the financial implications. Fitch thought that twenty-five sisters were needed, but the Board had a budget for only ten. Suddenly, some of the Board members realised that Damien had been working all these years without any compensation, without even so much as a present. He had just sent for repair the wheels of a cart he had bought from Van Giesen, at the latter's departure to Honolulu. The Board thought the cart a 'useless article' and presented him with a new one. Damien sent a warm letter of thanks, but also took the opportunity to ask *Papa Ole* not to infringe 'the moral law' any longer. Paedophiles and pimps were terrorising the children. He very much wanted to have the guardianship of them in order to protect them.

On 5 December 1881, Dr Fitch arrived, to everyone's relief. He had good news for Damien: nursing sisters would soon be coming. They were more than needed, because things were going wrong in Kakaako as well. The fathers in Honolulu hardly ever visited the hospital and it would be good if Damien could visit sometime. The patients were worried and resisted deportation. The bishop had another surprise, according to Fitch. The Catholic fair had raised $4,000. Köckemann wanted to give him part of the money in person and invited Damien to Honolulu for Christmas. Damien promised to attend the winter retreat, but wanted to spend Christmas with his parishioners. Montiton's skin disease was gradually spreading over his whole body and the irritation was driving him mad. He could not be left alone for the festivals.

Damien had also been given permission to solemnise a marriage, because the couple had had a child, an unusual event, since live births were rare among patients. On Boxing Day, 26 December, he gathered all his courage and climbed the *pali* to celebrate Christmas with the parishioners there. The journey was a torment, because he was in tremendous pain from his left foot.

He landed in Honolulu on 30 December. There were letters from home awaiting him. A long letter from Pamphile gave details of Léonor Fouesnel's visit to Damien's family in Tremelo. A letter from one of his nieces gave news of his mother, who was still active and in good health.

On New Year's Eve, Damien was sufficiently recovered from his seasickness to visit Kakaako. Dr Fitch discussed with him the work that the sisters would do if they came. Van Giesen, who was now steward in Kakaako, showed him the chapel he himself had built in his spare time. It was no masterpiece, but better than nothing. Damien said mass for the patients and preached about heaven, their ultimate goal. Afterwards, he answered as best he could the questions that the future deportees put to him.

That night Damien slept little, as he had done for months. He was kept awake by the fireworks and the sound of people's drunken laughter on the street. The worst thing, however, was his foot. He could draw a clear line between the part in which he had no feeling and the part where the pain was razor sharp. Sometimes, he felt like screaming. He had swollen lymph nodes in his left groin. He had scabies and he knew that he needed to burn all his clothes and bedding, if he wanted to be rid of it, but could not afford this. He was also suffering from chronic diarrhoea.

He must not limp, however, and certainly not when he was presented to Walter Murray Gibson. Damien regarded him as

FATHER DAMIEN

an ally: he had called Damien a Christian hero and doubled the
settlement's budget. During the pleasant conversation, the prime
minister asked the bishop how far he had got with the project
for nursing sisters. Köckemann made an evasive reply. Gibson
asked the party to accompany him to the royal palace to give
their New Year greetings to the king, but the latter was still
recovering from the previous night's festivities and they were
received by Queen Kapiolani. The queen expressed her concern
about the leper settlement. Her relative had leprosy and so she
knew how it felt. Gibson announced solemnly that nursing
sisters would soon be coming and the queen declared that she
was pleased.

The prime minister felt he had her support and on 4 January
he sent Köckemann a report of the last meeting of the Board
of Health. Nurses were needed. 'I thought that this valuable
assistance could not be found more willingly anywhere than in
the ranks of the Catholic nuns,' Gibson wrote. 'I am happy that
I have been given the authority to invite eight or more sisters
to come and help our sick. I shall be responsible for first-class
travel, for comfortable lodgings and maintenance.' Köckemann
was now more positive about the idea. He could do down the
Anglicans. The crux arose from the letter itself, however, because
Gibson spoke of 'the sick' and not about 'lepers'.

Waiting for the Sisters

Back in Kalawao, Damien preached on the theme, 'lepers today,
but not in heaven'. He continued his round of visits, conducting
funerals and the constant squabbles with Montiton.

He received an invitation to the coronation of King Kalakaua
on 12 February 1883, but Köckemann would not allow him to
attend, because he had only just been in Honolulu.

When Gibson sent Köckemann word that he wanted to
transfer money for travelling expenses and part of the accommodation expenses to the mission's account, Köckemann finally
started to take action. The choice of an emissary to the United
States was quickly made. He considered no one other than

174

Léonor Fouesnel, because he had already been responsible for finding French teaching brothers for Honolulu. If Fouesnel were successful in this scheme, he would acquire the necessary credit to become provincial, whereas at present he was too controversial.

The struggle to succeed Moncany, who was dying of tuberculosis, had already begun. Favens would remain titular provincial until his death, but he was now completely senile. The number of candidates was limited, because, with a German bishop, the order superior had to be French. Gulstan Ropert was one possibility, but there were rumours about him and he was too young. Fouesnel, who had made a good impression on the general during his trip to Europe, was the only other possibility. In his letters, Köckemann sounded as though Fouesnel was the only one he could get on with, despite one or two doubts.

Fouesnel was a controversial figure. Moncany, Bouillon and others had complained of his expensive tastes and luxurious lifestyle. Fouesnel seemed to be a 'lone wolf'. For him, only the best was good enough and he enjoyed the good things of life on his own. He could not bear mistakes by subordinates, but he could not take criticism. He hardly ever praised others for doing something well. He cared about no one and no one, apart from Köckemann, cared for him.

Moncany died in the summer and Fouesnel, who was still in the United States, was appointed his successor. He arrived back in Hawaii on 1 August with the news that the sisters of the Third Order of St Francis, from the Convent of St Anthony in Syracuse, New York, had agreed to care for the sick and to open schools in Hawaii. Mother Marianne Cope would help five sisters to get settled. The same boat brought news of Fouesnel's appointment as provincial. However, for the moment, he had to concentrate on preparing for the arrival of the teaching brothers at the end of August. The Board had also appointed Dr Edward Arning, a bacteriologist who had studied at the Berlin Academy under Professor Koch, to look for a cure for leprosy.

In the Molokai settlement, life was continuing as normal,

while they waited for the nurses to come. Damien continued to request guardianship of neglected children. Meyer replied, laconically, that he should make the orphanages more attractive and then the parents would let their children come. Damien asked Köckemann, who was temporarily combining the functions of bishop and provincial, to be allowed to use a gift for improvements to the home and this was granted, although the bishop thought he should use the money for religious purposes.

It took the exiles more than a month to realise that the sisters were not intended for them. The first indication was that there were no plans for a convent on Molokai. Further signs were that the money for existing projects, like the repairs to the road between Kalaupapa and Kalawao, dried up and money for new projects was not forthcoming. On 20 August the Board decided to review all projects.

Meanwhile, each group of new exiles told of the extension work in Kakaako. Dr Shobun Goto's son was in charge of the bathing therapy and it seemed to be effective, since the patients felt much better. A laboratory for Dr Arning was being built next to Henry van Giesen's office and another hut was converted into a building for the dying and an autopsy theatre. Van Giesen appended to the list of exiled youths an urgent request that Damien come to Honolulu, because there were serious matters afoot.

On 30 September Meyer wrote, 'I have received more money for the settlement, but Walter Gibson told me yesterday that he feared there was not enough money to keep the institution going. I think, however, that when the night is darkest, the dawn is about to break.'

Dr Fitch brought a full report. There was to be no further investment on Molokai until the sisters had developed a programme of work. A convent was being built on the Kakaako site, but until then they would live in rented accommodation. There were no plans for Molokai.

The Beginning of the War between Damien and his Superiors

It was clear from his description in his report to the general that Fouesnel had little time for Damien.

A good religious man, a good priest, an extremely zealous missionary, excessively dedicated to his lepers. He has no *sapere ad sobrietatem* (understanding of sobriety) and sometimes his indiscreet zeal causes him to say, write, or even do things for which the religious superiors can only reprimand him. He has married men and women who had left spouses behind, without first requesting the correct information. His unquestioning zeal means that he cannot be corrected. He is loved and held in high esteem, but he is led by his lack of reflection, not by his good will.

The comment on Montiton was much more positive. 'Despite his sufferings, he tries to follow the rules of the Order and directs his zeal to his soul.'

Various replies from Fouesnel to requests for information concerning the marital status of people in Wailuku are extant. Fouesnel's negative opinion was so strong that Br Bertrand warned Damien that the new provincial was pursuing him, but he did not dare to write down what he knew.

The first extant letter from Fouesnel as provincial to Damien was a scolding because Damien was asking for a private benefaction that he had been given. Other priests donated their gifts to the mission. Köckemann, Fouesnel wrote, thought Damien's tiny corner of the world was costing too much money. He should ask the Board for wood. In an aside, he reported that the sisters were expected on 8 November, but there was no word about Molokai and no explanation that the arrival of two nuns had emptied the mission's coffers.

On 8 November, the day of his landing in Honolulu, Dr Arning, who was a dermatologist, bacteriologist and venereologist, set to work at once. He calculated from the statistics that leprosy had a ten- to fifteen-year course. The incubation period was unknown. In order to prove that leprosy was not the fourth stage of syphilis, he looked for the bacillus, that the Norwegian doctors Hansen and Neisser had discovered, in the tissue of a patient with leprosy, which he took from patients and, with the help of Van Giesen, from two corpses as well. If there were a connection between the two diseases, then, in his opinion, it was necessary to develop syphilis colonies, not leper settlements. He said straight away that the theory was dangerous, because it stigmatised the patients, who must have contracted the disease by improper behaviour and debauchery. Foreigners seemed to have developed some kind of hereditary resistance to leprosy.

Unintentionally, the realisation of Damien's dream had produced the opposite effect. Fitch cancelled his trip to Molokai because he had to help the sisters, and Meyer had no more money and feared he would not get any.

Fouesnel wrote a blazing letter to Montiton, in which he hit out at Damien concerning the sisters. The letter is not extant, but Montiton must have shown it to Damien, because the latter wrote to Fouesnel that he had not expected to meet with such a lack of confidence from the provincial. He did not regard himself as better than the provincial and repeated that he had neither said nor written anything, nor even raised a cheer, when the sisters arrived. He had, in fact, given up all hope. If the mother superior or one of the other sisters wanted to come to Molokai, they would live comfortably in the midst of a small, but completely Catholic village. Since his presence might disturb Fouesnel, he would withdraw, if he were given prior warning.

Damien had never suspected that he had fallen so low in his superiors' esteem. Fouesnel realised that he had gone too far. He blamed Köckemann and the senile Favens, apologised and added that he hoped it would be the last time he would have to humble himself before a subordinate whom he had insulted by using inappropriate language.

At the end of December, Fouesnel was once again angry with Damien because he was spending too much money, just when the mission was short. Maigret had deposited money in

Paris, but the mother house had used it for other purposes. The war between Damien and his superiors had begun.

14

Damien a Leper
(January 1884–January 1885)

Damien's Leprosy Diagnosed by Superiors

Since the arrival of the sisters, the Molokai community had not seen a doctor and, once again, Damien found himself obliged to amputate a foot with a butcher's knife. All the patients were hoping to be removed to Kakaako, but in the meanwhile, everyone was waiting with mounting excitement for a visit from Dr Arning, which never happened, or from the sisters, which likewise did not take place. Dr Fitch wanted to book a passage for the sisters on the *Mokolii*, but Fouesnel put a stop to this idea. He told Gibson that the boat was too small and dirty. Fouesnel did invite Damien to the winter retreat. 'We shall be happy to see you,' he wrote.

On the last day of the retreat, 21 January, the new St Philomena's Chapel in the Kakaako hospital was consecrated. Queen Kapiolani and the prime minister, Gibson, were present and a choir of lepers sang Mozart's Fourth Mass, accompanied by Van Giesen on the piano. Both he and the bishop seemed very moved. Gibson thanked the sisters for their noble self-sacrifice. Damien was hoping to be introduced to them, but Fouesnel wanted to prevent him speaking to the mother superior and so kept them occupied with a succession of different people. The next morning, the mother superior and two other sisters sailed to Maui Island to set up a school and hospital in Wailuku. Four sisters remained in Kakaako.

The arrival of the sisters had major consequences for Molokai. The deportations were stopped until the hospital was organised. For four months, advanced cases had the opportunity to undergo the Goto therapy. They were treated by several doctors and three nurses. Because Molokai, where there was no treatment, was little more than a dumping ground, the patients in Kakaako begged the king and queen not to be sent there, because the situation there was becoming even more harrowing. There was no money for anything. The *Lehua* missed the food supply delivery twice in a row, despite the fact that the sea was not rough. The reason was that not a single bill had been paid since the arrival of the sisters. The 800 exiles were facing an acute food shortage and feared they would be left to starve as the cheapest way of being rid of them.

Fouesnel did not mention Molokai in his long report to Paris. He did speak about Grégoire Archambaux. Archambaux, whose leprosy was common knowledge, was upset because his church was empty. There was open warfare with Burgerman.

In March 1884, people were sent into exile for the first time since the arrival of the sisters. Because the sisters fought to keep their people, Van Giesen was given the blame and feelings ran so high that it came to a murder attempt. A group of Hawaiians, under the leadership of the half-Irish MP Tom Birch, forced their way into his bedroom, bound him to the bed and poured paraffin over him, screaming 'Burn him! burn him!' The men were arrested and imprisoned, despite the sisters' protests.

Queen Kapiolani, whose relative was married to Van Giesen, and Gibson came straight away to assess the situation. They spoke to the patients in a conciliatory tone and the queen spoke of her 'heavy heart' and endlessly repeated her good wishes. When the carriages had disappeared in a cloud of dust, Dr Trousseau called out the names of forty-two people who had to go to Molokai. This was a fifth of the total number of patients.

Because a doctor was now required to accompany the exiles, Molokai received its first medical check in more than four months. Princess Liliuokalani complained sharply about this neglect. Gibson sensed the royal irritation and once again urged a visit to Molokai by the sisters, before the opening of parliament

Honolulu harbour, where Damien arrived on 19 May 1864

The church of Halepua'a, on the island of Hawaii (Big Island),
which was built by Damien in 1865

Father Léonor Fouesnel

Damien at the age of 33

Patients in advanced stages of the disease

The eastern settlement of Kalawao, at around 1900

Three patients in front of a cottage, with the
pali in the background

Kind David Kalakaua

The American quarter master Joseph Ira Dutton, who came to
help Damien, pictured in his office

A dormitory in Bishop House, Kalaupapa

Léonor Fouesnel (third from the left) and Bishop Herman Kockemann (second from the right) in front of Mission House

Saint Philomena, Kalawao, following the completion of
reconstruction work in 1889

Damien, shortly before his death in 1889

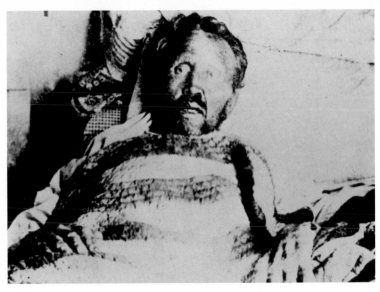

Damien on his death bed, 1889

The British monument sent in honour of Damien in 1890

on 16 April. He argued that such a visit would help to push through the decision to entrust all the hospitals on the islands to the Franciscan nuns.

Fouesnel tried to calm Damien by reporting the worrying situation. The Board wanted the Franciscan nuns for Molokai and promised them all the islands as well. Mother Marianne was not afraid of the lepers, but it was discouraging for her group, which had counted on taking over all the hospitals except the Queen's Hospital. This was why Fouesnel had urged that the sisters should first take over Wailuku on Maui Island, Hilo on the Big Island, and Kauai. Molokai would be the last on the list. He wondered whether there was a house in the settlement where three or four sisters could stay comfortably when the mother superior made her visit to look for a site for the convent. He was amazed that Damien did not drum up all the priests who had been opposed to Fouesnel's appointment and have him removed. The post of provincial was getting to be too much for him, anyway.

Dr Arning had understood what was intended by the message that Molokai was part of his territory. He landed in Kalaupapa on 7 March with Dr Fitch, the secretary of the Board and the forty-two new exiles. He had been ordered to take Clayton Strawn, the *luna*, back to Kakaako, for eye treatment. Ambrose Hutchison was designated his successor.

Damien had welcomed the new exiles and had returned to Kalawao. A short time later, a tall, pale, blond man with a pince-nez knocked at his door. Dr Arning introduced himself. The conversation turned to leprosy. Damien wanted to know whether cowpox vaccination could have transmitted leprosy. Arning was not sure. He was experimenting on an ape in his laboratory, to see if leprosy could be transmitted from man to animal or vice versa and he wanted to find out how long the bacillus remained active after death and whether a corpse in the ground could be a source of infection. Dr Arning was hoping to find a cure. Damien had a sense of déjà vu.

Then came the painful moment. The superiors had asked for Damien to be examined. Arning examined Damien's foot and the leproma in his groin and officially diagnosed leprosy.

Only the superiors would be informed – Damien's illness would remain secret for the time being. The opening words of the letter that Köckemann wrote to Damien a few days later were friendly. He sympathised with him. Then came the real announcement. The bishop was pleased that Damien realised that he was infectious and that he had decided not to infect the other priests. He must go on serving 'topside', however, because the bishop had no one else. It was as if the life of these parishioners was of no importance.

When Damien finally got to Kaluaaha in April, Dan McCorriston wanted to shake his hand, but Damien refused. He maintained a safe distance, too, when he baptised the baby.

During one of his subsequent visits, Arning was able to persuade Damien to go secretly to the churchyard after curfew had sounded and open a grave, so that he could take some specimens. Damien agreed, as long as the body was that of a Chinese victim and not a Hawaiian. However, when the grave was opened and Arning was taking specimens by the light of Damien's lamp, the latter realised that the corpse was, in fact, the corpse of a Hawaiian. Damien was horrified, but fortunately no one noticed the desecration of the grave, which was the worst of crimes in Hawaiian eyes.

Molokai for Hopeless Cases

After yet another disagreement, Montiton had rushed off to Honolulu. This was a disaster for Damien, because he once again had to put off his visit to 'topside' for a month, at the last minute. It took courage to climb the *pali* with his painful foot. From Honolulu, Montiton sent instructions about how his garden was to be kept up and what Damien might and might not eat from it. He briefed him about all the rumours that were going around in the Mission House. It was said that the government was thinking of buying some land near the Pearl lochs where all the lepers, those from Kakaako as well as those from Molokai, would be brought together. The sisters had 'won' he said, but did not mention what the battle had been about.

Damien had other sources of information. Clayton Strawn dictated to Tom Birch a letter saying that two armed Chinese would be among the next batch of deportees. They would join the armed band of scoundrels. A few days later, he told Damien that all the lepers would soon be free, except himself, because he was totally blind. In mid-July, he addressed Damien as 'My dearest and best friend', and wrote, 'I want to hear a letter read aloud from my good old friend Damien.' Strawn had also now heard about the plan to establish a new settlement near Pearl. On 17 July he wrote, 'Father, I have confessed several times and been to communion. I have changed completely since I left Kalawao. I am much more steady and feel better both in body and soul.' Damien was pleased.

Kakaako had done wonders for Strawn. The hospital was running well and this was largely due to the firm hand with which Mother Marianne had been directing it since 29 March. She had threatened to return to the United States if all the promises that Fouesnel had made in Syracuse were not kept. She demanded the direction of the hospital from the Board and this was granted on 2 April, together with the title of agent. The sisters received a salary of $25, a trifle in comparison with what the doctors received. Van Giesen was transferred to Molokai, at her express demand.

In Kakaako, Arning prepared a report that would be presented to parliament on 16 April. He summarised his six months' experience in Kakaako and added information that he had gathered during his two flying visits to Molokai. Leprosy was infectious, but had nothing to do with syphilis. He had already found one case where leprosy was not the consequence of a debauched life, but he did not name the patient, since Damien's illness was still a secret. He had been able to isolate the bacillus of Hansen and Neisser in leper tissue, both from living and dead victims, and hoped to be able to determine whether the disease could be transmitted during mass vaccination. Until now, he had had to confine himself to animals. It was clear that he wanted to experiment on humans.

Arning had one major point of criticism. Molokai was 'inhuman'. It was outrageous that a country called a disease incurable and then dumped the patients in a remote place. This was 'medieval barbarism' and any doctor must oppose it. This was a disastrous example for a people that was having Western culture imposed on it and looked up to the *haole*. Hygiene on Kalaupapa was poor, but that was not surprising. Gathering hundreds of people in an isolated spot could only encourage their inherent indifference to hygiene. A brief monthly visit from a doctor was far too little. He argued in favour of a resident physician-surgeon, who could carry out electro-therapy.

The epidemic was not under control. Samples taken in schools had shown that 7.5 per cent of the children had leprosy. These should be placed in an attractive home where they could continue to go to school. He proposed that all patients should be brought together in one place, with all facilities on hand.

The king opened the parliamentary session. He announced the renewal of the treaty with the United States. The US Navy was to be permitted to use Pearl Harbour as a coaling station. The main problem remained the health of the Hawaiians. Kalakaua hoped that segregation would help to restrict the epidemic and thanked the sisters who had come to help the country. Gibson announced that 10 per cent of the kingdom's budget was for health care.

In mid-April the Board decided to invest in Molokai again. Meyer must give them an estimate of the wood that was needed for houses. There would soon be fresh deportations.

Arning's tirade about the inhuman conditions on Molokai had made various people sit up and take notice and the Board once again decided to look for a resident doctor. Princess Liliuokalani proposed a young Briton, named Arthur St Clair Mouritz. He had come to Hawaii to work with lepers after hearing about Damien at the University of London, but had taken a post as government doctor on Oahu. During an excursion he had come across a remote hut, where a man was sitting on a tree trunk. Too late, he saw the rifle, and the man who had leprosy threatened to kill him. Mouritz saved his skin by promising a medicine. The man's wife must come to the surgery and make the sign of the cross with her finger. She did so every month and collected the medicine. One day an unknown man came into Mouritz's surgery. It was the 'leper' and he was cured. Mouritz took him to Trousseau and he also confirmed the miracle. This story came to Liliuokalani's attention just at the moment when a resident doctor was sought. Mouritz was obliged to accept the post.

He landed, after a dreadful voyage, on 8 May, along with Fitch and sixty new deportees. Mouritz noted Damien's appearance: tall, upright, muscular and strong, tanned and good-looking, hatless and with calloused hands. He was an outdoor type.

Mouritz was shocked at the filthy state of the settlement. The place was crawling with vermin. The majority of the patients had scabies or diarrhoea. He immediately ordered that the hospital be given a thorough cleansing.

Montiton was also back. Now that he had partially recovered from his skin irritation, he initially behaved more calmly and Damien once again had time to prepare his sermons.

Visit by Queen Kapiolani and Princess Liliuokalani (July 1884)

Leprosy remained on the agenda throughout the parliamentary session. The future president, Sanford Dole, who was at that time the leader of the white planters, tabled a motion of no confidence against the prime minister, on the grounds that he was wasting money. In the businessman's opinion, too much money was going to the lepers. Gibson survived the motion, but he knew that, if he was to succeed, he needed more sisters. He asked for reinforcements, even though the mother superior had not yet visited Molokai.

Princess Liliuokalani did visit Molokai, for the second time, this time accompanied by Queen Kapiolani. She wanted to hand out to the exiles in person the first articles of clothing from a charity festival in the Iolani gardens. Prominent ladies, who were members of the *Hoolu Lahui*, the Mothers' Union, there, had sewn various articles of clothing for the patients.

The visit took place on 22 July 1884. The royal party came ashore after lunch and were greeted by the people. They made their way to Montiton's house and took their places on the *lanai*. The queen declared, 'I have heard so much about your misery, my dear people who have been taken away from all that is dear to you. I wish personally to inspect your homes, to speak to everyone individually and see your living conditions with my own eyes. I want to give a report of your needs to the king.' She had brought clothing and she said, 'Father Damien, my faithful friend whom I truly admire, will distribute them to those who have asked for clothing.'

Thereupon, various men stood up. They had complaints about food, housing and loneliness, but above all, about the lack of medical care. Finally, Hutchison, the superintendent, spoke. The nice houses, he said, belonged to the wealthier exiles. The poor lived in leaking shacks. He asked the queen to put the case for better housing and a water supply for Kalaupapa, because the village had only brackish wells.

He was in the middle of his description of the undrinkable water, when his daughter, aged about three, ran up to him. He picked her up and tried to go on, but then turned to the queen and said that his daughter and other children in the settlement did not have leprosy. They had been born there. He asked if it were not possible to do something to save such children from infection. The queen promised vaguely to do what she could.

There followed a thorough inspection by the royal party of the whole settlement. The queen and princess entered each home and spoke freely with the people. When Hutchison asked them if they were tired, the queen repeatedly replied, 'We must finish this.' They even visited the people who were living in caves in the Kauhako crater.

They visited the hospital and sat cross-legged on the floor by the patients. When Kapiolani saw the dying-shed, she was shocked and ordered its closure.

They visited the shop, where they were appalled at the quality of the provisions, but the abbatoir received their approval. The tour was extremely thorough – the party even went to the

Waikolu valley, where they inspected the stream from which water was brought to Kalaupapa.

At supper, Arning insisted to the queen that she must put pressure on the sisters to come to Kalawao. The queen remarked that they would need a convent and added that Van Giesen should begin work next day.

Arning and Damien did not spend the whole time with the royal party. They detached themselves from the group for a painful examination. Arning wanted to be as formal as possible and requested Damien's permission to examine him. He took several samples from the lepromas and confirmed the leprosy that he had already diagnosed in March. He asked a number of questions about how Damien might have become infected and the progress of the disease. Unobtrusively, he also looked for syphilis chancres. Arning also examined all the children. He determined that all the twenty-six orphan boys had leprosy, but that four of the sixteen girls were healthy. Damien was not allowed to examine girls.

Liliuokalani's critical report was presented to parliament. Kapiolani sent Damien a list of the patients' wishes that she had noted. She asked him to go from house to house to make sure this was correct and see if there was anything else. Damien advised her that each person should receive a separate parcel, to avoid jealousy and quarrels. In September, 408 parcels were sent and 250 were in preparation. As he made his house to house visits, Damien noted how hard things were for the *kokuas* and asked that they be given a new set of clothes.

Stoddard Writes a Bestseller about Damien

Meanwhile the retreat had begun in Honolulu. Montiton, who was no longer officially segregated, took part. Dr Arning had declared that he did not have leprosy. Nevertheless, Köckemann was not pleased about his presence, although he was primarily relieved that Damien was not there. Even so, he remarked, sarcastically, 'We had been expecting you, but you didn't turn up.' Fouesnel, who had learned from Gibson that the queen valued Damien's work, sent him a case of wine. What he really needed, however, was shoes.

In the autumn of 1884, Damien's problem was with Van Giesen. He had been sent to Molokai at the wish of the mother superior and was written off as a difficult man. This was no doubt partly because of his character, but also partly because of his disappointment that he had been expelled in spite of all his efforts and was stigmatised as an enemy of the sisters. The whole settlement was convinced that the sisters would not come as long as he was there. So he had to go.

Despite all the criticism and rumours, Van Giesen did achieve things. He was superintendent of works at the new docks at Kalaupapa, the excavation of a channel and the dynamiting of the submerged rocks. He had the visitors' house brought over to Kalaupapa for use as a warehouse and supervised the building of a new house for the doctor. He also managed to install a telephone line. It was a simple matter from the doctor's house to the visitors' house in Kalawao, but getting it over the cliff was a dangerous job. Despite all this, the hostility to Van Giesen was so strong that few people sympathised with him when his wife Carolina died, a woman whom he had followed to Molokai, Kakaako and back to Molokai. Only Montition gave him some religious tracts. Van Giesen thanked him and said they were a comfort in his grief.

A few months later, Van Giesen got to know a girl who was visiting her parents in the settlement. He invited her to come again and this gave his rival, Hutchison, a reason for complaint, because her presence was illegal. When his complaint was upheld, Van Giesen considered the matter settled, according to Hutchison. He left the settlement an angry man.

In another version of the story, Damien had a hand. He wrote to Kapiolani, 'Van Giesen is not a father to the suffering people. He is a hireling. If he refuses to build a house for the sisters, then the chairman of the Board of Health must give him another task. I will build it myself.' When Damien told Van Giesen what he had written, the latter was so angry that Damien wrote to the queen, 'He must be expelled. I have reported the case to the Board and they will probably do so.' Kapiolani replied, 'As for the *haole* who flies off the handle so easily, it is better that he go and leave you in peace. I have transferred the matter to the competent authorities and they will probably take the necessary measures.' Damien should be assured that he could approach the queen with any problem.

This did not solve the medical problems, however. Mouritz spent July in the settlement, but in September, he asked not to have to return. The patients thought he was lazy and lacking in enthusiasm. This was not surprising, since he was working on Molokai against his will. Dr Fitch took up his monthly visits again and Damien doled out the medicines in the doctor's absence. He knew well enough that the white powder was morphine sulphate and the yellow one was podophyllin.

On 7 October 1884 three doctors arrived at once on a visit, but this was more in the nature of a holiday trip. Dr Mouritz and Dr Fitch were familiar faces, but the third doctor, Charles Stallard, was new. He was later to become personal physician to the Prince of Wales, the future Edward VII. The fourth visitor was a professor of English Literature at Notre Dame University in Indiana, Charles Stoddard. Stallard and Stoddard had got to know one another during the voyage from Australia to Honolulu.

In Kalawao, Damien was just coming out of the church. Stoddard noted: worn soutane, youthful, calloused hands, healthy appearance. When they had declined his invitation to supper and invited him to join them instead, he fetched maize from the kitchen and made a clucking sound. Chickens came fluttering up from all directions and perched on his arms, shoulders and head. He caught one of them, and that was his contribution to supper. That evening, they sat talking in the doctor's house until late.

The two doctors got on with their work the next day, whilst the visitors went with Damien on a visit to the huts. They were struck by Damien's popularity. Of course, he had just handed out the queen's gifts, but the visitors were not aware of this. They were greeted warmly everywhere. The professor noted the typical horror moments. A boy fanning his friend, who was a small heap of suffering beneath a blanket. Stoddard saw an eye like a burst grape and a tongue that lay like a fig on the lips that had been eaten away. The swollen, waxy face looked as though it were covered with mould. Four patients were playing cards near the dying boy. The people tried to brighten up their surroundings. They had hung pictures from *Harper's Weekly* and the *Illustrated London News* on the wall and did not glance at the pile of coffins, lying behind the carpenter's hut.

Moved, Stoddard played the organ in St Philomena's, which was a gift from Boston. He became completely absorbed in the music, and when he became aware of his surroundings again, the church was full of people who had come to listen. Embarrassed, he looked out of the window and saw Damien, surrounded by sick children, woodworking in a yard. The angelus sounded. The men all took off their hats and prayed, a lovely scene.

The professor wanted to write about this man. The contrast with his previous visit was striking and he put all the improvements down to Damien. Damien took them in his buggy to Montiton's house. The latter showed them his beautiful house, his neat garden, his loud, garish church. He played a waltz on the organ. They walked cheerfully through the churchyard. On the other side of the fence, they could see children romping in the sea. They were laughing and their voices echoed across the graveyard, where other children lay. Once again, Stoddard was overcome. When they were taking their leave, he wanted to see Damien's decoration. Damien removed it from the dusty leather case and showed him the cross. 'I didn't come for this,' he said. 'I never wear it.'

The guests left via the *pali* and turned the climb into a jolly race. That evening, in a house in Kaunakakai, they discussed the things Damien had said, such as, 'Lepers here, but not in heaven.' They wondered why the priest, who seemed so happy, kept repeating, 'I have kept my three vows, whatever anyone may think.' Stoddard was so impressed that he did indeed write a book about Damien. It became a bestseller and was translated into many languages.

Despondency

Leprosy was a problem, particularly since no one knew how it was transmitted. Damien had no one but Arning to whom he could speak about his illness. The doctor was concerned, asked if Damien was taking his pills and advised him, now Mouritz was in fact going to stay, to make his illness known to him. Mouritz was planning to set up electro-therapy and that would help Damien.

Damien replied, 'I have taken the arsenic pills every day. I stopped for a few weeks because my foot had become completely red, but I have started again. It doesn't really make much difference. I am still healthy. I can hardly wait to use electricity every day, as soon as the machine is in order. Dr Mouritz will help me to stem the progress of this incurable disease.' Yet he still did not really believe that he had leprosy, for he wrote, 'Let us wait and see how the disease develops and whether there are new symptoms which confirm the verdict of real leprosy.'

His foot was the problem. The nerve was swollen and inflamed, but he still had to visit Pelekunu. The outward journey by boat was all right. When he returned, there was a deluge and the waves were like walls. The captain put out a sloop, so that Damien could go ashore at a small cape. In shallow water he jumped into the sea, but he lost his footing in the current and had to swim, with heavy strokes, to the shore. He had to walk a long way in his wet clothes and the rivers and river beds were full, so that he had to go through cold water again. He caught a cold which he was unable to shake off throughout December.

He had a sore throat when Montiton came raving on that he was going back to the Puamoto Islands, whatever the bishop might say, since he was a free man. Meanwhile, Köckemann was writing to Paris that Montiton had never been at peace in the Order. He should be allowed to do as he wished immediately. The bishop had a plan.

He summoned Grégoire Archambaux to Honolulu, to be examined by Dr Arning. His neck, face, limbs, trunk – everywhere was a mass of lepromas. Arning established by the use of electric shocks that half his face, in fact half his body, was without sensation. According to Arning, Archambaux had had leprosy for at least ten years and must be exiled. The old man accepted his fate with resignation: God's will must be done. The next day, however, he cried long and hard and had an asthma attack. Köckemann now had to decide what to do, but he found every option difficult and in the end left Montiton where he was. Archambaux went to Molokai as a voluntary exile, but he continued to be extremely distressed and could not come to terms with the situation.

Damien also did not know how he was going to cope. The nerve in his knee was affected just when he received a distressing letter from Dr Fitch. The Californian doctor had received 'the order to resign' on the 'grounds of refusal of salary increase'. The patients on Molokai sent a petition to keep him, because Fitch had done more for them than the others, but their request was ignored. There were many rumours going around. The *Kanaka* in Kakaako were supposed to have wanted him to go because he was too slow in his work. The sisters were said to find him slapdash and perfunctory and, above all, arrogant. Köckemann and Fouesnel did not want this convinced Protestant in post. One report spoke of $10,000, promised by Gibson to Köckemann, but nothing more is known of this. It was the case, that, after Fitch's departure, the bishop managed to have his salary transferred to the sisters.

There was also an issue with Arning. He had asked Fitch to allow him to experiment on two patients. Fitch had refused and Arning had then asked the Hawaiian government to permit him to vaccinate someone, who had been condemned to death, with leprosy. This person would then be kept in solitary confinement, to see whether he developed the disease. What was to happen if he did not is not clear. Keanu, a giant of a man, who had committed a crime of passion, was willing to undergo this experiment. Arning vaccinated him in his cell in Lahaina. He chose the technique used for smallpox vaccination. Keanu developed the disease so quickly that it was feared he already had leprosy before he was vaccinated. He was an easy victim, of course, weakened as he was by solitary confinement, lack of exercise and sunlight and poor diet. He was a complete wreck by the time he arrived on Molokai to die, just before Damien's death.

Fitch's parting letter to Damien was emotional and difficult to read. 'I am a broken man,' he wrote. 'I shall never see you again, my good friend, but be assured that you will remain etched on my mind like a jewel. I hope to hear from you. Those poor wretches, among whom you live, have so many reasons to bless your dedication.' Fitch wanted to pay one final visit to the settlement, but he could not face descending the *pali*. He wanted to see Damien, but he also wanted to collect money owed to him by Henry Wright and Van Giesen, both of whom were refusing to pay.

Damien attended the retreat in January. Köckemann had summoned him to Honolulu in order to have him examined by his own doctor, Dr McGrew. Damien was hoping that Dr Arning had made a mistake and that McGrew would pronounce him well. Trousseau was also called in and the two doctors gave Damien a thorough examination. Then Damien discovered, to his horror, that the doctors were not looking for signs of leprosy, but of syphilis. They asked him direct questions about his sexual life. Damien answered in a shaking voice that he had always strictly kept his vow of chastity.

Köckemann realised the pain and insult he had caused Damien and, despite all his precautionary principles, he had a long – and final – private conversation with him. Arning had suggested that he should be sent back to Europe and Köckemann supported this view, but Damien rejected it. What would happen to his patients? Who would look after them? He had only one wish: Archambaux was so intemperate, could he not be placed somewhere else? Montiton was difficult enough. The bishop reassured him: Montiton would soon be returning to Tahiti. The next day Archambaux received permission to return to his parish in Lahaina. Since he had voluntarily gone to the settlement, the superiors were not breaking the segregation regulations.

During the retreat, Damien wrote down his confession in note form.

Angry on Sunday 3 times before mass. Impure thoughts, nakedness, contact, the furies. Listened to tittle-tattle and gossip and did the same myself. Neglect of self-examination and prayer, distraction during prayers (partly intentionally), *ahia* [insults] to the Mormons, 2 or 3 times allowed someone to die without the sacraments, vanity, hatred, too brief and too little teaching of the catechism, not strict enough with the children, nakedness, grumbling at others, inflexibility.

He was despondent. His superiors suspected him of having venereal disease. He had pain in his left leg. Sometimes a warm footbath helped. He put a kettle on the fire and poured water into a basin. He put his foot in and waited for the pain to ease. He looked into the basin and saw pieces of skin floating on the water. He drew his foot out of the basin, looked at it, and found it was badly scalded. Damien had not felt the scalding, so he must have leprosy. He screamed. Priests came running to him and asked what was the matter. Damien could say nothing, except, 'I've scalded my foot,' and, 'I'm a leper.'

He was in pain, but he tried not to scream when Trousseau bandaged his foot with cloths soaked in oil. He lay in bed for some days, for Köckemann had given him leave to stay. He received few visitors, because he was infected. He was still limping when he got back to Kalaupapa. Hutchison asked him what had happened and he replied, 'I scalded my foot. I am a leper.'

On his return, Archambaux left the settlement and soon after rumours started to go round about binges and huge rows between Archambaux and Burgerman in the presbytery at Lahaina. As soon as the general gave his permission, Montiton would be leaving for Tahiti and Damien would be left alone. He could celebrate the mass but had to sit down to preach: Meyer and Fouesnel both asked if he needed anything. Meyer would continue to do so, but Fouesnel was too busy with the preparation of the Provincial Council. His proposal was far-reaching: the members of the Order must avoid all physical contact with lepers. Henceforth, they must not touch any object that had been handled by a leper, and must inhale camphorated spirits before hearing a leper's confession, or giving the sacraments. Any part of the body that had been touched by a leper must be washed in a solution of carbolic acid or other disinfectant. Members of the Order who had leprosy must consider others. They must not touch others nor hand them any infected object.

Köckemann proposed Burgerman as a companion but Damien replied, 'I shall never be able to live with him, neither as his father confessor, nor as his confessant. You know why.'

Pamphile sent him a boring letter in English about grammar and how he had nearly died of a lung infection. Damien replied that there were worse things. He had trouble 'with a sort of nerve disease in my left foot. I can no longer conceal from you that I am threatened by a more serious disease than tuberculosis.' His beard was grey, but apart from his left foot, he was still well. They were now burying people one above the other in the churchyard, because of lack of space. He hoped to stay in Kalaupapa until his death.

That night, a storm destroyed the harbour wall. The reservoir burst because of the excess water and Damien's roof was blown off. He wondered how he would be able to repair it. He was dragging his leg. It had only cost him ten minutes to go to the hospital and back, but he had cried with pain all night.

15

Damien Officially Segregated (February 1885–June 1886)

Pain, Loneliness and Another Examination for Syphilis

Sometimes, Damien had to bite his pillow, in order not to scream. The scald on his foot had formed a scab, but the inflamed nerve continued to cause him pain. He really did not want to visit 'topside'. He feared he would be unable to climb the *pali* and was frightened of infecting other people, but he had no choice. 'If I really have been attacked by this terrible disease, then I must recognise that death is approaching by slow degrees,' he wrote to Köckemann. 'Without being too preoccupied by my body, I must think above all of my soul. I ask you for a good father confessor.' On 25 February the Nunc Dimittis, the farewell of many years' duration, had begun.

A few days previously, Köckemann had given Montiton permission to leave Molokai, but Damien begged him to stop Montiton going. He was a difficult person but he was a good father confessor. They surely were not going to leave him alone with his scalded foot and the leprosy which had already affected his knee.

Köckemann was moved by this appeal and ordered Montiton to stay. When the latter received this news, he was angry, declaring that Damien was an egocentric intriguer, who was trying to imprison a poor old man in such a hell-hole. The general was his superior and he had given him permission to leave. If the bishop refused to give him the fare to go to Europe, then he would go to the French consul and create a fuss.

Damien hoped that the crisis would blow over while he was on 'topside', but when he returned he found Montiton with his bags packed. He left the settlement on 19 March.

Damien had to rely on other priests for his confession. The first who came was Gulstan Ropert, who stayed for two days. It was the last time the two men met. The next priest to come was the German Columban Beissel, who remained only while the boat was in harbour. Dr Arning also came and brought news that four sisters had arrived but it was not clear where the mother superior planned to place them.

Arning had orders from the bishop. Because it was a delicate matter, he had asked Dr Mouritz to come along as a witness. At ten o' clock in the morning, Arning was sitting at the desk in the dispensary; Mouritz was standing by the dusty window. Damien was on time and Arning politely requested him to undress. The two doctors examined his mouth and throat and felt his glands. He had to show them his feet and they carefully examined the inflamed nerve in his left foot. Only then did they explain the real reason for the examination: Damien had to remove his underpants, because the bishop was once again asking whether or not Damien had venereal disease.

Damien was upset. He exclaimed that he had always kept his vow of chastity and had never had relations with either a man or a woman. He said he was being persecuted. Arning remained calm and reminded him that many doctors regarded leprosy as the fourth stage of syphilis. Damien snapped back that Arning himself rejected this theory and Arning confirmed this. Leprosy was an infectious disease, transmitted by a bacillus. He picked up his magnifying glass and said that it was best to get the matter over with as quickly as possible and make the situation clear.

He examined Damien and found no signs of syphilis and then called Mouritz to confirm the situation. Mouritz was extremely embarrassed and Damien was angry and reproachful, because he suspected Mouritz of being responsible for some of the rumour-mongering about him. Mouritz swore that he had never spread gossip of that sort about Damien, although he had said other things. He also admitted he knew there were rumours about Damien and Julia, the matron of the girls' home, but Arning told Damien to get dressed and announced that he had found no sign of syphilis.

That evening the three men sat together and Arning decided to have the matter out. He told Damien that he (Damien) himself was partly responsible for the gossip. His presbytery was known as 'Hotel Molokai, Lepers' Rest'. His door was always open, people were always wandering in and out, he had no curtains and there was always an inviting light burning at night. Damien defended himself. The orphans sometimes woke up in the night, they had nightmares, which was not surprising, given what they had been through, and they had to be able to come to him.

Dr Hyde (September 1885)

During his week-long visit, Arning examined all the patients, to determine those who would benefit from further treatment in Kakaako and those whose case was hopeless and who should be left to die on Molokai. Queen Kapiolani had asked him to examine all the children of parents with leprosy and to make a list of those who were still healthy. The plans for a home for healthy girls at Kakaako had been approved. Arning also took many photographs during this visit.

The visit took place before the hurricane hit Kauai Island. There was also damage to buildings on Molokai. Dr Fitch arrived to estimate the damage. Dr Charles Hyde, the head of the Congregational mission, had pleaded for his reinstatement. Fitch was pleased to hear that Damien's foot was no longer giving him pain, but shocked at the condition of his right ear, which was swollen and covered in lepromas. Fitch asked Damien to assist Dr Hyde during his visit. Hyde was a decent man who wished to work sincerely for the welfare of his fellow human beings.

In early September 1885, Damien got to know the friendly, polite and well-educated American. He was in his mid-fifties, an elegant, fair-haired academic. He was a graduate of Princeton and had afterwards worked in New England, where he had combated alcohol and drug abuse among the working class. His work had got him into trouble and an uncle had been able to get him the commission to reorganise the Theological Seminary in Honolulu. He had been in Hawaii since 1876. He thought Hawaii dirty and was afraid of catching leprosy, particularly when he developed a skin ailment in 1884.

Despite his fear, he wanted to consecrate the new Congregational Chapel on Molokai, and arrived on 31 August 1885, loaded down with gifts. To his great joy, Catholics also participated in the festivities. He spent two weeks in the settlement and consulted with almost everyone who had a position of authority. With Damien, he discussed the medical as well as the psychological and moral aspects of the situation. Although the conversations were friendly, he declared in his report that the orphanage buildings were unsuitable and needed replacing by modern, spacious and well-ventilated buildings.

Nursing was even more important. Since the Franciscan nuns, who had been in Hawaii for almost two years now, had still not visited the settlement, he suggested that the Protestants should try to recruit nurses. Hyde did not know where to look for nurses, but he could raise the money. He decided to approach two important members of his congregation. Charles Bishop, the widower of Princess Bernice, might be able to do something, and Henry Baldwin, a planter, was well known for his generosity.

Hyde and the doctors also brought news, because there had been no visits from members of the Order since Ropert and Beissel. Damien had not made his confession for four months. He protested to Fouesnel about this, but the latter defended his colleagues. Beissel and Archambaux both suffered from seasickness and so it was preferable that Damien, who also had no sea legs, should travel to Maui. Fouesnel does not seem to have realised how ill Damien was, but, to his friend, Professor Stoddard, Damien wrote the true state of affairs.

The leprosy germs have finally established themselves in my left foot and ear [sic]. One of my eyebrows is beginning to fall out. It is impossible for me to go to Honolulu, because my leprosy has manifested itself. I expect that my face will soon be deformed, for I do not doubt the true nature of my illness. I am calm and even happier with my people. The Good Lord knows what is best for my salvation and, in that conviction, I say every day a *fiat voluntas tua*.

No one congratulated Damien on the twenty-fifth anniversary of his perpetual vows on 7 October.

Double Murder at the Departure of Girls Without Leprosy

A few days before the Kapiolani Home for the healthy daughters of parents with leprosy was to be opened, Hutchison received instructions to send the fourteen healthy girls to Honolulu. His own three-year-old daughter was among the girls who had to leave their parents for the rest of their lives. Hutchison was pleased that Damien was to travel with the girls. His daughter would be in good hands and perhaps Damien would be able to persuade the sisters to visit Molokai. Just before their departure, however, Köckemann forbade Damien to come to Honolulu, because of his leprosy. The Provincial Council had decided that he could not stay in the mission and no mention was made of Kakaako. Damien, who, as he himself said, was dying a little more each day, was isolated. The bishop had asked him not to communicate directly with the Board any more, but to deal with everything through himself.

Outwardly, Damien took this news calmly, but he could not accept the lack of opportunity for confession, since it was required by the Order. He had not made his confession for six months, yet when Köckemann reported to the general, he said that he and Fouesnel were concerned that Damien was only visited every two months.

The departure of the fourteen girls caused emotions to run high. They had to gather in the harbour depot at Kalaupapa in the afternoon, in order to see that their papers were in order.

Ambrose Hutchison had to write each of them an exit permit. One *kokua* per child was allowed to accompany them and they, too, needed permits. It was an extremely emotional time, since parents were saying goodbye to their children for good. One father, a man named Momona, was extremely upset. He had not wanted his child to go and had sent petitions to the Board to allow her to stay.

It would turn out that, on this day of all days, the steamboat *J. I. Dowsett* was late and the tension of departure continued to mount. Finally, at around four o'clock, when the girls were ready to go on board, an incident occurred and Momona stabbed three men, who were busy carrying cargo from the steamboat to the settlement. Two of them were fatally wounded, as Dr Mouritz confirmed when he examined them. Damien spent the night with the dying men and conducted the funerals next day.

Hutchison had travelled with the girls to Honolulu to report the incident. The prime minister, Gibson, immediately travelled to the settlement, accompanied by the chief of police and his son-in-law, Fred Hayselden, who was secretary to the Board, and arrived on 2 November to investigate the situation. They concluded that the authorities in the settlement bore a share of the responsibility. Meyer should have been present and Damien should have realised that emotions were likely to run high. They both accepted the blame. Mouritz defended himself on the grounds that his only task was to examine the girls. Hutchison was reproached for his 'stubbornness' and 'stupidity'.

The girls were taken to the new home in Kakaako, which was run by the nuns. They were to be kept apart from the persons with leprosy in the hospital, on the one hand, and from the rest of the population, on the other. They were disinfected, and then prepared for their role at the formal, royal opening of the home. During this ceremony, the king presented Mother Marianne and Fouesnel with honours. The news of the festivities gradually filtered through to Molokai.

On 5 December 1885, Damien's problems about confession were resolved of themselves, when the fifteen witnesses of the double murder were summoned as witnesses at the court at

Lahaina. Sheriff Everett and several officers were waiting for them on their arrival, because the seven segregated witnesses had to go straight to gaol.

Damien, who was not yet officially registered as a leper, was allowed to stay with Archambaux and Burgerman in the presbytery. The only advantage of this was that Damien was able to make his confession, for otherwise the tension between the two priests was unbearable.

The other witnesses had an even much harder time, for at least Damien had food and a bed to sleep in. The witnesses were locked up as though they were criminals. They were given salted salmon in a dirty bucket, as though they were pigs. They were not allowed to go near the crazy Keanu, the condemned man who had received leprosy vaccination as his punishment. The only good thing was that David Kaau, a *kokua* who was a witness, brought them food from restaurants. He also informed Fred Hayselden, who was in Lahaina for the trial, about their conditions. Hayselden gave him $5 for food 'for the boys'. Hutchison was pleased that Burgerman and his own family came to visit him in prison.

When it came to it, no witnesses were required, because the accused pleaded guilty. The judge sentenced Momona to ten years and his son to five. The sentences were comparatively light because of plea bargaining. Momona gave the authorities details of the armed rising he and others had been planning, of which Strawn had warned Damien, in return for a shorter sentence, particularly for his sixteen-year-old son.

Damien Officially Declared to Have Leprosy. Segregated By Superiors

During the trial, Hayselden had given Damien permission to go to Honolulu, but Fouesnel immediately prohibited this, the danger of infection being too great. Damien was also not allowed any money. The teaching brothers and nursing sisters were a heavy burden on the mission's budget. In his bitter New Year's letter, Damien complained that that day two children had died of lung complications and another girl was at death's door. He wrote, 'Father Léonor [Fouesnel] is constantly threatening to take away a small allowance that I do not ask him for every month, as was agreed, but every two or three months, when I need it.' He also complained, 'I must protest against the somewhat tyrannical manner in which the good father seeks to lock me up here. As long as my health permits and the Board does not oppose it, I may travel. Why should my superiors deny me the freedom of movement that I sometimes need?' He threatened to write to the general about the matter.

Damien would have liked to attend the winter retreat, because he wanted to go to Kakaako to study the amazing Goto method. As has already been noted, this was a system of herbal baths, with an accompanying regime of medication. People who came from Kakaako spoke about the new bathhouses that had been built, because the treatment was successful. Dr Arning wrote the experiment off as quackery. He wanted to apply exclusively scientific methods and believed that some people had an inherent susceptibility to the leprosy bacillus. In that sense, leprosy was hereditary. In mid-January 1886 Arning resigned, because the Board rejected certain far-reaching experiments. He remained on the islands for a few months as a tourist. Perhaps he hoped that he would be reinstated, like Fitch, but he had trodden on too many toes.

Damien, too, was under fire. On 10 February Fouesnel wrote,

Once again, I have heard rumours that you want to come here. It is my duty, my dear father, once again to refer you to the decisions that have been made, not by me, but by the Provincial Council. *Hoomanawanui*, be patient. There are only two places in Honolulu you can come to: the Mission House and Kakaako. In the Mission House, you will be shown to your quarters and you will not be allowed to leave until your return. If you were not to do so, the mission would be put under quarantine by the *haole*, as soon as they got to know that there was a leper in the convent. They would even be frightened of us, and we are not lepers. If you go to Kakaako, then you will have to pray in the chapel for lepers. You cannot say mass, because Clément [Evrard] and your humble servant would not be willing to celebrate mass with the chalice and in the robes that you had used. The sisters refuse to receive communion from your hands. Your behaviour, my dear father, would show that you lack sensitivity or charity toward others and think only of yourself. Your egoism is too great and I should gladly believe that you do not harbour any such thoughts. Mr Gibson told me that he would permit you to come but that he first wanted to speak to Monseigneur. He must, because he wishes to prevent your visit. You must clearly see the consequences, not least for Kakaako. I have this directly from him, not from hearsay. You should know that I have been watching the Japanese treatment closely. If it produces a cure, I shall let you come straight away, as you have requested, for, my dear father, we all hope for your cure, if it is possible.

Was the publication of Stoddard's book *The Lepers of Molokai* the reason for this attack? Damien was receiving increasing amounts of fan mail. What reason could there be for not allowing a leper to visit a leper hospital – he could bring his own chalice and robes – unless it was intended that he should have no contact at all with the nuns? He had already threatened to write to the general and now he asked permission to communicate directly with the Board. Did his superiors not trust him? Was he not doing good work for the Board? He was spending all his spare time compiling a report on leprosy, at the Board's behest. He went over his diaries, correspondence and files, in order to outline the history of the last thirteen years in the leper settlement as accurately as possible. He was not confident, however, because he asked Gibson if he was approaching it in the right way. It was difficult, too, to work with inflamed eyes.

In his report, Damien declared that a good diet and perfect hygiene were the only means of retarding the progress of the disease. There was a lack of dairy products in the patients' current diet. He had not yet won the battle against drunkenness and the sanitary conditions, particularly in Kalaupapa, were extremely poor. In Kalaupapa, there was not even a water supply. Housing could be better and $6 per annum for clothing was insufficient. The permits for *kokuas* who were married to lepers should be maintained, because this reduced debauchery. The problem with the *kokuas* was that they asked to be paid for their work, and yet they ate the patients' rations. Moral standards were at a low ebb and people were still practising witchcraft. They needed a resident doctor, because it was his task, not that of the priest, to dispense medicines. In an appendix, Damien dealt with the transmission of infection. He considered that there were two forms of leprosy. Syphilitic leprosy was transmitted by sexual intercourse or it was hereditary. Even small children could develop the disease. Bachelors of various nationalities admitted that they had a venereal disease before they got leprosy. Promiscuity must be combated, therefore. Vaccination could also transmit leprosy and wearing the clothes of a leper, the particles of moisture on the breath, the saliva on a pipe that was passed around were all enough to effect transmission. The incubation period was two to ten years.

Damien sent the report for Meyer to read. The agent did not agree with all the points. Money, instead of rations, seemed to him a better idea, and he thought $6 a year for clothes adequate. The water supply in Kalaupapa was a priority for Meyer and he added pages of suggestions on the subject. Meyer thought the section on infection the most interesting.

When he had read both reports, Gibson was determined to do something for Molokai, but he had no money. He wrote to Damien, 'We are minded to send a man in a few days to see what can be done about a water supply.' The section about infection would not be published, but he did not give the reason.

Segregated by his superiors, Damien had contact with a different outside world. He sent a copy of the report to Charles Stoddard and E. H. Hudson, who were responsible for the periodical *Ave Maria*. Köckemann received two copies of Stoddard's book, one of which he was to pass on to the Sacred Hearts' Mother Judith. Damien made his excuses for the praise with which Stoddard spoke of him – this came from the author, not from Damien himself. Indeed, he received too much fan mail.

During the opening session of parliament, Gibson spoke about Damien by name: 'The case of Father Damien, as described in the reports by the Doctors Arning and Mouritz, is the most interesting and valuable, in relation to the question of infection.' During the *luna* crisis of 1877, Damien had promised to do everything he could for the sick and for the Board. Gibson quoted a passage from that letter, 'I have sacrificed my health and everything I have in the world and so you must trust me.' In high-flown words, Gibson referred to the vow of chastity that Damien had made. For this reason, his case was so interesting. For thirteen years, he had been in close contact with the sick.

This speech drew attention to Damien. It was no longer possible to avoid placing his name on the register of lepers. This was done on 30 April, the day on which the French missionary periodical *Missions Catholiques* published a letter by Köckemann, full of praise for Damien.

A Visit to Honolulu After All?

Damien worked hard to make the Corpus Christi festival a special occasion, as always, and received help from the residents. He was now an invalid himself and no longer needed to make allowances for other participants. He was weakened by lack of sleep, because every time he turned over on to his swollen right ear, he was woken by the pain.

Around this time, he received a letter from an Anglican vicar, Hugh Chapman, who lived in Peckham, in South London. 'I ask God every day that it not be long before you receive your crown and despite the fact that I shall never be close enough to you to see you wear it, I rejoice in your coronation, although I am an outsider.'

The letter had begun like all the others by those who had read Stoddard's work. 'The Holy Sacrament means more to me since I have read about a voluntary leper.' One sentence stuck in Damien's mind. 'If money can relieve in any way any of the necessary requirements of the lepers in your care, I shall do all I can to raise £500.'

If Damien had money, he would be able to introduce facilities for the Goto method to Molokai. Dr Mouritz continued to urge that, despite the prohibition, he should go to Kakaako for a cure. The daily baths and a change of surroundings would do him good. Convinced of the need for such a visit, the doctor wrote to Köckemann, 'Father Damien's life is so hard and joyless that a little relaxation and a little nursing by the sisters would, in my opinion, do him good.'

Beissel had visited Damien in the middle of June and thought that he had become much worse. He was weakened by pain and insomnia. The lepromas on his right ear were terrible. His hands were affected and his face was swollen. Things were not going well psychologically, either. He was worried about what would happen to his parishioners after he was gone. Beissel reported all this to the bishop, but he did not add that Damien had shown him the letters he had received from Fouesnel. Beissel, who was an older man, was deeply shocked and reported to the general, 'Léonor embitters the pills that he ought to sweeten.'

Köckemann suggested that Damien should be allowed to come to Honolulu, after all, but Gibson did not think it an appropriate moment, since he had to exile his political opponent, William Pilipo. He did promise to do something for Damien on Molokai, but did not say what. It could not be the Goto method, because if he were to provide the money for that, he would also have to provide the money for a second doctor to supervise the treatment. Mouritz, who avoided all extra work, had refused to have anything to do with the matter, because he did not believe in it. Damien did want to supervise the treatment, and Mouritz agreed, as long as he had nothing to do with it. He was pleased that the mother superior had promised to visit Molokai in July 1886. That would give people hope.

Damien knew that his friends were urging that he be allowed to visit Kakaako and he wrote himself to Köckemann, 'Last

year, when the disease manifested itself, I expressed the wish to
be allowed a room, a sort of resting place, in Kakaako. I would
be able to rest there for a few days if my conscience or some
other reason required me to visit Honolulu.' He continued,

> The absolute refusal [of Fouesnel], expressed in the tone of a
> policeman, not a religious superior, and that in the name of
> the bishop and the prime minister – to the effect that the
> mission would be placed in quarantine if I should even dare
> to show myself in Honolulu – caused me more pain than I
> have ever felt since my childhood. I answered with complete
> submission, on account of my vow of obedience.

When the news went round that Damien was to go to Kakaako,
there was a wild panic among many of the exiles. They feared
that Damien, who, when it came to it, was white, would go to
be cared for by the sisters, now that his illness was serious. Who
would look after the orphans? Damien assured them that he
was only going to learn the Goto method and would be back
in three weeks.

On 1 July Meyer urged, in his turn, that Damien should be
allowed to go to Honolulu. Damien pleaded with Köckemann,
'I hope that you, Monseigneur, will rescind the strict command
that my provincial has laid on me.' No reply to this letter is
extant. Dr Mouritz continued to urge that Damien be allowed
to go and, on 8 July 1886, Meyer wrote,

> I sympathise with you in the highest degree and am certain
> that in the present circumstances a visit to Honolulu to see
> what can be done for you is a duty that you owe yourself,
> but my advice is that, despite all this, I cannot say how best
> you might go. You must go on your own responsibility, and
> risk possible consequences. As agent of the Board, I do not
> have the right to give you a permit. These are granted by the
> Chairman of the Board. If you do go, you would be best to
> go on the *Mokolii*. Then you will run much less risk that
> something will be said or written than if you were to go on
> the *Likelike*. On Saturday, there is a sailing in the late afternoon

and one at midnight. I am going to Kaunakakai on Saturday. If you have come up in time, I shall accompany you with pleasure and we can discuss things. It is possible that the *Mokolii* will leave a little after midday, because there are no cattle on the ship, only sheep.

P.S. Mr Gibson said that he did not want you to go to Kakaako. He is rather unwilling that you should go. If we see one another, we can discuss this better than I can do in writing.

On Saturday 10 July Damien took the least steep path up the *pali*. He had to rest frequently and had throbbing in his painful ear. Meyer was waiting for him with his most docile horse. Not so long before, Damien had been accustomed to ride horses to death. Damien rested at Meyer's house and as they left, looked around at the Monterey cypress, which he would never see again. In Kaunakakai, he boarded the transport steamer to the forbidden city of Honolulu.

16

Triumph in Honolulu
(July–December 1886)

Triumphal Visit to Honolulu

Damien stumbled from the boat onto the quayside at Honolulu and up the hill to the cathedral. He was not welcome in the convent. The fathers and brothers were startled at his arrival and looked at him with anger, outrage and fear. No one spoke, no one offered him a hand. Damien had broken the segregation regulations. Worse still, he had disobeyed his superiors. He was not allowed to stay. He was only permitted to rest for a while on an old chair that would afterwards be burnt. Köckemann telephoned Gibson and made clear that this was Damien's own headstrong action, and the mission was not responsible for it.

Gibson telephoned the mother superior. They were both aware that their conversation could be overheard, not only by the operators, but by other users, and so the conversation remained formal. Mother Marianne spoke the historic words, 'Send him to us, we shall look after him. Do nothing that may hurt his feelings. I do not think that any of us can imagine how much he has suffered. I promise you that he will feel more comfortable than he has done for the past few years.'

The Mormon butcher, Waller, was on his rounds, when one of his customers told him about the telephone conversation. The woman could not understand why Damien was not welcome at the mission. Waller drove his cart to the Mission House and asked to speak to the bishop. He offered to build a hut for Damien in Kakaako and to take him there. He expressed the feelings of the people of Honolulu: Damien had a right to medical care.

On Sunday 11 July 1886, Damien finally got to meet the nursing sisters in Kakaako. He had first asked the general to send sisters to Hawaii thirteen years before, and, since 1883, when the sisters had arrived in Honolulu, he had been hoping to see them on Molokai, yet they had not had (or made?) time even for a visit. Because time was short for the dying, Damien had felt it necessary to disobey his local superiors. He wanted to know about the treatment his own people, the second-class lepers, were missing. He was encouraged by what the mother superior had to say. The Goto method did involve extra work, but the sisters were happy to do it, because the patients made rapid progress and the doctor was even considering releasing some of them, which had not happened before in leprosy cases.

On Monday, Gibson paid a visit and the mother superior gave the official pronouncement in the presence of her assistants. They were deeply moved by Damien's suffering. In the afternoon, Gibson visited Damien. The conversation was difficult. Damien spent half an hour arguing that the Goto method should be introduced on Molokai. Gibson thought him a chattering bore, although he meant well. The mother superior had had enough of his questions as well. On 15 July, when he had been in Kakaako for three days, Gibson noted in his diary that she would be relieved when Damien left.

Others seem to have warmed to him, including the Dutch sister, Crescentia, who prepared his meals, and Olinda Gomes, the young Portuguese maid. Sister Leopoldina later gave testimony to the beatification process that Damien had foretold that she would come to work in the leper settlement, when he encountered her one day in the hospital dispensary. He played with the children in the hospital, who came to look at him out of curiosity. He also visited the healthy girls in the Kapiolani Home, most of whom he had known on Molokai. They needed comforting and news from home. Gibson noted that the mother superior had told him, 'You should see him with the girls from the Home. He is like an old playfellow. He has a bad influence on them.'

The purpose of Damien's visit was not social, although he did hope to persuade the sisters to pay at least one visit to Molokai. His aim was to learn the Goto method and that was why he asked everyone, including the mother superior, for information. The doctors were very co-operative. He spent hours discussing dosages, side effects and the results with the young Dr Goto, who assured him that the method had effected many cures in Japan. The therapy was quite simple: two warm baths a day, pills after meals and an hour later a tincture of a Japanese bark.

The Kakaako hospital was overwhelmed with visitors. Everyone who was anyone in Honolulu wanted to speak to the leper priest. Damien was the social event of July. One of the visitors was Mother Judith, the superior of the Sacred Hearts nuns, who had travelled to Hawaii with Damien twenty years before. To her, Damien confided his true unhappiness. He could live with the pain, but not with the isolation of a pariah. Not to be able to confess, to be rejected, dumped because you were sick, that was what was intolerable.

Mother Judith asked him how he made his confession and he told her that he knelt before the large cross in the churchyard, on the spot where he hoped to be laid to rest. Sometimes, he confided, he felt more at peace after this than when he had really received the sacrament. Judith asked if he liked Kakaako and Damien replied, 'Not really. As soon as I know the method, I shall be off.'

On 16 July the king paid an unexpected visit to Damien in Kakaako. The mother superior hastily telephoned the prime minister and the bishop. Meanwhile, the king discussed the Goto method with Damien and, when the prime minister arrived, the king informed him that he wanted facilities to be set up in Molokai. In the king's presence, Damien asked Köckemann to send him a colleague and this was granted.

Now that Damien had got his way, he left Honolulu immediately, despite Dr Goto's wish that he should stay and complete his own course of treatment.

Gibson Jeered on Molokai: Rebellious Girls

Damien boarded the *Mokolii* on the evening of 16 July. He could have travelled more luxuriously, because Gibson was himself sailing to Molokai that evening, but he chose the freighter on which he had come. He enjoyed his last sunset outside the leper settlement.

On his return from the convent, Gibson had telephoned the four other members of the Committee of Five that dealt with the combating of leprosy and asked them to set sail for Molokai straight away. He wanted in person to promise the exiles they would receive the Goto method. He informed the press of his intention, since this was a political move, given that Honolulu high society had shown its support for Damien.

Damien arrived an hour before Gibson. The king's promise was greeted with warm applause, especially when Damien said that he felt better after only five days. When the politicians arrived, they ceremoniously took up their places on the terrace of the harbour depot in Kalaupapa, in order to address the people. Gibson stood up and made as if to still non-existent applause.

He began to speak, but was immediately interrupted by someone in the crowd, who demanded to know when the Goto method was to be installed. Gibson replied that this was a major decision, which required all aspects of the question to be considered in advance. The patients jeered, but he went on and told them about the king's visit and of the monarch's respect for Damien's dedication and his deep interest in their lot.

The crowd's disappointment burst out and the five politicians were overwhelmed by complaints and negative remarks. Gibson concluded that this was the work of the opposition. If it had such a hold in the settlement, then he saw no need to speed up the installation of the Goto method or the arrival of the sisters.

Back in Honolulu, he went straight away to Kakaako, to complain to the mother superior. Gibson was sorry for her and noted in his diary that she did not know what to do with the girls in the Kapiolani Home. Since Damien's visit, they had become rebellious.

Joseph Ira Dutton, Former Quartermaster

Damien believed the promises Gibson had made and asked Hayselden to send him a supply of the herbs and pills used in the Goto method. He himself had brought a supply of the necessary articles with him from Honolulu, which he was storing in the temporary dispensary, the guest room of the presbytery. He calculated how much wood he would need for a men's bathhouse. He felt stronger and was better able to do his work. On Sunday, he was able to say two masses without having to sit down.

Köckemann had promised a second priest for the settlement. Elated, Damien asked him to send Pamphile or the Belgian Louis-Lambert Conrardy, both of whom had been asking for years to be allowed to work on Molokai. Köckemann quickly replied that Pamphile was a good idea, but that the final decision rested with the general. Two days later, the bishop wrote to the superior general, 'I prefer a simple, good religious man, not so clever as an old scholar. We already have more knowledge than docility here.' To Pamphile, Köckemann wrote that Damien had brought the problems on himself. Montiton had left the island because he could not get on with Damien, another father (Burgerman) was willing to go but Damien would not have him and a third (Archambaux) had an unconquerable horror of the place. All the other missionaries were indispensable to their posts. He was happy with the idea of Pamphile for the post and had heard much good of him, but the mission needed younger workers. The decision rested with the general. The postscript to the letter was distressing. Either the bishop was lying, or he was not aware of the situation. 'I forgot to say that the Rev. Father Damien is not so unfortunate as you imagine. The Rev. Father Columban visits him every two months. Your brother can communicate weekly with Honolulu and with Maui. He was lately in Honolulu. He was not badly disfigured and was very cheerful.'

Providence sent Köckemann the American former quarter-master, Joseph Ira Dutton. He had come to assist Damien. He had sinned and he wished to do penance by cutting himself off from the world. At the age of forty he had converted to Catholicism, and he had hoped to find consolation in the Trappist monastery at Gethsemani in Kentucky, but the contemplative life did not suit him. He got to know some Redemptorists in St Louis, who sent him to New Orleans. There, he heard about the settlement on Molokai and thought that this was the penance he was seeking.

Providence, according to Köckemann, had sent Dutton the day after Damien's departure. The bishop telephoned Gibson immediately to tell him of the American's arrival. Gibson invited Dutton to his home and when the latter spoke of devoting the rest of his life to the lepers, Gibson decided that he was a religious fanatic. Since Köckemann regarded Dutton as the solution to the problem, Gibson tried to gauge his motives and his abilities. Fred Hayselden and he decided that Dutton was an odd man. He asked only for board, lodging, clothes and a daily paper. He even wanted to pay his own passage to Kalaupapa. He did insist on having the right utensils and spent several days looking for the most up-to-date cooking apparatus. He also visited Kakaako several times, which disturbed Gibson. Delighted, Köckemann informed Damien that Providence had solved his problem of solitude. Dutton wanted to devote himself to the lepers and seemed sincere. He was coming as a penitent.

Dutton arrived on 29 July 1886. Damien asked him to take care of the two churches and Dutton also took over the administration of the orphanage. He was also to serve at the mass. The first day, Damien showed Dutton around the villages and showed him the churches. He also showed him around the presbytery. Dr Mouritz asked Dutton, with a smile, whether he had been shown the Belgian photographs: this was, apparently, a sign of trust. Dutton was struck by Damien's poverty and quickly got the impression that he was impulsive and disorganised.

After only a few days, Dutton knew the routine. When Damien had started on something, he would say, 'I'm off, brother Joseph. You can finish this off. I'm the carpenter and you are the engineer.' Dutton did not mind this, particularly if he was helped by John Gaiser, a German-American patient, who was a trained mechanic. They asked themselves how it was that things that were put together so badly still worked. In that respect, Damien was a genius.

Dutton told everyone who spoke English about his past life. He had been born in Vermont, but grew up in Wisconsin. He had joined the Union Army as a quartermaster, in his teens. He married, but his wife had left him, because of his drinking and gambling. On 27 April 1883, his fortieth birthday, he had converted to Catholicism from Episcopalianism and had taken the name Joseph. Damien asked if he wanted to become a priest, but he said he had no calling.

Dutton had his suspicious about Gibson. Experience had taught him that once a budget was assigned, it was difficult to have anything extra added. He suggested to Damien that he should make a detailed proposal and helped him draft four points.

1. An ordinary hospital on the level ground to the west of the churchyard in Kalawao, where all hopeful cases are brought together to follow a course of treatment as in Kakaako, strictly regulated and with a stern discipline.

2. The buildings must consist of a boiler house (10' × 20') and two bathhouses (each 36' × 10'), a refectory (36' × 12') and a cookhouse (12' × 20').

3. Two dormitories: one for men, one for women, with a wooden fence between them, with accommodation for fifty people (both for men and for women), three buildings (18' × 40') with a verandah within. All this surrounded by a good strong fence, as in Kakaako. This institute must be placed under special management, but the Board of Health must instruct the superintendent of the settlement that he must aid this institution with all the means at the disposal of himself or his assistant.

4. Choose from the lepers who are currently in the settlement, or who will be coming later, those who are judged to have the greatest chance of success.

Outside these two dormitories, but close by: a good bathhouse, connected to the boiler house by pipes, for the use of those lepers who wish to avail themselves of the Japanese therapy, not in the hope of cure, but of alleviation. The existing hospital must be a place of refuge for the hopeless cases, with one or two large baths which can be used as I currently do in my own house. This can be done anywhere where the water supply is adequate.

Damien estimated how much wood he would need. Dutton advised him not to speak of an 'estimate', in the official letter, but of a 'first estimate', then it would be easier to add things to it. Damien also asked for official permission to carry out the work. While they were waiting for a response, Damien, Dutton and John Gaiser converted one of the rooms in the presbytery into a bathroom. A bathtub with a built-in heating system was soon to be delivered.

When, by 24 August, only some of the medicines that had been ordered had been delivered and the Board wrote that the decision on the project would be taken when the parliamentary session was over, Dutton sensed that something was up. He therefore suggested that Damien should respond in the affirmative to the letter he had received from Hugh Chapman, the London vicar who had offered to raise £500.

Damien acted quickly. On 25 and 26 August he wrote three important letters. To the general, he confirmed that he had received the cross of the Royal Order of Kalakaua. He also bore the much heavier but more honourable cross of leprosy, with which the Lord had stigmatised him. His general state of health was good, but the disease was undermining his system. He was working, but had to rest now and then. He had disobeyed his local superiors, because he had to study the Goto method, with which the sisters were having success. He needed a companion and asked the general, on the grounds of article 392 of the Order's rule, to send him his brother Pamphile.

The second letter was sent to the London vicar, Hugh Chapman. Damien was praying for Chapman and his co-religionists, 'that we may all have one faith, all may belong to the same true and Apostolic Church and all be one in Christ Jesus'. The final paragraph was the most important.

> As far as the collection you propose for the lepers for whom I care is concerned, I will state that any sum, however small, will be gratefully received for the assistance of the 600 unfortunates. Since I have made the vow of poverty, I myself have few needs. A remittance from the Bank of England to Bishop & Co., Bankers, in Honolulu, would be the easiest way of remitting the money.

A translation of Damien's letter to the general – with a few omissions – was sent to the Rev. Mr Hudson at Notre Dame University.

Damien also copied his letter to the general to Pamphile and added that the disease seemed to be going away, as a result of the Japanese treatment, which he had now been following for five weeks. He had no time to write to the rest of the family, because the government had commissioned him to establish a large hospital, in which hundreds of sick people would be treated under his direction. He not only had to work as a priest, but as a doctor and architect as well. He did not forget his sick mother, who was now eighty-three, when he stood at the altar. At the time Damien wrote this, his mother had, in fact, been dead for several days.

Gibson Reneges on His Promise

In the middle of September, it began to be extremely doubtful whether the hospital would indeed be built. Had the project been nothing but election propaganda for the prime minister? Damien's letter to Hayselden was cutting. What was he supposed to do with thirty-three iron bedsteads for boys? Where was the coal for heating his primitive baths? The supply of medicines was diminishing, despite the fact that Dutton doled them out sparingly. They were approaching the cold season and then it would be difficult to transport fragile items like the promised baths. Damien was now certain that the patients needed the treatment, because his own hand was so much better. He was no longer limping and was able to help in building a cottage for Dutton next to the pandan tree. He asked Fouesnel for one or two small items and also mentioned that he would like to make his confession, since he had, once again, not done so for two months. This comment went unanswered. Damien's impatience that the chicken feed had not yet arrived annoyed Köckemann. He considered Fouesnel a good provincial and Damien must be patient. This was rewarded: on 29 September Beissel remained ashore long enough to hear Damien's confession.

In mid-October, Damien received the news of his mother's death. Pamphile told him that hearing that Damien had leprosy had broken her health. Damien said little to Dutton about his mother's death. She had had a long life and had been well until the end.

Meanwhile, the wood for the bathhouses still had not arrived. As a test, Damien, in a sarcastic way, ordered wood for a refectory for the boys.

> Despite our poor installation, the Japanese therapy is working well, despite the fact, also, that I cannot rely on the help of the local or medical authorities, except for one or two medicines. I have started to set up this therapy here at the special request of His Majesty the King and the chairman of the Board of Health. I hope I shall not be let down by the authorities. Even if the medicines are used extremely sparingly, we shall soon be out of Japanese medicines and even Epsom salts . . .

He also needed a stove.

Lack of nurses remained the chief problem. November 8

was the third anniversary of the arrival of the sisters in Hawaii, but they had not even visited Molokai. In Kakaako, ten sisters were looking after 100 patients.

Not that there was no nursing care on Molokai. A hut between St Philomena's and Damien's house was used for the bathing of suppurating sores. The patients soaked their hands and feet in bowls of warm water with disinfectant. Damien cleaned the sores, put ointment on them and bandaged them up. In November, Dutton took over this task.

It was at this time that Molokai became really famous. Stoddard's book was a success and, in London, Hugh Chapman published Damien's letter, to which Cardinal Manning provided an introduction. Miss Agnes Lambert, a leprosy expert, described Damien's many-sided abilities and called on readers to cut out colourful prints from the *Graphic* or *Harper's Weekly*, to send to the patients. A wave of support went through the British public and Chapman was overwhelmed by prints, but also by financial contributions. The £500 was quickly raised and young women, in particular, were eager to volunteer as nurses for Hawaii.

The Belgian newspaper, *Courrier de Bruxelles*, translated the British article, but carried the additional information, so it said, that Damien was dead. Pamphile read this on 21 October. There was now no reason for him to go to Hawaii.

On 6 December Gibson no longer needed to take account of a parliament in session and wrote an arrogant letter to Damien. It was impossible to accept Damien's plans for new buildings at the present time, because of the heavy costs involved. However, if Damien could find some way of converting existing buildings, so that the Japanese system could be put into practice, then the authorities were willing, as always, to come to an agreement.

Damien was furious. Gibson was going back on his word. He scribbled the draft of a reply on the reverse of Gibson's letter. If necessary, he would use existing buildings. 'The existing hospital, with a good bath, will continue to be available for the hopeless cases, as I provide at present in my own home. This can be done anywhere with sufficient water.'

In the full text of the letter, he copied his previous four

points and concluded, 'I should like this institution to come under the separate management of the Board of Health, which must give all possible help. The director can choose from all the lepers who are in the settlement at present.'

This plan meant war and Damien considered the consequences. He decided that his response was too sharp and altered the draft of his letter accordingly. The second version was considerably more polite. The letter now concluded.

If I had been asked to keep the costs down, when I was requested to list the materials required for the proposed plan, then the costs would have been half as much. I was, however, asked to continue and make an estimate of the costs for the materials for the plan that had previously been presented, with the promise that the matter would be put in hand immediately.

Damien suggested that Dr Goto and Hayselden should visit the settlement to choose a site. If they were unable to come, he requested a permit for a short visit to discuss the matter. He was out of medicine and the supply of coal was low.

Damien had learned in a letter from Köckemann about the Belgian report of his death. Köckemann added, 'It is amazing that you did not die during your first week on Molokai, with work that was too much for a dozen sturdy men. I find it regrettable that the admiration for your work distorts the truth.' Damien replied with the suggestion that his name should be placed on the list for prayers for the dead as 'Josephus Damianus de Veuster, the leper priest who seldom confessed'. On 9 December he sent his New Year's wishes to the bishop, in which he made it clear that he expected no further correspondence.

By Christmas, the supplies needed for the Japanese method were almost exhausted. Köckemann's Christmas gift to Damien was that he could expect $25 from Paris. The bishop had also read in the *Pacific Commercial Advertiser* that there was a large sum of money in the offing, but said that he did not believe this report. He concluded, 'I take this opportunity to wish you true happiness in the New Year, but suffering will only end with life itself.'

Damien replied that he only received the *Weekly Advertiser*, in which the article had not appeared. The periodical *Ave Maria* had collected $1,000, with which they wanted to buy tabernacles. Hugh Chapman had opened a subscription list, with the permission of Bishop Manning, but he knew nothing more. He received letters from England and America almost every week. 'Please pray that my head is not turned by the praise of these sympathetic people.' He wanted to use the small sums he had received from Paris and Brooklyn for fire prevention. There was another small sum on the way and he was receiving lots of coloured prints. 'With my wishes for the New Year, I send you a St Charles Borromeo and, if you want it, a St Herman! If you do not want to keep the former, just send it to Charles in Hilo.'

He did not wish to cause trouble, but the fact remained that he hardly ever made his confession. He had done so only three times that year. This was an even heavier cross than his disease, which was spreading. His abdomen, chest and arm muscles were affected and he had lepromas on his legs. The patches were hardening and going yellow. He could no longer scrub them away. His nose was blocked and the bridge was collapsing. His mouth was also affected and he was hoarse. He had brown patches on his cheeks, forehead and chin and was losing weight rapidly, so that his clothes were too big for him. His feet were swollen and he frequently fell over.

17

Dispute about the Money
from London
(January 1887–May 1888)

One Thousand Pounds

Around the turn of the year, Gibson was discussing the building of a new chapel in Kakaako with the mother superior. The Hawaiian state would pay for this scheme. The mother superior was delighted with the proposal and wrote enthusiastically to Köckemann about it on 3 January 1887. He replied that he had already approved it on New Year's Day. He saw no difficulty in using part, or even the whole, of the budget for the Goto baths on Molokai for the chapel. After all, Damien was going to receive a large sum of money from England.

Fouesnel had not been involved in this plan. He only returned to Honolulu from Maui in the middle of January, a new man, having lost three stones in weight. He immediately rejected the plan. It was too showy, too extravagant and the money was intended for Molokai. He had also heard stories about large sums of money, but all he had seen so far was $25. He spontaneously sent Damien $50 and, for him, that was the end of the matter.

It is not clear whether Gibson, the prime minister, realised that Hawaii was on the verge of a revolution. White men were training with the Honolulu Rifles under Volney Ashford. This was, apparently, a kind of citizens' militia but, in fact, it was a cover for more dangerous activity. Important trading houses such as Castle & Cooke and E. O. Hall & Son had been secretly importing arms and ammunition for some time and there were secret arsenals throughout the city. A group of legal experts, headed by Lorrin Thurston, had drafted a constitution. They learned the text by heart and then destroyed it. Gibson felt the threat and tried to dissuade the king from his latest plan. The king wanted to buy a warship, as the first step towards a Polynesian Federation, which would cover the whole of the Pacific.

Tension always rose when the Mauna Loa erupted and this occurred again in January 1887. Some of the tremors were felt in Kalawao.

On 17 January 1887, Damien received a letter of credit for £995 from the banking house of Bishop & Co. The money had come from London via Sydney. Damien was beside himself with joy. He had never expected to receive so much. He immediately drew up plans for some of the money to be spent on adequate clothing for the patients. One set of clothing for wear and one in the wash seemed to him a good rule. He asked Meyer to arrange for this, since he himself could no longer travel. He also wrote straight away to thank Chapman for his generosity.

Damien wrote to Köckemann, asking for permission to allow a sister from Loretto and a nurse from Liverpool to come over to work in the settlement, since he had long ago given up hope of seeing the Franciscans there. He then announced the arrival of the money from England and said that the donors had made clear that he was to have sole management of the money. He said that he had not yet decided what he wanted to do with it, but would decide the following week whether to send it to the bishop or put it in the bank. He asked to be allowed to retain a substantial amount under his own name, so that he could pay the bills for the things he had already ordered. 'I think that such a course of action would avoid suspicion of the Catholic mission, because the money does not come from Catholics, but principally from Protestants.' Some Protestants in Britain had already raised objections.

Sisters on Molokai After All

Köckemann supported the plan to bring over the sister from Loretto and suggested it to the mother superior, but she rejected it out of hand. The sister would first have to undergo the novitiate in Syracuse and then the Order would decide where she should be sent. Köckemann knew that Damien would be ill-pleased with this news. This was a nuisance, because the bishop had to persuade him to transfer the money to the mission, which was the usual procedure. In any case, according to the bishop, the mission needed the money far more and Damien would receive a share. He told Damien he should discuss with Fouesnel how he would be able to keep to his vow of poverty. He went on, 'Permit me, after all the poetry that has been written about the lepers of Molokai, to add a few prosaic remarks.'

The bishop repeated that he and the government had contributed to Damien's fame, but if he were to believe the newspapers, Damien did everything alone and his superiors served only to allow him to shine. This was an insult to the king and Gibson and it might happen that a jealous enemy would make people believe that Damien had extorted the money under false pretences. Moreover, now that Damien did have so much money, he might as well pay Dutton's costs himself. One sentence stood out, 'There could be a change of government at any moment.'

Around the same time, a surprising rumour went round. Dutton had heard that the whole Chapman business was a way of getting Anglican sisters of the Order of St John to take over the leper settlement. Mouritz, who was an Anglican, was supposed to be in the plot.

Damien warned Gibson and asked Köckemann not to prevent the Franciscan nuns from coming to Molokai any longer. He was bitter in his letter to the bishop. 'After having received frankincense and gold from every quarter,' he wrote, 'I receive now from my bishop bitter myrrh.'

Köckemann replied that Damien's letter was not flattering, but candid. Perhaps it was that candour which had long not been in evidence. The bishop had always known that the sisters would one day go to Molokai. Initially, there were too few of them and they had not come exclusively to care for the lepers. The invitation from the king had referred to the 'sick'. The mother superior had never gone to Molokai and the bishop had let her go her own way. She had set up Kapiolani Home and again he had let her do as she pleased. If she wanted to go to Molokai, he would let her go, but Damien must know that the sisters in Kakaako did good above all by enforcing rules and keeping the sexes apart. How could this be done on Molokai?

In his letter of 5 February the bishop sought to set everything out calmly. Damien only considered the leper settlement, while he as bishop had to direct the whole mission and, after all, they were still living in a hostile country – one could never be too careful. He would certainly speak to Gibson and the mother superior. He then referred to Damien's remark. 'After the gold and frankincense, the myrrh did not please you. You have spewed that, together with an old quantity of gall, in my face. Let us hope that it goes no further. For my part, I have never ceased to make your heroism known whenever I could and it was proper to do so.'

A few days later, Köckemann was furious. A newspaper had reported that Damien's superiors had forbidden him to go to Kakaako for treatment. Fouesnel was convinced that Damien had prompted this. Fame had gone to his head. Instead of arbitrarily buying clothes for his lepers, he would have done better to ask his superiors' advice first. Now, he had insulted the government, and what was more, he was treating Fouesnel like an errand boy.

In his restrained report to the general, Köckemann wrote that everyone was doing something for the lepers: the government, the mission, Damien. The sisters would go to Molokai when there were more of them. A few days previously, the bishop had written to Damien that he did not really know what the sisters were all doing in Kakaako. Damien was a problem, Köckemann informed the general. He had received a large amount of money and when the bishop had tried to give him advice, he had flown off the handle. Köckemann was convinced this was evil.

Gibson feared that Mother Marianne would take her sisters to Kalaupapa, even if it were only to prevent the Anglican nuns coming. He was determined to do all he could to prevent this.

On 14 February Köckemann seemed certain that the Anglican nuns were coming to take over the leper settlement. A letter from Chapman, now lost, apparently indicated this. When he sounded the mother superior out as to whether she could set out straight away, she said she was ready and would willingly go. This was apparently in earnest and Gibson sent his son-in-law Hayselden to Kalaupapa, ostensibly to look for a site for a convent. A few days later, the secretary to the Board returned with horror stories. The sisters could not go to such a place. Implicitly, of course, this meant that Damien needed help, because it meant that Kalaupapa was not as well equipped as the government had always proclaimed. Hayselden did, in fact, immediately order baths and heaters. An old barn could be converted into a bathhouse.

The departure of the sisters had been prevented, but according to Gibson's diary, he was very upset, because the mother superior would not move to a house in Queen Street that he had had done up for her and the sisters. She had said he was only a friend. She had also said that she would go to Molokai in a few months.

Köckemann had allowed Dutton to make temporary vows a few days before this situation. Damien was his superior, but if there were a disagreement, the brother could appeal to the bishop. Fouesnel had thought about Damien's money. He did not say it straight out, but they had to sort out what was to happen to the money after Damien's death. Splashing it about, as he had done on buying clothes for the exiles, was not appropriate. Damien was also no longer to write uncensored letters. Once again, he must present all letters to the provincial for approval, except those to the general.

The situation became more and more complicated. The general wanted a letter from Damien for publication. Fouesnel's tone now altered. If Damien had his letters home checked, he would be showing humility. Fouesnel had never wanted to be the superior and now he was obliged to inform a temperamental man like Damien of matters which were invariably badly received. Like the ungrateful person Damien was, he had asked Meyer to do his shopping. Less than a month before, Fouesnel had reproached Damien for treating his provincial like an errand boy. For his part, Meyer was pleased that Damien took no account of religious allegiance when he was distributing gifts, only of need.

In March, the situation was still unclear. Gibson tried to win back the mother superior by giving her a ring, inscribed with the text Ruth 1:16–17, and the entwined monograms W and M, to mark the anniversary of their friendship. Mother Marianne kept the ring.

Gibson also publicly went on the attack against Damien. In an editorial for the *Pacific Commercial Advertiser*, he wrote that distributing clothes was really a serious criticism of the Board and he questioned Damien's honesty. Damien should give an account of the English money, because the public had questions about it. He wanted to know all the facts.

Gibson and Köckemann thought that the solution was obvious. If the sister from Loretto and the nurse from Liverpool took on the nursing duties on Molokai, then the mother superior would not have to go. Damien's dream would be realised and perhaps he would then accept the proposal that Hayselden had drawn up on the Board's behalf. This stated that Damien

as an honest and faithful priest and a loyal man, who acted in the interests of the people, should elect that the Fund be used in an official manner, to the greater benefit of the lepers for whom the government was caring. He [Gibson] proposes that you place the whole matter of the use of the money in the hands of your bishop. He would then spend it with the Board of Health, to some extent in accordance with your ideas, and this for the good of the suffering people. In that case, the government would send a formal letter of thanks to the generous donors in London, as a result of which your good work for the cause of the lepers in the kingdom would be recognised.

This might have worked, if the mother superior had not once again opposed the arrival of outsiders as nurses.

Anonymous Press Articles and Political Tension

The general became involved in the disputes. He had realised that Damien was not able to go to confession often enough and opened fire on Fouesnel, who defended himself. Whereas in the past, he had asserted that the transport connections were good, it now turned out that a small steamboat did not call in as often as once a fortnight. Beissel already had a hard time with his Portuguese parish and he also served 'topside', where you had to beat your way through the jungle with a stick. These arguments showed either that Fouesnel had no idea what Molokai looked like – though he had visited topside and the settlement – or that he was simply lying.

No one could live with Damien, the provincial wrote. Burgerman and Archambaux refused to go there and yet they were both lepers. The sisters would soon be going there and their sacrifice would be much greater than Damien's, because they would look after the lepers and they would receive communion from a leper. In Fouesnel's opinion, Damien was a liar who was forcing the poor sisters to sacrifice themselves.

Articles continued to be written about Damien and one, in the journal of a girls' club in Soho, was read by the British painter Edward Clifford, whose interest it engaged.

For three months, the English nurse Miss Martin was in the settlement. She stayed with Dr Mouritz, but then left.

Political Tension Concerning the Leper Settlement

In the spring of 1887, Damien's communications with his superiors were confined to the strictly essential. The bishop cleared three letters Damien had written to England, with minor alterations.

Gibson wrote an anonymous article attacking Damien in the *Pacific Commercial Advertiser*, arguing that the Board of Health ought to spend the money Damien had received. Fouesnel called the article 'shabby' and tried to prevent another attack. He was still defending himself to the general in Paris. There was only one excuse left: no one was willing to go.

On 21 April Fouesnel sent Damien various items for the mass and drew his attention to a long article in the *Advertiser*.

The long article will not please you any more than it does us. It shows that we are not entirely wrong and that you must put a stop to your correspondence with the outside world as far as possible. This matter can have much more serious consequences than you imagine. Gibson is extremely upset about it. We cannot go into town without being spoken to about it and without people asking for information about it.

The article in the *Pacific Commercial Advertiser* was harsh. The anonymous author began, 'There is something odd about the English Aid Fund of Father Damien of Molokai.' A letter had been published in *The Times*, in which Damien said he had used the bulk of the money, without specifying how. But parliament had approved a budget of $100,000 for Kalaupapa, which surely meant that the lepers there were being looked after. In the last fiscal year, $34,000 had been spent. It was impossible that the people suffering from leprosy were in a miserable condition. The newspaper quoted Damien's last letter to Chapman, in which he thanked his sponsors. Because the cold season was approaching, he had bought material. The rest of the money he would keep for future needs. The sentence that 'the perfume of the flower of English love was greatly appreciated by the many poor and destitute sufferers, whose cold and withered limbs would once more feel the comfort of warm material' also caused comment.

A patient from Kalawao was the next anonymous writer, who continued the discussion in the *Pacific Commercial Advertiser*. He pointed out that the people who had contributed to the

Fund wanted Fr Damien to manage the money as he saw fit. 'Does the Board of Health in Honolulu know what the lepers really need?' the patient wondered. Perhaps he, or she, wanted his own share of the cake. 'Parliament did approve $100,000 for the lepers, but $6 a year for clothes is too little. And that money, moreover, has to be spent in the shop, where often high prices are charged for poor quality.'

On the day this article appeared, the official statistics for health care for the kingdom were published in the *Hawaiian Government Gazette*. The total amount for the 609 lepers in Kalaupapa and the 102 in Kakaako was $120,819.70 to 31 March 1887. This total included the following items: Meyer's salary $1,800; Kapiolani Home $1,495.24; Dr Goto's salary $2,335; Dr Mouritz's salary $3,000.; costs of Dr Arning's return journey $5,000. The printing of reports cost six and a half times as much as the amount of money Damien had received. It was also notable that $4,049.22 had been spent on clothing for the lepers and $275 on medicine. Fouesnel sent a copy of the figures to Paris. Damien criticised Hayselden, who thought Molokai too sinister a place for the sisters, but a paradise for the lepers.

Businessmen had analysed the budget and considered that $4,000 for clothing for 711 people was excessive, even though this amounted to less than $6 per person. The *Pacific Commercial Advertiser* took up the defence of the authorities and declared it 'not extravagant, but certainly sufficient'. Gibson hoped these figures would break Damien's popularity.

On 31 May the *Hawaiian Gazette* published a letter in which Gibson's departure was demanded. There was a revolutionary atmosphere. Fouesnel supported Gibson and did not want to offend him. He decided not to send any of the five new priests to Molokai. As for the five crates of gifts that had arrived, Damien must describe their contents 'clearly and on a neat piece of paper'.

Damien was busy with correspondence. He answered the letter from Dr Goto, who was going to England to study and had asked him for addresses in the United States and Britain. Then he wrote to Edward Clifford, the English painter, who

wanted to visit him. Damien thought Clifford's suggestion that
he should bring a magic lantern with him was wonderful, because
the children would enjoy watching the projected prints. Knowing
quite well that Fouesnel would read the letter, he wrote,

> Someone who allowed himself to be influenced by jealousy
> and dirty politics has tried to drag English generosity to the
> lepers through the mud in a local newspaper. If I gave this
> person the chance to get hold of the rest of the Fund – he
> has asked me to so indirectly – he would publish a letter of
> praise in the name of the Hawaiian government. Please note
> that this letter is not for publication.

Damien was making clear to Fouesnel that he knew Gibson
was responsible for the anonymous articles.

Gibson also defended himself and instructed Hayselden to
get Meyer to find out who the anonymous patient was who
had attacked him in the newspaper. He suspected it was Damien,
but it turned out to be someone called George Horan, a man
who often hung around at the presbytery.

Köckemann was an administrator, who had little feel for
politics. He chose just this moment, when political tension was
gripping Honolulu, to make a tour of the islands. Before he set
out, he sent Damien instructions on headed notepaper as to
how to make his will. He was to copy out the following text
Köckemann had enclosed.

> I, J. Damien de Veuster, Catholic priest, resident in the leper
> settlement on Molokai, being of sound mind and memory,
> do hereby make my last will and testament and declare that
> I bequeath all my possessions, joint and several, that I may
> possess in the Hawaiian Islands up to the moment of my
> death, to Monseigneur Köckemann, bishop of Olba and
> apostolic vicar of the Hawaiian islands, and to his successors.
> I name and designate Joseph Dutton as executor. Witness
> my hand and seal, this fifteenth day of May, in the Year of
> Our Lord eighteen hundred and eighty seven. J. Damien
> de Veuster.

A few days after the bishop had left Honolulu, the ministry resigned in order to prevent a revolution.

Successful White Protestant Coup

In the early morning of 30 June 1887, the white militiamen of the Honolulu Rifles collected their weapons and made their way to the arsenal, where a meeting had been called. The city was alive with rumour. The militia was going to force Gibson to resign. King Kalakaua was ready to take flight via a secret passageway and his supporters were going to plunder the homes of the whites. Gibson was aware of the danger and made a hurried farewell visit to the convent. He emotionally urged the mother superior to return to Syracuse, because the new leaders might harm them. He sent his daughter and grandchildren to his summer residence and asked Lieutenant Colonel Ashford for protection. Just before the meeting was due to start, he rode to a cabinet meeting. Meanwhile the young barrister Lorrin Thurston had demanded Gibson's resignation. Ashford placed the prime minister under house arrest. If he tried to flee, he would be shot. An angry crowd surrounded his house, but confined itself to shouting insults and slogans.

After daybreak, Ashford stormed Gibson's house. The prime minister just had time to swallow a note from the mother superior. Gibson and Hayselden were handcuffed and had to walk down the street with nooses around their necks. They were led to the depot of the Pacific Naval Company on the quayside. The excited crowd demanded their execution and the two prisoners were made to sit on soapboxes beneath the gallows. They were insulted and pelted with rubbish. Gibson began to cough up blood. At sunset, his daughter Talula forced her way through the crowd. She had brought water for her husband and father and shouted to the crowd that their behaviour was shameful. Gibson summoned up the courage to ask on what grounds he was being held and was told it was embezzlement. Later in the evening, they were removed to the police station and locked up. Detectives went through all the papers in search of evidence against Gibson and Hayselden. The Kakaako accounts were also seized. The luxurious coach in which the sisters went about, and other items, fell under suspicion. On 11 July all the charges were withdrawn. Gibson was requested to leave the islands, ostensibly on grounds of health.

Fouesnel tried to calm his nerves with wine. He was worried about the sisters, who had lost their protector. Other priests, such as the newly arrived Fr Sylvester Küpper, thought Fouesnel was pathetic. The sisters were not his responsibility. The two men quarrelled and insults were exchanged. Fouesnel asked Damien to be careful, because the patients had lost their father, Gibson, and their mothers, the sisters, 'for it was to be feared that the Protestants would not want anything more to do with the sisters'. It was a question of waiting until the king had issued a new constitution.

The king appointed four ministers on the nomination of the leaders of the coup. The proclamation of the new constitution was delayed because the Supreme Court and the foreign diplomats first had to examine the English text. Only when the text had been signed was it translated into Hawaiian. The king had lost his power of veto and the ministers were now responsible to parliament. All whites and the majority of half-whites received automatic suffrage, but only the wealthier Hawaiians could vote. Gibson left the islands two weeks after the 'bayonet revolution'.

Around that time, the first reforms took place. Dr Trousseau was appointed chairman of the Board of Health. Dr Mouritz advised Damien to take advantage of the power vacuum to undertake one or two items of capital expenditure. The dormitories were too full and badly ventilated. Damien presented a plan for two dormitories, of thirty-six by twelve feet each, surrounded by a covered verandah. In the letter to Meyer on this subject, he referred to 'our new Board of Health', and wrote, 'I hope that our new Board will not take away the treatment from us, because it gives relief, and even alleviation of the symptoms of our terrible disease. You have seen our bathhouse, which is now working well. It would be regrettable to have to stop using it because of a lack of medication.'

The sisters in Kakaako received instructions to prepare thirty-one people for deportation. They regarded this routine measure as a bad omen of impending persecution, because 'good' children were also to be exiled. Damien was to take good care of one young man in particular, who wanted to leave his inheritance to the sisters in gratitude for their care. When they arrived on Molokai, this new group said that the sisters were to be sent back to America.

Three weeks after the coup, Trousseau promised to send Damien Japanese medicines as soon as they arrived. He confirmed Meyer as manager. In agreement with Mouritz, Damien transferred his supply of medicines to Dutton, who now held daily consultations in the hut where he bathed sores. Given the disturbances, it was not surprising that Damien had received no visitors, but in August it was more than four months since he had last made his confession. Küpper had got as far as the top of the *pali*, but then he had become dizzy and turned back. He asked Meyer to telephone Damien and get him to come up, but Damien was no longer able to do so, because his illness was too far advanced. Küpper, therefore, returned to Honolulu to take part in the retreat, along with seventeen other members of the Order. Everyone there agreed that Damien seldom made his confession, but no one could suggest a solution and the discussion widened to the whole leprosy issue. Trousseau was demanding that all incurable cases should go to Molokai. After the elections in November, there would certainly be a new round-up. Burgerman and Archambaux would be exiled and then Damien would be able to go to confession. Damien could not wait another two and a half months, however, and Köckemann designated the German, Fr Wendelin Möllers, as his confessor. Möllers had been expelled from the Marquesa Islands, after seven years of hard work, because he had quarrelled with almost everyone and this had led to difficulties with the government. He was a sincere, but sour-tempered and strict man.

In Molokai, Damien was waiting for Möllers. He rode to

the wharf and halted his buggy on a stretch of grass, so that his horse, William, could graze. He got out of the buggy with difficulty and while the boat was tying up, he discussed with the hot-tempered American, Alfred Carter, how to blow up the massive rocks by the quay. It was now many years since Damien had proposed that this should be done. Trousseau, who knew Kalaupapa well, had immediately given orders for the work. Carter asked for 'white food' to be ordered for the white lepers, because, after all, the immigrants paid the most taxes. Damien agreed with him as far as food was concerned. Everyone should be allowed to eat what they were used to. Whites paid more taxes, but they also earned more, so that, in percentage terms, it might even be that *Kanaka* paid more.

Tensions with Dutton

The leper settlement felt the changes. In the autumn of 1887, 200 patients arrived. The hospital, which was twenty years old, was renovated. It was high time, because the doors and windows were rotting. Damien hoped that a mortuary could be built, because now that the dying-shed had been closed, people were dying on the wards and the bodies were sometimes left lying there for hours. He was hoping that this wish would also be fulfilled, because for the first time since the arrival of the sisters in 1883, the Board was paying bills quickly and was responsive to suggestions. He suggested that there should be a closed section for the mentally ill and the purchase of a covered ambulance with good suspension for taking invalids to and from hospital. The most urgent matter was a water supply for Kalaupapa.

As usual, none of the visitors who disembarked from the sloop was wearing a soutane, and so Damien went home, where he estimated how much a boys' dormitory would cost. If he did the work for nothing, the Board was willing to send him materials to the value of $400. Mouritz said that if the Board did not keep its word, he could always use the English money. When Damien shook his head, he became angry and spat out that Damien had sent a blind boy to the hospital, because the youth had not wanted to be baptised. Damien countered that the boy had needed extra care and he had no nursing facilities in the orphanage.

If Beissel or Möllers had come, Damien would have been able to discuss his problems with Dutton, but now he could only approach the bishop, and this did not solve anything. Dr Mouritz did not like the new Board and it was he who insinuated to Dutton that the new management did not trust him. Mouritz advised him to place himself completely in the service of the Board, because otherwise he could be dismissed. As a result, Dutton gave up his work in the orphanage in order to take up nursing in the hospital.

Damien complained to Meyer that he needed Dutton in the orphanage and suggested he should work part-time in the hospital. Meyer proposed trying to find a solution acceptable to both parties. This proved difficult, because Dutton claimed that he was sick of these conflicting instructions: Gibson had taken him on as a nurse, Köckemann as Damien's sexton. Dutton had asked to be allowed to work as a nurse for a few hours a day, but now that Mouritz was offering him the post of hospital director, he wanted to take it.

Damien hindered the discussion by putting pressure on Dutton. He reminded him of his vow of obedience. Moreover, Köckemann had instructed Damien to make the penitent's life difficult and to keep him humble, and a position such as hospital director was in conflict with that.

When Köckemann involved himself in the matter, the discussion degenerated completely, until he proposed a compromise that Damien and Dutton finally accepted: Dutton would continue to be responsible for the boys' home, but would work for three hours a day at the hospital. Damien was to be much less demanding and allow Dutton more freedom.

The fuss and bother seemed to be over, until Köckemann confided to Damien that Dutton had difficulties with him as a person. He found Damien's familiar manners – he called everyone by their first name, in Hawaiian fashion – terrible. He found it dreadful to receive communion from the hands of a leper and could no longer stand the sight or the stench of the disfigurements. These wounding comments destroyed the relationship between the priest and the brother and it was never restored. The dispute had a further consequence. Dr Mouritz, who did not enjoy working in the settlement, made use of the rejection of his recommendation in relation to Dutton as a pretext for his resignation.

To people like Dr Woods, the specialist in leprosy who had visited him in 1876, Damien said what he really thought, but he asked him not to publish the letter. The reply he received must have been important, because Meyer asked him for permission to show the letter from the doctor, who had seen cases of leprosy throughout the world, to influential people.

Despite the fact that he was a leper, Damien did his work as he had always done, and he wrote, 'I am happy and content with my lot. It has pleased Almighty God to choose me as a priest and a nurse to the lepers. May our souls, after they are freed from these infected bodies, together with you, the pure, true children of Holy Church, be in paradise.'

Nevertheless, he was hurt and used work as a tried remedy. The water pressure for the bathhouse needed to be increased. The dormitories for boys were overcrowded – he had boys sleeping in his house because there was no room – and yet he had to wait for wood for a new dormitory. And there were new people arriving all the time. 'Our hearts are aching because so many patients are being snatched away from us. We love them and do not want to see them go,' Mother Marianne wrote. Fortunately, the road up the *pali* had been improved after an earthquake had swept away a Portuguese man. Immediately, $1,000 was paid out for improvements to the path.

Perhaps a priest was waiting until the path was finished, Damien thought, because he had once again gone four months without a visit. Fouesnel fumed and threatened, but he did not get anyone to go to Molokai. On 1 October he suggested going himself. he would telephone from Meyer's and then Damien would just have to climb to the top. He had done all of Damien's shopping, except for the rice, because the Chinese supplier was out of stock. During all these months, the repugnance for leprous fingers had been keeping Dutton and Damien apart.

Dutton worked things out of his system by writing hundreds of letters. He was feeling guilty, because he could see that the bridge of Damien's nose had collapsed. The leprosy had also affected the bones. Damien realised that he would soon have to start looking for a successor, a healthy priest. Fouesnel declared that the sisters were only prepared to receive communion from healthy fingers and they were so badly needed. Since the Sacred Hearts Order was unable to make even one day free for the settlement, Damien began to look for a solution outside the Order. For eleven years now, a Belgian missionary who worked among the Umatilla Indians in Washington State had been putting himself forward. If Köckemann could allow Louis-Lambert Conrardy to come over, he would be able to succeed him and Damien would have a confessor. Four months without confession was too long.

Dr Emerson, Chairman of the Board of Health

There was good news, as well: Dr Nathaniel Emerson had been appointed Chairman of the Board of Health. He had become a friend of Damien's during his time working in Kalawao. Damien sent him a jubilant letter of congratulation, in which he immediately asked for Japanese medicines. Damien's superiors had forbidden him to have any direct contact with the Board, but he had no choice. When he had asked Fouesnel for Japanese medicines, the latter had replied angrily that even Kakaako had none. Damien wrote back to the provincial that once again he had spent four months without making his confession. Fouesnel had promised to come himself, but he had gone to the Big Island; and where were the other priests from the Order who had promised to come? Where was Beissel? Möllers? Fouesnel? Was Damien dead for them already? On 17 October Fouesnel wrote back condescendingly that he forgave Damien for his outburst, because he understood the sick patient's situation. Möllers was in Honolulu and was to set out the following day for Wailuku, which meant he could make a stop-over at the settlement. Damien should certainly not count on the sisters, because they had enough problems already: Dr Trousseau had the nerve simply to summon a number of patients and ship them off to Molokai, without consulting the mother superior. She did not dare to complain about the tyrant, and the new administration would blame her. Anyway, Damien need not worry: soon there would be a new provincial who would comply with Damien's whims straight away. Poor old Fouesnel, who never did anything right, would be freed from his *pilikia*, his problems and everyone would be rid of him. Damien did not know that the general wanted to replace Fouesnel by Ropert, but he did realise that the superiors in Honolulu, in particular, were afraid of the new administration. The election campaign was in full swing and it was not clear what the future would hold.

Damien felt hopeful when he read Emerson's letter.

I am happy to be able to reassure you that I insist on doing everything I can for you and since the Japanese medicine helps you, I am very happy to be able to do it. At the moment, there are no supplies, but the Board is hoping for a new delivery soon. When it comes, you will be resupplied.

Since all whites, most half-whites and only a few Hawaiians were allowed to vote, The Reform Movement won the elections by an overwhelming majority. Dr Hyde rejoiced: 'It is absolutely clear that the Hawaiians have now lost their prestigious position and influence, that was guaranteed by the old constitution. These islands will no longer be governed in the interest of the Hawaiians, but in those of the new, cosmopolitan population, the Chinese excepted.'

The elections made little difference to Molokai. It was news that a shipping line in Honolulu had brought four crates of *gurjun* oil free, a gift from the British painter Edward Clifford. The oil did not effect a cure but it did keep the skin clean and brought relief. At the end of November, Damien received a gift of cases of salmon and preserved apples. All of the material that had been ordered for the dormitories was also in the cargo, except for the nails. The Board gave its approval for the building of a cookhouse and a recreation room for the boys and sent kettles, a coffee pot, a frying pan, fifty iron bedsteads and whitewash for the dormitories.

These extensions were necessary, because, according to Fouesnel, large groups were to be exiled. On 8 November the provincial tried to sound friendly. He was really sorry that Damien was not getting any more Japanese medicines, because they made him feel better. A doctor in Honolulu was said to be hiding all the supplies. Fouesnel would try to get him some , although he was extremely upset himself. The Board wanted to get rid of the sisters, in order to eliminate all reminders of Gibson.

No Time for Visits, Except for the Will

Despite the fact that Fouesnel censored his letters, Damien again expressed his thoughts clearly and frankly on paper. He thanked Monsignor Cross, of Oregon, for his sympathy. He was in need of it now that the Reform Party was starting to hunt down persons suspected of having leprosy. He had fifteen boys under his protection. He asked Pamphile to pray for his parishioners, many of whom were suffering not only from physical but from spiritual leprosy. Although the newspaper had said that he was dead, God had unfortunately not yet called him from the world. He was still bearing his cross and would continue as long as he could, but he felt lonely. Not that he was bored – he was doing a great deal and did not have enough time. He asked his niece Marie-Justine to write more. He had just finished this letter when the post arrived. Hollister & Co. was a company that regularly gave the exiles damaged goods, but they refused to send them sparkling drinks, because the bottles became infected. Hollister could send sparkling drinks in disposable bottles, but then Damien would have to pay fifty cents a dozen. Damien showed this letter to everyone, not because of the contents, but because it was the first typed letter he had ever received. Dutton found it difficult to read and did not believe in it, but Damien thought that typing was the way of the future. There was also a message in the post that Beissel would be aboard the next boat. Möllers had visited a fortnight before and another visit seemed an unexpected bonus.

Damien wanted to wait on the quay, but the following morning, 17 November 1887, he was busy with preparations for the mass when someone rushed into the church and called him to a Chinese patient who had a severe wound to the abdomen from attempted suicide. Damien and Dr Mouritz arrived at about the same time and the doctor determined that the case was hopeless. While they were tending the man, Damien asked about Mouritz's successor. There were three candidates: Dr Kimball, Dr Curtis and Dr Petersen. Mouritz was unwilling to speak about his resignation, which he had tendered because Damien had opposed Dutton's appointment as hospital director. In fact, this was a pretext. He had always disliked working at the settlement, but what he really could not stand was all the administrative nonsense that Meyer landed him with. Now that he had saved enough to open a practice in Honolulu, he wanted to leave. Damien stayed with the Chinese patient until he died.

Only then did he have time for Beissel, who had been sent by Köckemann with a double, and, above all, a delicate mission. He had to warn Damien that the Board had decided to exile Grégoire Archambaux again. Archambaux was prepared to go to Molokai if he did not have to undergo a humiliating physical examination. The bishop wanted Damien to look after the older man.

Beissel also had to discuss Damien's will with him. The dispute between Damien and Dutton in September had led Köckemann to think that the one-time quartermaster was as untrustworthy as he had initially thought. He now wished to have Evrard named as executor. Damien had to rewrite his will and Dutton and Beissel witnessed it. Beissel then left straight away.

A week later, Fouesnel confirmed the news of Archambaux's exile. The 'enemy' wanted to lock him up. Damien was to find a nurse for him, because Archambaux was helpless. Not so helpless, though, that he was unable to clear out the presbytery in Lahaina before he left, taking even the chalices with him. When Burgerman returned and found the empty cupboards, he demanded that his things be returned.

Archambaux's exile was part of the strict policy followed by Emerson. Despite the mother superior's objections, he sent a boy of five and a girl called Katharina to Kalawao. The doctor bore a grudge against the nun, who behaved as though the patients were being sent to hell every time someone was exiled. She had been on the islands for four years and had never been there, whereas he had lived there. The next departure of forty exiles was delayed because of bad weather. Clayton Strawn had a premonition that the boat would be lost and wrote to Damien about it, and, indeed, his fears were fulfilled. When the boat did sail, it was sunk by a tidal wave after landing the exiles.

The weather delayed the work on the dormitories. At this time, yet another petition was sent, requesting that nursing sisters be sent to the settlement.

The Sisters Do Not Come

Damien first needed a healthy priest, since without one the bishop would never let the sisters go, even if they wanted to. Louis-Lambert Conrardy was anxious to leave Washington, because the white settlers thought he was stirring the Indians up. Conrardy knew that his life could be in danger when he made a complaint about two inspectors who forced Indian chiefs to sell their reservations without Washington's knowledge. The Belgian Bishop of Oregon, Charles Seghers, had just been murdered in Alaska. He and his successor, Monsignor Gross, advised Conrardy either to leave or to join a powerful Order, such as the Jesuits. Conrardy felt that he was too old for the novitiate, and once again applied to go to Molokai.

Damien's superiors were opposed to this because Conrardy was an 'outsider'. Finally, they worked out a compromise. Conrardy was given permission to visit Molokai, so that he could get to know Damien. If they got on, he would have to spend a year as a novice in Leuven or in Miranda, in Spain, or to Chile before returning, unless the general chapter, to be held in Paris in September 1888, were to send a letter to the Vatican College for Religious Orders to request a dispensation. With the full agreement of his superiors, Damien would then officially invite Conrardy to come.

He had a temporary companion. Archambaux arrived on 1 December 1887, and immediately asked for wine. Fouesnel, who had given Archambaux $40 a month 'drink money' in Lahaina, had given Damien strict orders that Archambaux was not to receive a drop of alcohol. Despite the fact that this caused one scene after another, Damien kept to this instruction, although he sympathised with the older man, sending him blankets and a jacket, because he was cold in Kalaupapa.

The sisters did not come. On 5 December 1887 the Board rejected the petition, despite the fact that all its members were favourable to its contents. It was the sisters themselves who had refused to go, unless they were accompanied by a healthy priest. The bishop had no missionaries who were free, and after all, there were two priests in the settlement already.

Meyer protested that the settlement needed nurses. In Honolulu, he threatened Fouesnel that he would look for another religious order, and he put this idea on paper. 'There are many good Orders who have members trained as nurses and probably good doctors, too. We would have to persuade four or five to come and do exactly the same work as the sisters in Kakaako. The best thing would be if they came with a resident doctor.'

In her note to Damien, the mother superior did not speak about the petition. 'We are sending you another of our good people. Our hearts bleed at the heartless manner in which they are shipped off. If it were God's will, how gladly would we not go with them, but our future looks dark. This time a good, poor man whom I strongly recommend to you is going. He is a good Catholic.' She also mentioned a carpenter and sent from all the sisters a warm *aloha*.

Meyer knew that the Board had no intention of closing Kakaako. The only problem was that the first thing tourists saw on their arrival in Honolulu was a leper hospital. For this reason, the Board was considering a new site, but this did not mean the sisters would be sent away.

When a priest of the Order of St Camillus of Lellis offered to come, Köckemann accepted him, on condition that he bring nursing brothers with him. Now it was the Board that rejected the offer, because the brothers refused to nurse women. The sisters still wanted their own chaplain and were refusing to go. This was the last straw for the Board. Because the Franciscans were so hard to please, they decided to look for a less touchy nursing order.

'Father Léonor is not really against the sisters' coming,' Meyer wrote to Damien. 'He sympathises with his friendly heart with the hopeless situation they would find themselves in here. It would be extremely harsh and unreasonable to make them live in the asylum. If they had wanted to do so themselves, no one would have stopped them.'

Damien still hoped that the mother superior would come one day. With this in view, he asked the British painter, Edward Clifford, to do a painting of St Francis for the convent. He hoped that he would live to see the sisters come but his disease was spreading. His ears were protruding and swollen, his nose was blocked and his right hand was covered in lepromas – this at the very time when so many new people were arriving. If the arrest of suspects went on at this pace, there would soon be 1,500 patients in the settlement. He already had sixty boys in his orphanage.

In December, so many people were exiled to Molokai, that the words 'over-population' started to be heard, just at the point when there was no longer a doctor to organise affairs. Although Petersen was only going to start work on 1 January, Mouritz, whose contract did not expire until 31 December, had already left. Emerson made an inspection tour in the middle of December in order to see how fifty newcomers a week could be accommodated. The fifteen houses that were under construction were already spoken for. There was also an increasing number of whites among the newcomers, who demanded bread. John Gaines had worked in the bakery at Lahaina for a long time and wanted to train boys, but he needed a good oven for this.

Meyer did what he could. When the Board sent thirty-four beds for sixty boys, Meyer offered to go and find the extra twenty-six. This trod on Fouesnel's toes, because he wanted to continue to make Damien's purchases, since this allowed him to keep a check on the money from the Fund. The last letter Fouesnel sent him in 1887 contains no wishes, only a decision: Conrardy would first have to do a year's novitiate and the sisters would not come to Molokai. 'I do not think they will ever come to Molokai,' he wrote. In short, it would be better for Damien to leave the issue of his successor alone.

Hysterical Father Archambaux 'Free'

The year 1888 began badly for Damien. He had stomach cramps, was hungry, felt sick and had pain in the chest. Nevertheless, he took part in the New Year festivities of the Board and ate heartily. The next day, he ordered shoes for his boys and informed the Board that the Kalawao reservoir – Kalaupapa still had no water supply – was leaking.

On 3 January Archambaux was beside himself with cold. He feared an asthma attack, refused to say mass and crept into bed. Then the ravings began. His shrill screams about the dirt and stench resounded through Kalaupapa. Sometimes, he got up and began to wash himself hysterically. If anyone dared touch anything he had brought from Lahaina, he cursed them as hired killers in Fouesnel's service. Or was it Burgerman who was whipping up the 'lepers' to infect him? The neighbours complained and Damien took Archambaux to Kalawao. The older priest was pleased, because it was loneliness that was making him go on. He went immediately to the supplies cellar underneath St Philomena and drank himself into a stupor. The next day he was ill. When Damien reprimanded him, Archambaux screamed that he was trying to murder him. He kept this up not only during the day but also at night. The boys in the home could not sleep because of the constant screaming and even the girls, who lived further away, and the patients in the hospital could not stand the situation after two days. Damien tried to explain to him that he had to stop, but nothing did any good. Archambaux went on hunger strike, because he was convinced the food was poisoned.

Fouesnel and Köckemann were agreed that Archambaux should have been left in Lahaina, because he could not cope with being confined. Therefore, they decided to ask the Board to let him go. There was little or no chance that their request would be granted, particularly since the patient was a Catholic priest. They were wrong, however, because Emerson had witnessed Archambaux's hysterical outbursts during his visit in mid-December and he knew that the crises were verging on insanity. Damien, seriously ill himself, was the one most at the receiving end and this was not fair to him. Emerson brought Archambaux's case before the Board and asked to be allowed to transfer him to Kakaako. The sisters had the time to spoil him. He certainly could not return to his parish, as the Catholic mission was proposing. There was some opposition, but Emerson gained the day. When the meeting was over, Emerson telephoned Fouesnel to give him the news that Archambaux could go to Kakaako. Shortly afterwards, the provincial received a note that stated that Archambaux was not allowed to leave Kalawao. Fouesnel exploded, but received an express letter which explained that Archambaux was allowed to go to Kakaako, but not to Lahaina. Fouesnel was to send this latest letter to Damien, who was to show it to Dr Petersen. Fouesnel described the confusion to Damien and went on about Petersen, whom he called an 'imbecile'. Confinement in Kakaako was not what Fouesnel had been hoping for and so he again thought that the Board was persecuting the Catholics.

Damien also got a lashing. Two large tabernacles had arrived in Honolulu and the provincial did not know what to do with them. Eighteen months previously, Damien had asked Fr Hudson of the periodical *Ave Maria* for the two tabernacles. They had to be robust and of stainless steel, able to withstand the rain and not too heavy. When Fouesnel saw the tabernacles, he could not believe his eyes. They were safes, with a huge decorative section on top. Each safe weighed 1,000 kilos. Fouesnel knew that Damien's wooden altars would be crushed beneath their weight. He suggested that Damien donate them to the mission and they would then put them in a more suitable place, such as the cathedral in Honolulu or the church in Wailuku. Fouesnel would see that Damien received some smaller tabernacles.

Damien rejected this suggestion. He did not give any explanation, because he was busy. He had to find accommodation for fourteen people from Kawaihae, twelve from Maui and eighteen from Kauai, whilst a group from Waipio, a group from Waiapuka and perhaps Fr Schäffer, who thought he had leprosy, were expected.

Nurses were urgently required. The Board was putting her under so much pressure, that the mother superior confided to Fouesnel the reasons why she did not want to go to Molokai. These have, to date, not been found in the archives. What is known is that Fouesnel was certain that the Franciscan nuns would not go. The only solution was to find another order, because the 'deliverance' of Archambaux had shown that the Board was not 'anti-mission'. Indeed, Emerson supported Damien through thick and thin. In order to retain the sympathy of the Board, the superiors had to find another nursing order. Damien heard vague rumours that the Order was looking elsewhere, but he did not mention this in his letter to Bishop Gross. He thanked the Bishop of Oregon for sending $218 and gave a picture of Kalawao as a happy place. They had received the Japanese medicines and the only thing they still needed was a mule cart for his sixty boys.

Conrardy wrote to Damien to say he was hoping to leave for Hawaii in February. He begged Damien to do all he could to secure him permission to share in his work. 'People from Liège are not lazy,' he declared. He would follow the novitiate later. The implication was: when Damien was dead. Conrardy realised that Damien's days were numbered.

Damien wrote to Köckemann, begging the bishop to allow Conrardy to come. He suggested that Conrardy should be allowed to take temporary vows, as Dutton had done, until the general chapter could regularise the situation. Damien was afraid that he was losing the use of his hands and then he would no longer be able to celebrate mass. At present work was continuing.

At the end of January, the fifteen new houses were almost finished. The work on the pipeline to bring water from the Waikolu valley to Kalaupapa was also making progress. Fifty-eight men and a foreman had been taken on for the work and Alfred Carter was also helping with it. As a white man, he, too, had received a permit to go to Kakaako, but his family had demanded that the hot-tempered man return to Kalaupapa. The unhappy man found it difficult to accept the triple exile and complained about the wages of $2.50 a day that the *kokuas* were receiving. He himself received only $50 a month, so some of the helpers earned more than he did. Carter, the father of ten children, was later to commit suicide. Quarrels like this delayed the work, but it was the *kona* storm, which hit Kalaupapa on 4 February 1888, that brought everything to a standstill.

Damien, Dutton, Archambaux and the sixty-five orphan boys and girls huddled together in the sturdiest dormitory. Archambaux was hysterical. The howling wind took his breath away and he had an asthma attack. When the wind dropped for a while, Damien crawled out of the dormitory to find wine for him. After a few glasses, the old man wept like a child in Damien's arms, as the real children looked on with frightened eyes.

The storm kept up and seemed to be circling round Kalawao. In the midst of the din, Damien heard a thundering crash. He feared that the spire of St Philomena's, that he had built in 1876, had fallen down. When they were finally able to go outside, Damien wept at the sight of the destruction. It was not just the spire, but a large section of the church itself that had been flattened. He wept because he feared he would not be strong enough to rebuild his church. He called to Dutton, 'Almighty God knows what is best for us. We must submit to the divine will, but I cannot cope with this any longer.' He raised his crippled hands aloft.

When Köckemann learned of the destruction of St Philomena's, he wrote asking Conrardy to come. He made this exception because of Damien's poor state of health. Fouesnel saw things differently, however. Damien had irritated him because he had lost a letter containing $80. Letters with money in them should be sent in the registered post. Moreover, Fouesnel still did not know what he was supposed to do with the tabernacles. What was more, no one concerned themselves with Fouesnel's opinion, but if it were up to him, Conrardy would have to do the novitiate in Chile.

Archambaux left on 15 March 1888. His hysterical attacks had been rewarded with a return ticket and he was now quiet and smiling. In Kakaako, his asthma attacks disappeared and so did his hysteria. He put everything down to the cold weather on Molokai and the care he received from the sisters. He was, of course, sorry for the trouble he had caused Damien, but if he had looked after him better, things would never have got so bad. Damien's superiors continued to spoil Archambaux, though. In their eyes, Damien, who had not taken care of Archambaux, was extremely difficult and egotistical.

Emerson Wants to Push Through Nursing Plan for Molokai

The prime minister, Lorrin Thurston, accompanied Emerson on a visit to the settlement at the end of March. It was not his first visit and, unlike Gibson, he had not invited the press. He was struck by how much needed to be done to make the settlement habitable. He therefore appointed a medical commission of inquiry of four doctors, plus Emerson as chairman.

On 19 March 1888 Meyer and Damien raised their glasses in celebration of the twenty-fourth anniversary of Damien's arrival in Hawaii. Meyer had just celebrated his thirty-seventh wedding anniversary and told Damien that it seemed like yesterday. Yet there had been many changes. Forty exiles arrived every week, but the death rate was more or less unchanged. It was estimated that around 1,500 leprosy victims were 'free'. There were 749 deportees in the settlement in the middle of

March. Damien was the only one looking after them, because Dr Petersen only came for a few days a month to monitor the situation.

Damien therefore had no patience with his superiors any more, and demanded that the tabernacles be sent, because they belonged to his parishes. Fouesnel was snappish and refused. Finally, he agreed, but a storm meant they could not be sent. They would come some time or other, but when the news came that the superiors wanted to comply with the mother superior's demand that, if the sisters came to Molokai, men and women would be completely segregated, it seemed like a joke. The Board was to build a wall between Kalaupapa, where the women were to reside, and Kalawao, for the men. Damien had joked about this idea with Dr Mouritz, but now it seemed to be serious. How could people now be expecting married couples to break their vow of faithfulness? Surely they ought to stay together, help one another, support one another, until death parted them. Damien was so shocked that he wrote to the prime minister himself, 'They are bound together by solemn bonds until death do them part and they must share their lives for better, for worse.'

Damien had urged the commission to continue allowing *kokuas* to enter the settlement. The doctors, however, had discovered that several healthy people were infected. It was criminal to tolerate their presence, but on the other hand, Damien's ideas about palliative care might be right. In his fifteen years on Molokai, he had seen that patients surrounded by love withstood the disease better and with fewer complications.

The medical commission of inquiry had asked to have all *kokuas* carefully examined for leprosy and to check on their general state of health. After a thorough analysis of all the examinations, the commission concluded that nursing was the highest priority. Since the Franciscan nuns were making no moves to work on Molokai, faith was no longer an issue. Anglican sisters would certainly do good work as well and an approach to them was the obvious solution.

The mission got to know something about this project and so the mother superior declared that she would go as soon as she received permission from her superior in New York. She had not yet written, because she had not yet received an official invitation from the Board.

Premier Thurston had the report of the medical commission of inquiry read to Charles R. Bishop, the widower of Princess Bernice. The banker, whose wife had left him a huge amount of landed property, was so shocked that he wanted to donate $5,000 for the building of the Bishop Home for single women and girls. Thurston used this gift as a means of putting pressure on the Catholic mission. Now that Conrardy was going to come, the sisters had a healthy priest. However, just around this time Köckemann was beginning to wonder whether Conrardy was the right person. Suddenly, he was saying that he must do the novitiate.

Damien's superiors were demanding that he use money from the Fund to build a house for Archambaux in the grounds of Kakaako. Damien refused and was again accused of egoism. Everyone pitied poor Archambaux. He played along with this and complained that Damien had not spent his whole time looking after Archambaux, but had been more occupied with his sixty-five boys: and Archambaux, sick as he was, needed so much love. Unaware of the problems he was creating for Damien, he wrote that it was good in Kakaako. He felt like a bird in a clean cage and prayed in a clean chapel where chaste sisters kept everything neat. He was not fortunate, but was resigned to his fate and was happy that Damien would soon have a companion.

Köckemann thought Damien must be egotistical, because he begrudged Conrardy the joy of the novitiate. He now wrote to the general that he did not need Conrardy. There were plenty of members of the Order who were eager to go to Molokai. The superiors concluded that Conrardy was only seeking glory in the leper settlement and, worse still, that he wanted to get his hands on Damien's money.

The bishop let fly at Damien, who was suspected of being the instigator of the search for nurses. The bishop argued that the members of the Board were against the Catholic mission again. They would certainly make false promises. 'I should not be surprised if Protestant ladies were preferred, or if impossible conditions were placed on the sisters,' he wrote. He did not at present wish to exert his authority, but asked Damien not to apply pressure, because that would put him in an impossible position. 'Many priests want to go,' he wrote dryly. 'We expect Conrardy any day.' Damien already knew this, because Conrardy had written to him from Santa Clara in California.

Köckemann alluded to the stream of complaints he had received. Suddenly, it seems that many priests did want to go to Damien. Köckemann's decision was fixed: not only because of the sisters, but also to calm the storm in his own Order, he would keep Conrardy in Honolulu for several days, so that the man could reveal his true nature. Then he would allow him to spend a short time on Molokai and then either send him away or require him to do a novitiate. Conrardy had no idea of the situation that would confront him when he landed on 12 May 1888.

Meanwhile, Damien was building his new church, and he made the new structure cruciform, with a stone tower and nave. The altar would be made to take the heavy tabernacle. The safes had arrived and Damien realised that there would have to be a new altar in Kalaupapa and that the roof would have to be raised, because the tabernacles were too tall.

18

Damien's Companion, Louis-Lambert Conrardy, The Healthy Priest (May–November 1888)

Conrardy's Arrival. Board of Health Wants Anglican Nuns

The young German missionary, Matthias Corneille led the protest. The general had sent him to Molokai, but on his arrival Köckemann had decided that he must first learn the language and customs of the country. This seemed reasonable to Corneille, but when he read in the newspaper that an outsider was going to take his place because no one from the Order wanted to help Damien, he thought it a disgrace to the Order. He went to Honolulu straight away to sign an official protest and suggested that Köckemann should circularise all the priests to see who was willing to help Damien. The bishop should then select one of them.

The replies came in steadily over the next two weeks. Most of them were furious. They had never refused to go to Molokai – they had never been asked. Some of them volunteered enthusiastically. Others thought that their vows required them to sacrifice themselves. Others, like Wendelin Möllers, promised to go, if their superiors asked them to, because this was required by the rules of the Order. There were one or two who did not want to reply, because it seemed to them quite obvious that they should go.

Even before Conrardy had met Mother Marianne, Köckemann had telephoned several times to say that he was totally unsuitable as a confessor. He spoke about the Indians with great sympathy, did not water down his wine, laughed and joked. Moreover, Conrardy had more engagements in those few days than Köckemann had in a whole year. He was obviously seeking fame. Köckemann assured the mother superior that she could decide herself whether she would accept Conrardy, but he would certainly not force her into the arms of the anti-Catholic government. If she ever felt she could accept the terms offered by the Board, he would send Wendelin Möllers with her. He was a realist, not a dreamer, like Damien, and, above all, thorough.

In order to keep a close eye on things, Fouesnel decided to accompany Conrardy to Molokai. Meyer had even received instructions to get Ragsdale's old house in order. The carpenter who was to manage the building of the Bishop Home was staying there. At the last minute, Fouesnel decided not to go.

The day Conrardy landed, Damien was waiting for him with his arm in a sling. His old hat only partially concealed his ravaged features. He had difficulty walking. Conrardy did not want to show his repugnance and put out his hand, but Damien shook his head. He was a leper, and Conrardy must avoid infection. Conrardy thought that Damien's welcome reflected the joy in his eyes.

On the way to Kalawao, Conrardy's repugnance welled up. He had prepared himself for disfigurement, but the sight and odour of his friend made him retch. He tried to look at something else: William, who was pulling the buggy, or the band of children who were thronging around him. When he arrived, he had to eat. He could not swallow a single mouthful. Damien assured him that the cook was 'clean' and so he swallowed one mouthful after another with downcast eyes. Damien persisted: Conrardy must eat well, if he wanted to keep going. It was too much when a scabrous mongrel appeared that looked as though it too had leprosy. Conrardy thought of giving up right away, but he did not get the chance, because Damien took him to his ninety-five boys. He introduced him to Dutton. Conrardy thought him a strange man, and his rhetoric immediately put him off. 'My life has no value to me,' the American said by way of introduction. 'I have been here for two years now and I think I have leprosy.' From the very first day, Conrardy concluded that Dutton was doing everything he could to contract the disease. He ate with lepers, and ate food that lepers had prepared.

The biggest shock for Conrardy was the number of funerals. Twenty people died in the first week. An epidemic of influenza had caused the death rate to reach unprecedented levels. Fortunately, the patients had a roof over their heads, because the fifty new houses were finished. There was even enough space for 200 new exiles.

The poor productivity of the Chinese coolies delayed the installation of the water supply on Kalaupapa. In May 1888, all the trenches had been dug. Meyer feared for the whole project, because in the winter a heavy sea could sweep the pipes away. He advised the Board to lay the pipes at a deeper level and also advised them to build a reservoir at a higher level in case something happened to the pipeline. Ideally, the abbatoir should be sited next to the reservoir, because then it could be kept properly clean. His final instructions were to choose a site in Kalaupapa for the building of the Bishop Home for single women and girls. Because there was so much work in hand, Meyer stayed longer in Kalawao. He got to know Conrardy as an open-minded man, without religious prejudices. 'He will soon be taking Damien's place,' Meyer wrote to the Board. 'The disease is spreading rapidly now.'

On 21 May 1888 Lorrin Thurston sent the mother superior an official invitation to care for the single women and girls on Molokai. Nothing was said about the other patients. Mother Marianne replied that she would transmit the contents of the letter, that Thurston had sent to Köckemann, to her superior in Syracuse. She needed his approval before she could extend her work to other islands. She herself was prepared to take on the work and she was sure that others would follow her. She concluded her letter as follows, 'Meanwhile, we shall pray earnestly that the good Lord will inspire us to work for these good unfortunate lepers.' The postscript was an attack on Damien. 'May I ask Your Excellency to do me the favour of not making the contents of this letter public? We wish to do the good that we can do in this world to help and support the suffering, in quietness, and we wish to do it unnoticed and unknown.' The mother superior wrote to her superior Lesen at the same time. She had learned that the sisters would be in physical, but particularly in moral, danger if they moved to Molokai. The mother superior's gibe amounted to an accusation that Damien did seek fame.

A Stream of Epidemics. Superiors Say Conrardy Must Go

On 31 May 1888 Damien was standing in front of his presbytery when the postman brought him some letters. One was from Pamphile, but the tiny handwriting was now illegible to Damien's inflamed eyes. Pamphile wrote at length about his health. He was fatter than ever and had a cold, the result of the bad weather: rain and no sun. The painter Edward Clifford, who was hoping to visit in October, had read somewhere that a certain Dr Neve in India combined iodine pills with baths and was having success with this method. There were other letters. As he read one of them, Damien grew pale. Dutton was playing baseball with the boys in the churchyard. He stopped because he could feel the tension. Damien called out to Conrardy in French and the latter came running. Together, they spoke indignantly in French and Damien beat his breast with his fist. Dutton realised that someone had stabbed Damien to the heart. He went over to him and Damien said, almost in tears, that the bishop had ordered Conrardy to leave the islands. He must either do the novitiate or go away. Damien did not show the least respect in his reply to the bishop. Conrardy was his man and Köckemann would have to get used to it.

Köckemann's reply was authoritarian. He had his reasons for sending Conrardy away, but since Damien was not going to obey him, he saw no reason to give them. As bishop, he had to take care of the spiritual welfare of the settlement, even if that meant he had to hurt people he was fond of.

A few days later, Köckemann wrote again about reasons he did not wish to talk about, because Damien would not understand them. Damien could rest assured that he would remain priest for Kalawao and Kalaupapa until he dropped – only then would Möllers take over. 'I was too optimistic when I allowed Conrardy to come,' Köckemann went on. 'I invited him to travel to Europe as soon as possible to do the novitiate there – a year and a half, perhaps a little longer – and then he would come back.' Conrardy could stay until the bishop had received a reply from the general. Fouesnel was less tactful: without mincing his words, he called Damien a bad man who had made the mission a focus for gossip. 'I don't want ever to have anything to do with that Conrardy,' he raged. He would rather never have written to Damien again, but he continued to do his duty. The mission had to pay 10 per cent import duty on the value of the tabernacles, which had been assessed at $1,000. Damien must sort it out himself, because he had 'shocked and insulted all his colleagues without any reason'. Fouesnel had no plans to remove him from his post, because elsewhere he would be even more of a nuisance. 'But a little meditation on humility' might be a good thing, Fouesnel thought. 'Accept and remember what I have told you already: as soon as you can no longer administer the sacraments, someone will come to live with you. There are many who are willing to come as soon as the bishop or I ask it.'

There is no reply to this from Damien extant. He concentrated on the $100 import duty for the tabernacles. Fouesnel would certainly give him no help and so Damien wrote an irritated letter to the Board. The kingdom had a customs treaty with the United States and the tabernacles came from there. Meyer sorted the matter out for him, but warned him in the same letter that there was a certain amount of rivalry between Conrardy and Dutton. The newcomer was pushing Dutton aside.

Fouesnel had not expected William G. Ashley, the secretary to the Board of Health, to speak to him about the duty on the tabernacles. Ashley accused him of upsetting Damien unnecessarily. Damien could count on the Board, even in religious matters, since Fouesnel would not do it. Ashley had had the duty lifted. In order not to end matters on an unfriendly note, and because this was an opportunity to set matters straight, Ashley asked about Fouesnel's plans for Molokai. The provincial said that Conrardy had to leave and that Möllers would go there when Damien was no longer able to work. The sisters were waiting for word from Syracuse. Ashley reported to Emerson that the sisters would go when Damien was dying or dead. Emerson feared that the sisters, whose arrival Damien had been urging for fifteen years, were trying to avoid Damien, hurt the physician and he got in touch with the Anglican Bishop of Honolulu, with the clear inquiry whether he knew of an order that would work on Molokai. Emerson skilfully allowed this news to leak out, so that Fouesnel got to hear of it.

The influenza epidemic was followed in June by a serious gastric infection, causing high fever and diarrhoea. Meyer was one of the victims and, despite the fact that he was a healthy man, it took him several days to recover. Dr Petersen thought that it was a type of food poisoning, because quite a lot of Damien's boys were sick and they had all eaten tinned salmon. He went to the shop to examine the suspected food and decided that it was not fit for consumption. Hutchison regarded this as a personal insult and criticised Dr Petersen so violently that he resigned. The patients were not concerned about this, because the doctor had not won their confidence. *Haole* medicines did not help, and so they went back to consulting their *kahunas*.

Conrardy estimated that since his arrival, three weeks before, some ninety of the 800 inhabitants had died. At the beginning of May, Damien had had ninety orphans under his protection. In June, there were sixty-five. Both priests had so many funerals to attend to and so many dying people to support that they had no time to carry out their administrative duties perfectly and Fouesnel carped at this. In any case, Damien did not know how he would have got through the month without Conrardy.

There was a deep air of sadness in the settlement. There was no longer any music during funerals, because too many of the musicians, who played in the band, had died. Everyone was grieving for at least one person and the oppressive weather drained people of energy. Dutton, who saw that Conrardy had taken his place, sank into a deep depression, as Meyer had foreseen. He even contemplated leaving the settlement, but finally decided that he must stay and support Damien.

That summer, Damien's eyes were badly inflamed. He was in pain and questioned himself about the future. Again and again he confided to Dutton that his superiors were right, he was not worthy to go to heaven. Dutton reassured him that, after all he had done, he would go straight there.

The new doctor, George Swift, could not really help Damien. This Protestant from Dublin was pleasant and jolly. He was the first doctor to bring his family with him to the settlement – he had a German–American wife and a baby. She did the administrative work, so that he could give more attention to medical affairs. The patients were not allowed to enter his home. The patients called Swift *Makani*, 'wind', because he was always in a hurry. His modern approach was noted, in particular. Because three female lepers were heavily pregnant, he asked the Board to order rubber gloves for him from the Goodyear Rubber Company in San Francisco. He worked with a Galo battery, because he, like Fitch before him, thought that electric shocks could bring relief. Moreover, he was thrifty. When he had time, he would search in the woods for discarded medicine bottles. Good observers, however, and the Hawaiians were good observers, recognised signs of morphine addiction in him.

In the summer of 1888, Damien spent as much of his spare time as he could with his eighty boys. He taught some of them to do carpentry and bricklaying, so that they could help him with the rebuilding of his church. He had drawn a plan, but did not send it to Köckemann. Since Köckemann could not give him the reasons for Conrardy's departure, he did not have to tell him everything either. He was not able to ask the bishop for money for the rebuilding, therefore, nor could he use the money from the Fund, although there was more than enough. He had just received another $265.42 in gold. That money was to improve the quality of life for all the exiles. He approached the English vicar, Chapman, and asked him to ask Cardinal Manning for help with the rebuilding of the church. He thought the costs would be around $1,000, including the reinforcement of the altar for the tabernacle. He asked Fr Hudson of *Ave Maria* for a bell, weighing around 125 kilos. Only E. O. Hall had bells in stock, but his largest weighed only forty-eight kilos. Someone from Boston wanted to send one weighing seventy-five kilos.

The building site was not a peaceful place, for the boys quarrelled, played, sang and sometimes were simply plain naughty. The Irish mason, Jack McMillan, played with them. When Damien was not around, he taught them special songs, which always stopped when the priest arrived. Sometimes the priest acted as though he were really angry, because this increased the fun. Then he looked at the work and said, 'Well', as he often did.

A new square tower was going up above the main entrance. Jack needed to be on hand all the time and often brought his half-Hawaiian little girl along, because she enjoyed playing with the boys. One day, Dr Swift brought his camera along. Jack posed proudly with his daughter, and the boys formed themselves into groups. Conrardy was willing to appear in four or five of the photographs, but Damien refused to appear in any of them, saying that he never felt comfortable being photographed.

He wondered whether he would be able to go on without Conrardy. His eyes were still inflamed and his right hand was contracting. He was hardly able to write any longer, and so he dictated a letter to the general, in which he urged that Conrardy be allowed to stay. He enclosed the original letters he had received from Köckemann. 'Conrardy is a practical man,' he dictated.

He can already speak *Kanaka* and behaves like one of us. He keeps the three vows. Would it be possible, when the general chapter meets, to accept him, somehow or other, without his having to do the novitiate? He has left his mission in Oregon, where he lived for many years isolated among the Indians. He cannot face conforming to the regular routine of a monastery for a long period. I need his help. He is becoming more indispensable each day. I need someone to help me with the leper settlement, and especially with the orphans.

At the end, Conrardy wrote, 'Damien is not feeling well and that is why he dictated the letter. If I must do the novitiate, then I would rather go back to my former mission.'

The general was faced with a dilemma, because Köckemann had asked him to send Conrardy away. Damien had so much money that the bishop feared that the two Belgians would go their own way. There was every possibility that they would quickly quarrel with one another, or with the government. Because there would certainly be scandals, the bishop's position was that Conrardy must do the novitiate or leave.

Fouesnel went even further. His dislike of Damien was increasing. He described him as a person whose international fame had gone to his head. He would soon no longer be able to administer the sacraments, because his hands were affected.

Damien was isolated. He could no longer get about and proceeded on the basis of rumours and letters – rumours such as that of 2 August 1888, that Kakaako would be closed. There was news of the death of Sam Wilder, the former chairman of the Board, and news from his benefactor-friends, Fr Hudson and Edward Clifford, and from a doctor in New Zealand, who had an exotic remedy for leprosy, or from the Norwegian-Swedish princess Eugénie, who asked him for information about the Goto method. These messages became ever more important to Damien, because his inflammation of the eyes meant that he had been unable to read mass for the first time in his life and could hardly read his breviary. Others could read letters to him. His own letters were no more than notes. 'I shall be happy as long as I have Conrardy with me,' he wrote to the general, and he thanked Pamphile for his letter. In the middle of August, he received news that Kakaako was not closed and that the sisters were coming to Molokai.

Franciscan Nuns Take On the Staffing of Molokai

Emerson's negotiations with the Anglican bishop about nursing sisters were dangerous for the mission. Fouesnel therefore explained to Mother Marianne that the 'staffing' of Molokai could no longer be put off. The provincial asked to be allowed to address a meeting of the Board of Health and presented his terms for the sisters to establish themselves in the settlement. A fundamental requirement was that a healthy priest should accompany the sisters. Fouesnel wanted to go, but Möllers and Corneille were already volunteering.

Now that the sisters were to come, the Irishman Charles Reynolds was appointed supervisor of the various projects. Reynolds looked carefully into all the details and there was a lively discussion as to whether the new abattoir should have a stone or a cement floor. The prison was to be removed from the hospital. The Chinese cafés that served alcohol had to be closed, to avoid shocking the sisters, but the Hawaiian drinking houses were not a problem. Damien urged that the cafés should be retained, because they were one of the few opportunities for relaxation for the patients. The care of the men and of the married women continued to be a problem, because the agreement was that the sisters would only look after single women in the home. The letter of application from the Irish nurse, James Sinnett, arrived at an opportune moment.

Damien had thought of solutions and now he would be able to explain them to Mother Marianne, for she had requested a permit from the Board for herself, Sr Leopoldina and the Portuguese maid Olinda Gomes. Emerson complimented her on her courage. He was to accompany them. On 20 September 1888 they all boarded the steamboat *Lehua*.

They only had three hours, even so they first took breakfast at Dr Swift's. Damien waited outside. After breakfast, he showed them the church, which was under reconstruction and pointed out the pandan tree under which he had slept for his first few nights. The air roots crept through the graves. He took the sisters to his boys' home and stressed that the orphans needed mothers. He said that he tried to be a good father to them. A Hawaiian woman looked after the girls.

The mother superior found everything dingy and dirty, however. She gave her opinion that the boys ought to wear a blue flannel uniform and was quickly gone, because there was scarcely enough time left to walk round Bishop Home. She inspected the narrow passage enclosed by the living room, reception room, dining room and bedrooms. She pointed to a small room and said that it would be the chapel. She had no time to inspect the outbuildings because the boat was about to leave.

The misunderstanding was clear: Damien thought that the sisters would look after the orphans, whereas their task was limited to caring for single women. A boy called Damien had arrived with the sisters. Damien first got Damiano Keoni Pepe from Kohala to tell him about the Big Island, and then reassured him. Mother Marianne would soon be looking after him. He made inquiries from Meyer as to the price of blue linen for uniforms, but Meyer, who realised the sisters would not be caring for the orphan boys, got round this by saying it was too expensive.

Because little that was out of the way occurred in Kalaupapa, waiting for things to happen seemed to last even longer. A former government doctor, Rolando Kuehn, wrote to Damien that he was still loyal to King Kalakaua. Damien replied,

Though we are both loyal to our King Kalakaua, whose name is seldom mentioned in the asylum now, I know that my days are numbered and I do not expect to remain for long in this wretched world. I can feel that the disease has gone to my lungs and I hope that in a very short while, when my body shall rest under the greensward, everything will be well. Our new priest, L. L. Conrardy, is with me. J. Dutton still looks after the sick boys well. There are eighty-eight now. There are 900 of us lepers and, despite the fact that we are ill, there is peace and joy on Molokai.

Everything went on as usual. Dutton tended sores and told the patients jokes. He and Conrardy played with the boys and their laughter warmed Damien's heart. They made kites and football was also popular. Damien supported the request of the teacher, Eli Crawford, a healthy *haole*, who wanted to stay with his Hawaiian wife until their child was born and the sisters arrived.

In Honolulu, Fouesnel wrote of the sacrifice of the sisters, but his letter contained a contrast. He sang the praises of the women, who, according to Fouesnel, did not want their good deeds praised in the press. Many priests wanted to work with Damien, who now had the support of Conrardy, but the sisters' chosen chaplain was Möllers. Briefly, he feared that his action had been premature, because Fr Lesen, the Franciscan superior, had warned Köckemann that the sisters had come to Hawaii to nurse curable people, not lepers. The mother superior had written to him that the sisters would be in physical, but above all, moral danger on Molokai. Moreover, he considered that the sisters would lack the comfort they were accustomed to as American women. He wanted to be certain that anyone who wanted to would be allowed to leave. And what if only one or two of the sisters were to survive this way of the cross? Köckemann assured Lesen that the sisters would have all the necessary comforts. To his own general, Köckemann expressed his anger at Damien, because Conrardy was still with him. Köckemann conceded that he had invited Conrardy to come, but when he had encountered the man in the flesh, he had had second thoughts. The mission had not abandoned Damien at all. The sisters' chaplain would also take care of him. The mother superior had rejected Conrardy as confessor, but Köckemann could not remove him because he was popular.

That day, Damien had difficulty reading the gospel. His voice broke and he frequently had to pause because he was having trouble with excess saliva and phlegm. During the offertory, he stumbled. His congregation was concerned. He muddled through to the Sanctus, started to feel dizzy and then fainted away. He came round, but about half an hour later, he was still feeling too ill to finish saying mass. Joseph Dutton reported this incident to the superiors and Br Bertrand informed Paris. Damien no longer wrote to his superiors. Köckemann wondered whether it was true. He was right not to dramatise this incident, because the day after his fall, Damien was on the quayside to welcome a group of children. He had more than one hundred children under his guardianship.

The three new sisters, who arrived in Honolulu at the end of October, brought with them the official decision of the superior in Syracuse. Köckemann went through everything once again with the mother superior in Kakaako. Then he paid a brief visit to Archambaux. The old man could no longer swallow, not even water. Fouesnel visited him for the last time on 5 November. Archambaux whispered something but Fouesnel, who was becoming deaf, could not understand him. However, he wrote to Damien that Archambaux was a model patient and he underlined the word 'model'.

Köckemann had arranged everything with the mother superior, but the issue of the chaplain still rankled with the Board. Conrardy was popular and was doing excellent work. When Köckemann once again raised the issue of expulsion, Emerson threatened to have Conrardy officially appointed as Damien's successor, in order to ensure continuity. He could only expel someone if he had good grounds for doing so. Köckemann thought that the appointment of a priest was exclusively a matter for the bishop. He did not even have to give any reason for rejecting a priest. In order to ensure that Emerson would understand him, he set out his position on paper. 'No priest may accept a religious or other mixed function on his own initiative, without the express permission of his bishop. This makes Conrardy's position illegitimate.'

Fouesnel had a more realistic view of the situation. On 6 November he wrote to Damien that Dutton had informed him about the incident during the mass. 'It pains me to learn of it,' he reported. 'There is a priest coming to assist you on Monday 12 November, but the sisters need him full time. I think, therefore, you would be best to have a hut built next to the presbytery for Conrardy. The iron sheets for your church were shipped yesterday.'

The roof of St Philomena's was almost finished, even though the work was not proceeding very fast. McMillan was having a lot of pain in his badly inflamed foot. Sitting on a chair, he gave the boys instructions for building the walls.

On 6 November the steamboat with sheet metal arrived, but the sloop capsized during unloading and the iron sheets ended up in the sea. Normally, it took four to five months to get them from England and Damien wondered if he would live to see that day.

Meanwhile, Mother Marianne and Sisters Leopoldina and Vincent were preparing themselves for their move to the island. Despite the greater risks, their salary of $25 a month was not increased. Meyer thought this was unfair to Damien, who had been working for fifteen years for nothing, and proposed that he should be paid the same amount. Dutton also worked for free, but he wanted to sacrifice himself and did all he could to catch leprosy. Damien now realised that the sisters were not coming for his boys and therefore proposed Conrardy as his successor. Meyer agreed.

So much and yet so little had changed. Dr Swift was trying the latest methods, while the patients still went to their own priests for remedies. Swift admitted to the Board, 'I know nothing about these cases, until I see the flag flying at half mast.' Damien approved of him. At least he worked hard and did not let things go like Mouritz. He visited the orphanages regularly and if Damien had him called out, he came immediately. His opponents thought he was paid too much – he received $3,500 per annum, whereas the sisters had to manage on $300. Swift called Damien a real priest, whose only concern was to fish for souls. Even though they were of different faiths, however, he admired his dedication, persistence and, especially, his sense of humour and his constant good temper.

It was assumed that the sisters would come on the fifth anniversary of their arrival in Honolulu, but this did not work out either. A heavy storm broke over Waikola and the rushing water washed away the pipelines, which had not been laid deeply enough. Meyer had predicted this would happen. Kalaupapa was without water, an inconvenience the patients had had to put up with for twenty years. It was too much for the sisters to cope with, however, in superintendent Reynolds's view. Their departure was therefore delayed until four or five iron tanks with a tap attached could be transported to Molokai. The cost of the relaying of the water supply was estimated at $35,000 and, instead of the sisters, workmen and engineers arrived.

Damien was permitted to continue with his building work. Waterhouse & Co. had galvanised sheets in stock and was prepared to sell them at a discount. They would be sent on the next sailing of the *Mokolii*. There was another problem. Möllers could not go to Molokai yet. The sisters could not go without a healthy priest and Conrardy had been rejected. Fouesnel considered travelling with the sisters, but when Fr Matthias Corneille chanced to land in Honolulu, he was keen to take over the position. He was also willing to take a letter, but did not know that it was a note full of hatred. 'Why do you dictate your letters to me, when you are able to write to your other correspondents?' Fouesnel raged to Damien. 'If you looked after your eyes, you would be able to go on using them for a long while.'

Damien filed the letter, as he had filed the letters about the *Gurjun* oil. This ointment was supposed to have cured leprosy on the Andaman Islands, according to Clifford, but Damien did not believe it. God alone, he was aware, knew a cure, but he was keeping it hidden from mankind for the time being.

19

The Franciscan Nuns
(November 1888–February 1889)

At dawn, Damien welcomed the sisters with a broad smile.
'Thank you, oh Lord,' he cried in English. 'I am so happy that
he has sent you.' He invited the sisters to attend mass. After the
service, Sr Leopoldina told Damien she was strong and would
do good work. The tall, slim nun was the jolliest of the three.
She was not particularly intelligent, but her enormously high-
spirited dedication was a gift. Damien then rode back to Kalawao.
He had invited Corneille to go with him, but the young German
had to build an altar in the small chapel in the convent. Only
on the third, stormy day did Damien receive an unexpected
visit. To his astonishment, Corneille found Damien, in high
spirits, instructing his boys how to fix iron sheets to the roof of
St Philomena's. He realised that Damien would keep going
until the end. When he saw his visitor, Damien climbed down
from the roof and proposed showing Corneille around the
orphanage. It was midday and the bell was ringing the angelus.
The children were running from every direction to the refectory,
but Damien shooed them out again, because he first wanted to
show what they had to eat. There was *poi*, rice and fresh fish on
the table. Damien then repeated the sentences his superiors
required him to say and that he now believed to be true.

The government looked after them well. The new government had increased the allowance for clothing from $6 to $10.
The people were living like the average *Kanaka*. After this,
Corneille rode back to Kalaupapa, where the popular Conrardy
was to give him a lesson in Hawaiian.

On Sunday 18 November Sr Vincent did not understand

Damien's sermon, given in Hawaiian. She noticed that the congregation looked nervous as Damien was thundering on. After the mass, she asked what he had been preaching about. It turned out he had been bellowing at them that now the sisters had come, the congregation had no more excuse for missing mass. Oversleeping would not wash with the sisters.

On St Elizabeth's Day, 19 November, Corneille consecrated the convent chapel and then rode to Kalawao. Damien's eyes were red and inflamed because he had spent the night with two people who were dying and had also read his breviary. Corneille wanted to give him a dispensation from reading his breviary – he could say a rosary instead – but Damien wanted to go on as long as possible. Corneille spent the whole day helping Damien and once again realised how much he would have liked to work with him. At 3 o'clock, he wanted to return to Kalaupapa, but Damien wanted him to stay for the funeral. Corneille had seen many of them, but Damien declared that if you had not seen this, you had seen nothing.

While he was waiting, Corneille read his breviary in St Philomena's. He was startled from his reading by the sound of drums and a band. He was astonished at the elaborate funeral service, but Damien knew that the Hawaiians attached great importance to it. He had organised his parishioners into four 'guilds', each having its own colour and flag, which competed with one another to produce the best performance.

After the mass, Corneille questioned Damien about the patients' needs. Damien said that their basic needs were met, although any extras were always welcomed. What they needed above all was love and affection. Every exile had only a short time to live and so needed love much more quickly. Then, as if it were the most obvious thing, Damien told him to tell the bishop that he had $2,000 in the bank. This brought them to the latest quarrel. Fouesnel thought that Damien ought to pay for the rebuilding of St Philomena's with the money he had been given, or else the Board should bear the costs, because it owned everything in the leper settlement.

A week later, Möllers made the descent of the *pali*. The 38-year-old priest had set out with strict instructions. He was to run absolutely no risk of infection and was also completely independent of Damien, since Fouesnel had appointed Conrardy as Damien's assistant priest. The situation was immediately difficult, because Möllers, Corneille and Conrardy all had to sleep in the small house that Damien had once had brought there for Burgerman, and there were only two beds. Möllers spent the first nights sleeping on three chairs and decided at once that he needed a new presbytery.

The three priests paid Damien a lengthy visit. There were now four of them in the settlement and, with Beissel in Kaluaaha, that made five priests on Molokai. Damien was so delighted when he heard this that he wanted to shout a greeting up the mountainside. He kept repeating that day that he was happy. He could no longer go walking about, but he remained active. Conrardy would later take over, and that was a reassurance.

'Even if that goes against the wishes of the superiors?' Corneille asked.

'Which of us only does what the superiors say?' Damien asked, and they all laughed, because everyone knew that it was sometimes necessary to be flexible.

Corneille left on the day the professional nurse, James Sinnett, arrived. The Irishman had applied for the post on the advice of Fr Hudson of the periodical *Ave Maria*. The Board jumped at the offer, because he could care for the men and, as a layman, he was not under Köckemann's authority. The copper-haired man had come for Damien and set out straight away for Kalawao. When Dr Swift came in late that evening, the nurse handed over his official papers and said that he was putting himself under Swift's orders. Swift looked at the man with the long beard and decided that he was a strange creature. From the first moment he did not like the newcomer, and so the doctor turned to Dutton and offered Sinnett to him as his assistant, since Dutton had been complaining of overwork.

Dutton and Sinnett both thought this was a good idea and for Swift the matter was settled. He thought Sinnett could do little harm in 'Damien Hotel', but by the very next morning, the nurse was wanting to turn everything upside down. The children must be given lessons, not allowed to play. The children did their business in the wood, which was unhygienic and could lead to immorality. Toilets must be installed. Meyer feared this could lead to quarrels, just when the orphanage was running smoothly. The allowance for the orphans' clothes was to be increased again and money had been approved for dormitories and refectories for adults. The only problem was that Damien still did not know what would happen to the orphans after his death.

Franciscan Nuns Settle and Take Over

After about a month on Molokai, the sisters planned their first visit to Kalawao. Damien was waiting for Mother Marianne and Sr Leopoldina at the garden gate. He was looking thin, ashen and ill, but he laughed happily and stretched his hands heavenward in thanks to God, because his long-held wish had finally been fulfilled.

Damien showed the sisters the rebuilding work on St Philomena's. It would be finished before he died. Then he took the visitors to the orphanage. The boys who had been in Kakaako ran up to them. With a lump in his throat, Damien asked the mother superior if she would look after his children. Sr Leopoldina was moved.

Julia, a Hawaiian *kokua*, looked after the orphan girls, the oldest of whom were making clothes for the younger ones. Julia showed them the dormitories. When they had finished, Damien called all the girls together. 'I shall die very soon,' he told the girls in Hawaiian. 'The sisters will look after you. Later on, you will go to Kalaupapa.' Two small girls threw themselves on their knees before the priest and clasped his legs, the Hawaiian posture of supplication, and begged him not to send them away. He promised that they could stay until he died.

Damien himself went to Kalaupapa on several occasions, but never entered the sisters' chapel. Sr Leopoldina thought this was a sign of reverence. She was certain that Damien was very pious, because otherwise he would never have been able to do what he did. He was a strange man, who showed her how to make boys' clothes. The children told many stories about him. One day, he was said to have climbed over a fence to take some potatoes. The owner caught him, but he paid for everything. His doors and windows were always open.

Damien found his equal in Sr Leopoldina. Sr Vincent could not cope with the settlement and became depressed. The mother superior concentrated on the management and administration of the Home. It was Sr Leopoldina who spent most time with the children and so she was most popular with the patients. She did washing with women in the river and took off her shoes to play with the children in the water. She took the children swimming, although that nearly ended in disaster when one girl was caught in an undercurrent and had to be saved by a fisherman. Sr Leopoldina was a sweet, simple, somewhat childlike woman, who had a tendency to enthusiasm. When she saw the handsome young engineer, Charles Reynolds, standing on the convent verandah, in his hunting clothes and with a rifle over his shoulder, she thought he was an angel. His blond hair was gleaming in the sun and straight away she decided he must be Irish, the finest people in the world. Reynolds gave Sr Leopoldina a bundle of feathers for the girls' hats. When she took them to the back garden to dry, she found Damien on his knees on the earth, leaning against the chapel wall, praying. She was moved to tears.

Damien had come for a meeting with Möllers in the church. The superiors had said that the chaplain was not to receive lepers in his home and he kept strictly to that rule. Damien fancied a hot drink, but would not get that in the church. Moreover, he had to be careful with hot drinks, because the disease had affected the inside of his mouth and so he could burn himself without noticing.

Möllers's message came as a thunderbolt. The sisters wanted a new church close to the convent. The old church was only five minutes' walk away, but Damien had to remember that the nuns were women and this was a long way for them. They also objected to the garish colours. Damien explained to Möllers that leprosy affected the eyes and many patients could no longer see pastel colours, but this objection was also brushed aside. The sisters also objected to the cruciform church, because it distracted the patients, who spent their time looking at one another, rather than the altar. Again, his objections were considered unimportant. He must get to work. He could use his money to build the new church, or, if he was still not willing to use that money for its proper end, he could rebuild the existing church in accordance with the sisters' wishes. After all, St Philomena's was almost finished, so it could wait.

Visit by the Painter Edward Clifford

Damien disregarded this order. He did not wish to embitter the visit he had been looking forward to for so long with a new quarrel. It was almost Christmas, when Conrardy, who had moved to Kalawao, and Damien rose long before dawn. Each had a lantern in his hand and they set out in different directions. Conrardy went on horseback to Kalaupapa, because he thought the *Mokolii* might land there. Damien had studied the pattern of the waves the evening before and looked at the splashing of the foam on the rocks and decided there were two possibilities. Either the boat would pass the peninsula by, or it would unload the freight at the promontory in the gulf of Kalawao. This was where he was going. He had to climb over rocks and wade through swollen rivers, but he had help. Twenty friends also wanted to welcome Edward Clifford, the painter and international traveller, doubtless because he came with many gifts. Clifford was a friend of the London Rev. Hugh Chapman and had been corresponding with Damien for two years.

Clifford was standing on deck and knew that the stumbling figure in the soutane was Damien. His face was shaded by a straw hat. Once he reached the promontory, Damien sat down. He waved to Clifford, who waved back. Clifford was distracted because, to his dismay, two small exiled boys had to jump into the rowing boat, in which a group of adults was already sitting. He knew that he would also have to make this leap and, in order not to have to look at the tiny sloop on the rough sea, he checked the crates which had to be taken ashore. He jumped and waded ashore, through the powerful breakers, towards Damien, who spontaneously put out his hand. Clifford could not avoid taking the leprous fingers in his own. The greeting was hearty and informal. Damien declared that Providence brought Clifford and he knew he would land at this spot.

Clifford quickly took in the broad, strong man, with the short, grey beard and black, curly hair. Once, he must have been good-looking, but Clifford did not find him so very disfigured. He had seen worse. His forehead was swollen and furrowed, the eyebrows were gone, the nose was sunken, swollen ears, lepromas. Damien was aware of the searching look and said, 'I'm feeling better. The Goto method works.' Clifford replied that *Gurjun* oil was also successful. He said that he had brought a large supply and asked Damien to try it. Damien, who knew that it did not work, promised to try it all the same.

Because the case with gifts was too heavy to bring ashore, the items were landed separately, and ended up being unpacked there and then, including Burne-Jones's watercolour, the *Vision of St Francis*, which he had sent Damien for his own room. There were gifts from various members of the British aristocracy, such as Palmerston's widow, Lady Mount-Temple, Lady Caroline Charteris and the Hon. Maude Stanley. The patients particularly liked the barrel organ, which had a repertoire of forty tunes.

The return journey was difficult. The river had been swollen by heavy rain on 'topside' and they had to carry all the packages over the rocks. Clifford did not mind. He was young, healthy, equipped and, above all, pleased because he had found Damien better than he had expected. He was so happy that he wanted to swim, but Damien advised him against it, so he splashed about in the waves, to the astonishment of Damien and the patients who looked on.

Edward Clifford was to be Damien's last visitor, but this did not alter the routine. Damien showed him St Philomena's and pointed to the places where he would hang the drawings that

Clifford had brought. He told him about the pandan. When they left the church, there was a change of plan. Damien said, 'Wait!' and signalled to the man carrying the barrel organ. The man sat down and started to play it and people came from all over the village. Clifford asked to be allowed to draw Damien and he agreed, and they spent hours sitting on the upper terrace, while Damien posed.

Clifford liked Damien's easy manner. He called everyone by their first name and wore denim trousers under his soutane. As they sat for the picture, Damien told Clifford about his mother, whom he described as 'a serious and devout woman'. Clifford sometimes sang hymns, such as 'Brief life is here our portion', or 'Art thou weary? art thou languid?' or 'Safe home in port'. Clifford asked Damien if he had a message for Cardinal Manning. Damien was not sure it was appropriate for him to send messages to a cardinal, but he finally agreed to send his humble greetings. He said that he could not accept the blessing of the Bishop of Peterborough, because he was a heretic. Then he expressed aloud his doubts. He had seen so many signs of devotion among the sick exiles, whether Protestant or Catholic. Dedication to serving others and devotion in the heart were what really mattered. He hoped that marriage partners would not be separated. It caused so much misery and made it more difficult to bear their illness. It encouraged them to throw themselves into immoral behaviour. If they could stay with their partner, they accepted their fate without complaint. They created a home in exile and went on with their lives. He went on about accommodation, clothing and food, but what struck Clifford was that the words 'go on', 'normality', 'love', 'sympathy', 'joy', and 'friendliness' constantly recurred. There was no cure for leprosy, perhaps there would be in the future, but not in December 1888. Damien knew that he would not recover and, if the price of recovery were leaving the island, he would refuse it.

When the picture was finally finished, Damien looked at it for a long time and sighed, 'What an ugly face. I did not realise the disease was so far advanced. There are no mirrors in Kalawao.' Clifford asked if he should send a photograph of the picture to Pamphile, but Damien said that it would shock his brother too much.

An American Christmas. Disobedience by the Sisters

Conrardy wanted to give the children an American Christmas, but he needed sponsors for this. He asked Emerson to launch a drive to collect toys from wherever possible. Damien added a few lines of praise for the work of the Board, in order to put them in a favourable frame of mind.

Emerson knew that this would be Damien's last Christmas and so he backed the project. Unfortunately, because of the weather, the gifts could only be distributed on 5 January.

Meyer also had a surprise. It was the custom for Damien's boys to process through the streets of the village, beating drums an hour before midnight mass on 24 December. Meyer, his family and staff, stood ready at the top of the *pali* and when they saw the torches and lanterns passing through the village, they threw down burning branches. Damien was called from the church to look, and enjoyed the spectacle.

After the dawn mass, Damien had to lie down and rest, because it was going to be a tiring day. Dutton had rehearsed a devotional play with the boys, and the sisters were to accompany the girls, who were well enough, to the festivities. Just before they arrived, Damien opened the personal gifts that Clifford had brought with him, including Faber's hymn-book, from Lady Grosvenor and her three daughters, inscribed, 'Blessed are the merciful, for they shall receive mercy.'

Mother Marianne had stayed with the sick children and the two sisters came with the other girls. They were reminded before they set out that they must not eat or drink anything served by Damien, for fear of infection. It was a fine day and they walked singing and laughing to Kalawao. They were embarrassed when they arrived to see the table set out for six in front of the presbytery, and wondered how they could avoid joining the meal, without hurting Damien's feelings.

Damien wished them Merry Christmas and introduced them to Clifford. Just then a cart came up and the driver handed Damien a package. It was a gift from Honolulu, pipes and tobacco from the firm Hollister & Co. Meyer announced an even better present, new clothes and shoes for the 100 orphans. Köckemann's gift would have been the best, if Damien had known of it. He had asked the general to admit Conrardy without a novitiate. He did not wish to inform Damien of this until he had received official permission, however. This reversal was not simply caused by concern for Damien. Pressure from the Board had been decisive.

The play was about Daniel and Belshazzar and was quite a spectacle. Dutton and McMillan had built a stage for the performance and, despite some stage fright, the performers got through their parts and were given warm applause.

After the performance, Damien wanted to show the sisters the dormitories, which had been spring-cleaned. Then he took them to his house. The dreaded moment of the meal was approaching. Soon they would have to sit down at table with this dirty man, although they had to concede his house was clean: sober, without any luxury, but clean. Damien then told them that James Sinnett, who was clear of infection, had prepared the meal and that the crockery and cutlery came from Dr Swift, so it was clean, too. There was no danger, because he would not eat with them.

The sisters had to sit and eat and it was an enjoyable meal. Clifford told so many stories and when Conrardy began to talk about the Indians, it was really exciting. The sisters returned home, singing with the girls, where they were immediately required to make a report and, when they admitted that they had eaten, because everything was safe, the mother superior thundered that they had been disobedient and lodged a complaint against Damien with Möllers. The chaplain sent a note to Damien, saying that he must go to the convent immediately. The mother superior covered him with reproaches and made him ask forgiveness on his knees. She insisted that he do penance.

It was night when Damien returned to Kalawao. He lit a

lantern, because he had to check the dormitories. Most of the children were asleep, but here and there there was one who was still awake, and he went to sit by them for a while, listened to their fears and told them a short story. He had a few apples in his pocket, and he gave one to the frightened child and made a sign of the cross on its forehead. He was proud of his hands, because in the places where he held the host, the top joint of his thumb and index finger, there was no leprosy.

Damien made mistakes, but many forgave him, or saw him as an irreproachable man. Sr Ignace Cavanagh, who lived in the Paridaens Convent in Leuven, sent him a painting for Christmas. The Paridaens Convent was right next to the Sacred Hearts Monastery, and she saw Pamphile regularly. The painting was not really good, but it was something from home.

Gifts arrived from the strangest quarters. Dr Hyde, the head of the Congregational Church, sent Damien $10 for the school. Damien decided to buy frames for photographs with the money. Most of the money he put in the bank, even though he was not sure what would be done with it after his death. Of course, he had to thank the benefactors and so he asked Conrardy to make a list of the names of the boys in the home. Clifford burst out laughing when he read it. Some of them had English names, such as Peter, Ann and Jane. The Hawaiian names meant Ratseater, Widow, Heaven Has Spoken and so on.

Clifford stayed in the leper settlement for a fortnight and Damien gave him a parting gift, a print he had received from Jerusalem, decorated with dried flowers. He wrote on it, 'To Edward Clifford from his leper friend J. Damien'. Clifford asked Damien to write something in his Bible and again he wrote, 'I was sick and you visited me. J. Damien de Veuster, Kalawao, Molokai, 30 December 1888.' He leafed through the volume and looked at the prints: Dürer's *Hands* and a photograph of Broadlands, Palmerston's country seat.

There were no fireworks on the *pali* on New Year's Eve 1888, because all the patients wanted to see the arrival of the *Likelike* early next morning. The banker Samuel Damon had chartered the boat for family and friends of the lepers, a thoughtful New Year's present for the exiles. Reynolds had just been appointed as superintendent, and the organisation of this visit was his first task. Like Dr Swift, he brought his family with him.

It was still dark when about a thousand Hawaiians and half-Hawaiians, together with the six British and Irish lepers, the two Germans, the Pole, the Russian, the Micronesian from Raratonga, the twenty-three Chinese and the Belgian, gathered on the quayside. Clifford, who was to leave on the *Likelike*, was shocked when joy turned to despair. First a sloop landed, carrying Damon and the Reynolds family. They were loudly applauded. Damon handed Damien some papers. Köckemann wanted some changes to his will. He was to name Möllers and Damon, not Evrard, as his executors. This was urgent, given Damien's condition. Damon set off for the convent, because he was on a tour of inspection. According to the superiors, Mother Marianne, after six weeks in Kalaupapa and two short visits to Kalawao, was the only one who knew the true situation in the leper settlement.

No one noticed this, because a drama was unfolding on the beach. The sea was so rough, that the captain said it was irresponsible to allow the sloop to land. The men could swim the last stretch, but the women must wave to their loved ones from the rough sea. Tears of grief and hysterical cries replaced the joyful reunion. A girl jumped into the water. The sailors tried to catch her, but she had to get to her loved one and she swam on like a madwoman. Clifford would not have known how to paint such a scene. Those were his last words to Damien.

Impossible Demands From the Chaplain and the Sisters

When the boat was out of sight, Damien went home, because he had arranged an urgent meeting with Dr Swift about Sinnett. The nurse wanted to build toilets next to the dormitories. Everyone agreed that this was necessary, but Damien knew that the Hawaiian children would not use them. Moreover, the earth was too hard there to bore deeply and so there was a question of how the waste could be carried away. Swift feared that the toilets would create a source of infection. It was better to let everyone go into the woods. Sinnett himself was not satisfactory. He spent hours sitting in a chair preaching about how he would change everything, but he did no work. Swift thought of the huge case of *Gurjun* oil. The oil would not effect a cure, but it helped psychologically. Henceforth, Sinnett could treat the lepers with oil.

Humour forged a stong bond between Swift and Damien. They both laughed heartily at the letter advising them that dogshit mixed with molasses was the remedy. Swift declared that this would be just the thing for nurses like Sinnett.

Sinnett did write letters for Damien, whose eyes were deteriorating. Damien's hands were covered with suppurating sores that burnt like coals. For this reason, the correspondence that Damien dictated to the nurse was increasingly sparse. Even that was painful, because he could only whisper and his feet were one mass of suppurating sores.

On his forty-ninth birthday, he received greetings from Köckemann. He hoped that, if it pleased God, Damien would have many years of physical and spiritual happiness on earth, but he must be careful, for the devil was trying to sow discord among those who worked for the good cause. The bishop asked to be remembered to Dutton and Sinnett, but forgot Conrardy.

Damien dictated his reply to Conrardy – Sinnett did not know French. He asked Köckemann to dispense him from saying his breviary. 'I read at night now,' he wrote, 'daylight is too painful.' The letter was short and sweet. Those days mostly Damien talked to Sinnett, who had the time. He repeated to him constantly that Clifford and Chapman were good people and he hoped they would one day convert.

While Clifford was in Honolulu, waiting for his friend the Scottish author Robert Louis Stevenson, he received a letter from Chapman, who had collected another £1,000. He insisted that the money should be used for the restoration of St Philomena's. More money would follow.

Children, in particular, needed all the help available.

Reynolds thought that the fact that his predecessor, Hutchison, had allowed healthy children to remain in the leper settlement was criminal. He knew nothing about the murder which had occurred when they left, nor about Anna Hoopai, a girl who had been whipped by Gibson. He wanted to transfer all healthy children to Kakaako. This must be done before Dr Swift began his smallpox vaccinations, because this was a possible means of passing on infection. His other project also concerned the healthy inhabitants. All *kokuas* who had infringed the rules of the settlement, who had been wanton or drunk, were to be sent away. Mother Marianne wanted all *kokuas* to go, but Reynolds was still unsure about taking this step.

The mother superior had her list of priorities. She wanted a new prison in Kalaupapa. A lockup with doors that did not shut properly would not do. The cells had no windows and the doors were made of a single piece of wood. Once the door was closed, the prisoner was in the dark. Meyer thought that the mother superior sometimes went too far. A Chinese *kokua* had stabbed another Chinese and had been sentenced to four months' hard labour, because the wound was slight. The mother superior wanted him brought before the supreme court, which would have involved transporting infectious witnesses.

Damien also had difficulty with Mother Marianne and the bishop. They were both angry that he had not stopped work on St Philomena's straight away and started moving the church in Kalaupapa. The old church was ugly, badly built and too far away from the convent.

Damien had an excuse on this occasion. Köckemann had not yet given him the funds for a new church and presbytery in Kalaupapa. The bishop did not dare ask him to use money from the Fund, for he knew that he would refuse. Dr Emerson did not regard the re-siting of the church as a necessary project in which the Board had to get involved. In order to show his goodwill, he was prepared to pay for moving the church on wheels, but this was impossible, because Damien had laid the foundations too firmly, so that the building could not be lifted up in a storm. The mother superior and Möllers continued to put the bishop under pressure and on 28 January Köckemann wrote Damien a letter that was downright aggressive. 'You know that I have no desire to hurt anyone's feelings, but it is my duty to do this. I am imposing my decision on you. Neither Léonor [Fouesnel] nor Mr Damon came up with the idea of re-siting the church.' Damien had his own reasons for delaying this work, the bishop knew, but it was necessary and Damien must put aside sentimentality in relation to the old chapel. He demanded that Damien discuss the matter with Möllers and the sisters. He, the bishop, would give his support to whatever they agreed.

Once the sores began to suppurate, the end was near. Eye infections and breathing difficulties were other signs. Damien had these three symptoms. Fouesnel said mass in Kakaako twice a week and could visualise the disease, and so he wrote, 'Wendelin [Möllers] wants to move the church. It is his parish, not mine, not yours. Monseigneur does not want to pay for a new church. Let Wendelin solve his own problems.'

This brief moment of sympathy ended a few days later, because then Fouesnel ordered Damien to start on Möllers's church. The chaplain was, after all, the '*independent* priest of his own parish'. The mother superior had persuaded Mr Damon of the necessity and the Board was now willing to pay for everything. Fouesnel did not say that the mother superior had asked Köckemann to give her official resignation to the Board. The bishop had panicked and now wanted Damien to comply with all the mother superior's wishes.

It is in this light, also, that the permission to build a new presbytery for Möllers, on a site chosen by the nuns, must be seen. Meyer reported this dryly, but added that he saw no reason to move the church. 'I'm too practical a man to do unnecessary work. The sisters can furnish a room for their private prayer in the Bishop Home. The women who lived in the dormitories thought nothing of a short walk, even if, by mischance, it was raining *hard*.' Meyer does not seem to have known that Möllers had consecrated the St Elizabeth's Chapel in the convent.

On 11 February Köckemann came up with a new task. He did not say that the Board had rejected moving the church as silly. He gave the impression that he had decided to keep the church in the same place, but Damien must use money from the Fund to enlarge it. He explained to the general that he, as bishop, had the right to decide how money should be spent, because it was a religious matter. Damien was disobedient, because Köckemann had read in American and European newspapers what the new St Philomena's was to look like. Damien had never once informed him about this. Fouesnel was doubtful about the bishop's points and thought it was Köckemann's fault, because he never visited the missions. Köckemann remained angry and thought that it was not Damien who was really ill, but Möllers, whose dislike for Kalawao expressed itself in physical ailments. Once again, he could see no replacement for the bitter German, despite the fact that six months before, half the mission had been on the waiting list.

Despite the fuss in Honolulu, Damien spent the last weeks of his life surrounded by people who wanted to help him. Dr Swift got Damien a writing table in pinewood and a table with a central leg. Fouesnel asked around for furniture for St Philomena's. He found a screen for the choir and was hoping to find a statue of Christ, but feared that a pall would not be finished in time. Damien himself chose bright colours for his church, because these could be seen by lepers like himself. He chose bright reds and yellows.

His letters were an unexpressed farewell, because he urged people to reply. 'It is as if they are ashamed that I have the disease,' he wrote of his family. On 12 February 1889 he penned his last letter to Pamphile. 'Anyway,' he concluded, 'I am still happy and content.' He wished only that God's holy will should be done. He had received much help for the education and counselling of his more than one hundred orphans: two priests and two brothers. Three sisters were helping with the more than one thousand exiles. The English, both Protestant and Catholic, showed the greatest sympathy for his work. It was getting harder to say mass, but he still prayed for his family at the altar and asked them to pray for him, because he was being drawn gently to the grave. 'May God grant me strength and the mercy of perseverance and a good death.'

20

Nunc Dimittis
(February–April 1889)

St Philomena's Damaged by Storm.
Last Work

The 'devil wind' that lashed the settlement from Pelekunu in mid-February certainly hastened Damien's death. The storm tore off the new roof of St Philomena's and brought down several houses and hospital wards. In Kalaupapa, a girl was injured. Mother Marianne was standing in the middle of the garden when the storm struck. She was lifted up and plumped into the arms of a big, strong leper, who came running to help her. The new Mormon chapel was completely destroyed – even the seats were smashed. The school was blown away but – and this was the oddest thing – the controversial church was undamaged, despite the fact that all the houses round about were damaged or destroyed. For a week, the sea was so rough that no goods could be landed.

Reynolds immediately set his Chinese workmen to work and in a few days everyone had a roof over their heads once again. Swift reported to Honolulu that one or two people had been wounded. The doctor was, nevertheless, in a good humour, because a British Anglican nurse was taking over the direction of the hospital. The mother superior could not object to this, because she had made clear that it was not her task to care for men and married women.

Dr P. A. Morrow, the publisher of a New York medical periodical, saw some of the damage. He wanted to write an in-depth article about leprosy for a conference in Paris and had brought a professional photographer, Mr Bingham, with him. Dr Emerson and Dr Swift took the journalist round. St Philomena's was still surrounded by scaffolding. Damien was willing to pose for the photographer on this occasion and Bingham caught in his lens a frail man with a swollen face and a broad coat. He sat bolt upright, with his arm in a sling. He was surrounded by his boys.

The next day, 20 February, Damien visited Kalaupapa for the last time. Mother Marianne wanted him to come into the parlour, but he refused, because he was unclean. That evening, he did not have the strength to climb into the buggy. He did not dare to knock on any of the parishioners' doors to warm himself, although he was very cold. He thought for a moment of asking Möllers for shelter, but the German priest was already so depressed and was not allowed to take in lepers. Evening came on. Lamps were lit in the windows and suddenly the wandering priest had an idea. He would just take a rest on the sisters' verandah and then he would have the strength to return to Kalawao. He lay down and dozed off.

Sr Leopoldina found him there the next morning. He awoke, looked astonished and then frightened and ashamed. 'He is dying,' said a weeping Leopoldina over breakfast. 'Death is in his look.'

He could not cope any more. Damien read Clifford's letter, but no longer had the strength to dictate a letter, and asked Sinnett to reply. His strength was sapped above all by diarrhoea. His breathing was hampered by coughing. He no longer used *Gurjun* oil on his inflamed fingers, because the disease was in the bones and ointment could not touch it. Sinnett told Clifford that Damien's condition was beyond hope. He could not bear daylight, could not sleep at night, except just before dawn and yet he was still working. At the end of the letter, Damien wrote, 'My love and best wishes to my good friend Edward. I am trying slowly to complete my way of the cross and hope soon to reach Golgotha.'

Clifford showed the note to his friend Robert Louis Stevenson, who had just arrived. His comment was clear: 'People do not regard Damien as a hero, because he is cast in a completely different mould.'

He got a basket of fruit for Damien. Clifford remembered that Damien liked bread and butter, and so he sent him some of that as well. Meyer ate one of the peaches during his visit to Damien and took time to talk to him about what was going on. He told Damien that the prisoner, Keanu, who had been vaccinated with leprosy by Dr Arning, had arrived in the settlement and gave him some other pieces of news. Damien could hardly speak, because of his cough, but told Meyer that Möllers was still on about moving the church and building a new presbytery. He knew that Möllers, who was his executor, would use the Fund money for this after his death.

The mission sent Damien an alpaca jacket and cardigan, because Fouesnel knew that the dying felt the cold. Damien recognised this symptom and told Clifford and Chapman that now only a miracle could save him. 'I do not want to defy God,' he wrote. 'My heart is freeing itself from earthly love and growing toward the desire of every Christian soul, sooner or later to be united with him who is the only life.'

He spent much time with Clayton Strawn, who was now a pious Catholic, and they talked about the past and Damien recited poetry.

On 1 March Damien asked Dr Swift to visit a dying woman. The next morning he felt unwell. His hand was bleeding and drops fell on the paper. The message was,

Dear Sir, Could you please come? I'm afraid there are internal problems, in the abdomen. You would be doing your weak friend a favour. Jobo Puhomia brought up blood yesterday morning. Please give him a moment of your time. You will find him in the second house from Jack Lewis.

P.S. In the same house you will find the dying woman I was speaking about last night.

He put down his pen; his last letter had exhausted him.

Fouesnel feared that things were going wrong, because Damien no longer wrote and Möllers told him that he was going downhill fast. He sent him oranges and lemons and a cask of Australian wine: 175 bottles would keep him going for quite a while. He wrote a note with them, expressing his sympathy. 'It looks as though a terrible end awaits you, when you will no longer be able to say mass or read your breviary, or do the handiwork you enjoy so much. A life full of restrictions must be difficult for an active man like you.'

The bishop had also read Möllers's letter and he, too, was concerned, but, in his case, about the will. Damien had to make a new version. It meant more work for the bishop, but it would give a better guarantee. Damien just had to sign. The bishop wrote, 'As long as you live, I shall not touch your money and I shall ask you for nothing. I do not wish to, because everything is for the leper settlement. Make over whatever you have in the bank to Fr Hermann, Bishop of Olba.' This signature was the last Damien made, but he had to complete one more large task.

Dr Emerson had asked him to dictate the history of his leprosy to Dutton. This would be his final contribution.

He began on 10 March, 'I, Joseph Damien de Veuster, Catholic priest, born in Belgium of Belgian parents, aged 49'. There was no history of scrofula or syphilis in the family, all of whom were strong and healthy. He had served as priest on the island of Hawaii from 1864 to 1873. There was so much to tell. Sitting in an easy chair, with his eyes closed, he remembered his life. When he dozed off, Dutton put down his pen and went off to do his work in the boys' home.

Now that he was dying, Damien thought he should do something for his boys and he ordered two bags of marbles, costing $8.50. He used Fund money, because it was for a good cause. This was the last payment he made. His only hope was that the church would be finished before his death.

Fouesnel did his best and found everything except the statue of Christ, and there were only small candle-holders in stock. The sisters of the Sacred Hearts were embroidering a pall, but would perhaps not have finished the communion linen. For a while, Damien thought that the provincial had become calm, but even then, aggression boiled up. He began, 'My dear father,

I must say something that will cause you much pain, but you will see that it is not my fault.' He went on,

> A member of the Board will give a final serious warning about the letters which he [Conrardy] is writing to all corners of the world in order to become famous and admired at the expense of others. If he does not stop, he will be expelled at the publication of his next letter. You can see now for yourself that I am not the only one who complains. Why tell stories just so that people would talk about you? I wager that the gentlemen of the Board are now saying, 'Remove him and take the money.'

As far as Fouesnel was concerned, Conrardy could stay, because if he were removed, then they would have to sacrifice another priest. Möllers was not strong enough. There were a lot of priests who wanted to go, but Fouesnel could not take Corneille from his thousand Portuguese parishioners. It was Damien's task to make Conrardy keep silent, while Conrardy himself could expect a pasting from the Board.

Conrardy had no idea what letter Fouesnel meant. He supposed he was talking about his published report to the Bishop of Oregon. He could not really see what was wrong with it. He was more direct with his sister – perhaps the storm was coming from Belgium.

Gibes from the Superiors as Farewell

During this crisis, a *kona* storm struck the leper settlement, but there was a storm in Damien's house, too. He was deeply hurt when his friend Meyer also turned against him, when he had read the article in question, which seems to have been published in Birmingham. The secretary of the Board had passed the controversial article on to Meyer. Meyer wondered whether the 'living saint', as he called Damien, had dictated the letter, or whether it was exclusively Conrardy's work. Hawaii was a paradise infected by leprosy, that no tourist would want to visit.

The agent had a mind to write an open letter to the British newspaper.

Damien thought it was a forgery. Köckemann went on kicking him while he was down. He had forgotten to send a pastoral letter to Damien, because he thought it was no longer necessary. The note was cruelly brief, 'Please answer my questions about mixed marriages as soon as possible.' Damien dictated his reply and asked if everything was now in order with his will. The bishop responded immediately that he would not be bothering him with that problem any more.

On 19 March 1889, Damien should have celebrated the twenty-fifth anniversary of his arrival on the islands, but only Sr Judith, the superior of the Sacred Hearts nuns, and Sr Marie-Laurence sent him congratulations. He and Dutton did exchange greetings on their mutual name day and, from Fouesnel, he received a letter in which the provincial called him a 'hothead' and a creator of problems, even for people who wanted to help him. He, Fouesnel, had really tried to find a large statue of Christ, even in Wailuku, but no one was willing to give one up. In a postscript, Fouesnel said that the Board was extremely angry with Conrardy and Damien. The next day, Fouesnel wrote again about the statue, which was never to come. The pall was finished, but it was of the cheapest material. The sisters had no time for embroidery. The communion linen could not be made, and so Fouesnel sent the fabric. Lepers could embroider as well. Fouesnel could not understand why Damien, who had less than a month to live, was in such a hurry.

During his next visit, Meyer showed Conrardy the newspaper article that had caused such an uproar. They analysed the contents and concluded that it was a compilation of the letter he had sent to Monsignor Gross and information drawn from Stoddard's book. There was also a good deal of imagination. Meyer believed Conrardy and the matter was closed, but on condition that Conrardy should be more careful in future. Now that peace was restored, the two friends could sit together again. Meyer told Damien that his sons had found a statue of the Hawaiian god Kane. He had ordered plaster of Paris so they could make a cast of it. Eli Crawford's baby had died and now they wanted to send the white man away. He had just had a talk with the sick parents of children who did not have leprosy, but had not been able to persuade them to send their children to Kakaako. There had been problems getting the *pai-ai* ashore, and the food for the whites had not been landed at all.

During their conversation, Meyer observed his friend and thought that he looked better, now that the disease was attacking him internally. The sores were clearing up and he was coughing less. He knew that Damien was resigned to death, because he said time and again, 'I am so happy that I can celebrate Easter in heaven.'

The Death Agony

Damien still slept on a mat on the floor. On 28 March he had more difficulty than usual in getting up. He had to get on to his hands and knees, hold on to a chair and pull himself on to his knees and then upright. He was out of breath, panting and sweating and felt like lying down again. He dressed himself with great difficulty and stumbled out to the terrace. He walked to the steps, but when he looked down, he knew that he could not manage them. He felt a dead weight on his chest and his forehead was beaded with sweat. Sinnett saw him and led him to a chair. Damien would never descend the steps again. That day, he signed a transfer of all his money to the bishop. He was happy, because he had kept his vow of poverty.

His friends thought he ought to sleep in a bed, and one was brought up. Dutton looked in his cupboard for sheets, but the man who had received so much money had none. He had nothing, really. The cupboard was more or less bare.

On Monday 30 March Dr Swift received an urgent note from Conrardy. 'Father Damien wishes you to come as soon as possible. He does not want to eat until you come, so that you can make a better judgment. Yours sincerely, L. L. Conrardy.' Swift diagnosed fever and an ulceration of the tongue and palate. Damien had had a cold for two days and was sweating a lot. His pulse was 96 and he had a temperature of 102.9. At ten past eight in the morning, Swift gave him an antipyretic, but two hours later, neither the pulse nor the temperature had subsided. He had eaten a little raw mincemeat, because that was the only thing he could get in his swollen mouth. He could not chew any more. Swift was relieved that there were no signs of inflammation of the bronchial tract.

That afternoon, Damien asked Möllers to prepare him for death. Möllers remarked with surprise that Damien looked happy. Damien said that he was, because he could confess less than a month after his previous confession. Because it was a general confession, the two religious men first renewed their vows of poverty, chastity and obedience.

That day, Dr Swift visited Damien twice more. His temperature was constant and Swift added quinine to the antipyretic. He suggested that Conrardy, Dutton and Sinnett should arrange to sit with him during the night and if he had not taken the quinine at midnight, then they must give it him the following morning, even if they had to force him to take it. As soon as he had fever, they must give him an antipyretic. Swift hoped things would go well, particularly when the symptoms remained the same the following day. He continued with the medication, but Conrardy had Möllers called to give Damien the last rites. The sick man was relaxed. He showed his hands, which were scabbing over. That was certainly a sign of death. 'I have another wish,' Damien told Möllers. 'I should like to see Monseigneur once more, but God is calling me to keep the Passover with him. May God be blessed. Do you know what is so good?' he continued. 'I have been alone for so long, and now I have two priests and three sisters with me. Now I can say Nunc dimittis, I relinquish the world. The future of the work with the lepers is assured. I am no longer needed, I can go.'

Möllers asked Damien if he would remember his orphans in heaven, and he replied that he would intercede for them, if he had any credit. Möllers also asked for Damien's alpaca jacket, that he had only had on a few times. He said he wanted to take on his mantle, like Elias, to take over his great love. Damien asked him, with a sigh, what he would do with the jacket, which was infected with leprosy. Möllers asked him to give him his blessing instead. The day before, Damien had made his general confession to Möllers. In principle he had confided all the sins he had ever committed. Now, Möllers was asking him, with tears, to give him his blessing.

Because Damien's temperature rose on 1 April, Dr Swift increased the dose of antipyretic. Every hour, Damien had to take a few grains of chloral until he could sleep. He had to be sat with day and night. A little after eleven in the evening, Damien reminded Sinnett that it was time to prepare communion. The dying man prayed for half an hour. Sinnett woke Conrardy at 11.30 and they brought the holy sacrament from the church. Conrardy administered communion at midnight.

Damien's condition improved at the beginning of April and he was even strong enough to receive one or two visitors. He told Ambrose Hutchison that he would spend Easter in heaven. Meyer tried to talk about ordinary matters. The final farewell was too difficult. That evening, Meyer reported to the Board, 'Poor Father Damien is seriously ill. He has a high fever and my most important task can now only be to report his death, but, as you often find, perhaps he will get through.' Meyer spent the night in the settlement. The next day his report was less good. 'Father Damien is very ill. I hope that he can pull through. He was very bad this morning.' His temperature was 99.9 and his pulse was racing at 116. On 4 April Damien's temperature and pulse both went down and Swift wanted him to drink milk mixed with egg and rum, but Damien said, 'No more.' The doctor made as much time free as he could to be with his friend and wrote to Emerson that he had no time to write a commentary for the photographs for Dr Morrow. He had to attend Damien.

Only in the Mission House in Honolulu did people seem not to take the illness seriously. Evrard, who seemed to be unaware that Damien was dying, asked him to say fifty masses.

Perhaps he would be able to say them, because, despite the persistent fever, Damien felt better by 6 April. Swift gave him a thorough examination and concluded that he was suffering from 'dangerous malarial fever', something that did happen with advanced leprous tuberculosis. He would die of general exhaustion. Swift explained what treatment he wanted to give, but Damien refused to take quinine. It was as though he wanted to die. Swift urged him to take the medication to prevent attacks of fever, but Damien shook his head. Swift therefore asked Conrardy just to continue giving the antipyretic. The patient was weakening visibly and so the doctor wanted to give him nourishment via the rectum, but Dutton refused, saying it was undignified for a priest. Damien also rejected the idea. Swift did not understand and Conrardy explained that Damien had resolved to die on a particular day and it would be sacrilege to prevent this. Dutton had given orders for Damien's grave to be dug under the pandan tree. Jack McMillan poured concrete into the hole to strengthen it.

Möllers visited Damien as often as he could. Damien wanted to say the prayers of the Order and asked him to tell the general that it was good to die as a child of the Sacred Hearts.

On 8 April Damien's temperature remained high, but his skin was less dry. After the midnight communion, Damien agreed to take a grain of quinine, but the next day his temperature rose. Swift gave him a tot of whisky toddy, a mixture of warm water, sugar and whisky. That evening, his temperature went down from 104 to 100.9.

Köckemann wrote to the general that Damien was possibly already dead. He hoped that he would still be able to see him during his planned visit to the leper settlement. He also hoped that the death of the martyr would not create new problems. Damien had done everything he was asked. The Fund, $3,700, was in the bank in the bishop's name, but in a separate account. Möllers could use the money exclusively for the lepers. Conrardy had become more reasonable, while Möllers seemed to be a bitter, sour man, with a weak constitution. He would never survive alone in the settlement. Conrardy could remain for the time being. Once again, the real message was in the postscript. 'When the news of Damien's death reaches us, I shall praise him in public. We shall keep the problems to ourselves. I shall hold a solemn memorial service for him.'

Damien was not yet dead, however. On 11 April Swift gave Damien another whisky toddy to help prevent him feeling the cold and Damien also took quinine twice. Meyer gave this good news to the Board, to whom he also reported that he had given orders for the building of Möllers's presbytery and a dispensary for Dr Swift in Kalaupapa, as well as a cookhouse for the boys' home. There was also to be a new fence around the hospital, because the old one was completely rotten. The two new churchyards were further away from the village centre and the hearse for Möllers had arrived safely. Damien was better and Meyer even thought that he was not going to die. He added jokingly, 'Even saints and martyrs must sometimes exercise a little patience.'

Dr Swift's report to the Board sounded a different note. Following the medical passage, he wrote, 'Poor man, he has been a difficult patient and I have sometimes not known what to do. He is now fully aware of his condition and follows my directions willingly. I have not given up all hope of a cure, but it is not necessary to say that his condition is critical.'

Until 12 April, Sinnett and Dutton carried Damien to the verandah every day, so that he could rest in the sun. The children came to his house to greet him from the lawn, and the adults joined them. On 12 April Damien said, 'No more. I am bound to my bed.'

Despite the persistent fever, Damien's mind was still clear enough for him to ask Dutton to make all outstanding payments and to deal with the papers and bookkeeping. Everything was to be transferred to Bishop Bank, so that the account could be closed. Everything to do with the Fund, such as the letters from England, must be kept.

On 13 April Swift suggested a milk enema, but again Damien refused. He was willing to take a whisky toddy against the cold. At one o'clock in the afternoon, he took two quinine capsules. He wanted to rest until the sisters came. The first time they had suggested coming, he had refused, but this time he agreed.

When the sisters arrived, Damien raised his hand. The sisters saw at once that his narrow bed was badly made. He had tossed and turned and sweated, but he seemed cheerful. The sisters knelt beside the bed and asked for Damien's blessing. With his right hand, covered with sores, he made the sign of the cross. Sr Vincent wept and hid her face against the quilt, asking herself whether she could ever do so much for God. She asked Damien to pray for them in heaven and he said he would intercede if he had any influence.

They did not want to stay long. Any effort left him out of breath. When they got up, he raised his hand as though he wished to say something, but he had no voice. He tried twice to draw a deep breath and then whispered, haltingly, to ask if they would look after his boys. He repeated his question and they are thought to have given him their word.

That day, he began to have the diarrhoea that was to prove fatal. Dr Swift was now allowed to give a starch and opium enema. The doctor wrote to a colleague about this death agony: 'This was a man who ought not to have died. Here was a patient for whom we almost have a treatment. I have not worked on leprosy, because that was not the principal factor in this case and, if it had been, then I would not have been able to do anything about it.' Dr Swift knew how famous Damien already was and he decided to make a photographic record for the future. Dutton was opposed to this, but did help to sit Damien up. Semi-conscious, Damien looked at the doctor, who was setting up a tripod at the foot of the bed. The doctor ducked under the cloth, Dutton pushed Damien upright and moved out of the way just in time. Swift took several photographs in order to be sure.

Möllers remained as long as he could that evening, but finally had to leave because the morning mass was early on Palm Sunday. Damien was unconscious most of the time and when he came to, briefly, was largely incoherent, muttering, 'Congregation . . . child . . . *enfant* . . . Monseigneur . . . arrived Honolulu . . . Palm Sunday . . . *Adieu* Wendelin.'

He wanted to see his boys again and when they came he blessed small groups of them and addressed several of them by name. Shortly after midnight on Palm Sunday, he received holy communion for the last time. He was fully conscious and said that two people were with him all the time, one at the head, one at the foot of the bed. James Sinnett was so distracted, he forgot to ask who they were.

The next morning, Dutton said to Damien, 'Your wish is fulfilled. You came on Palm Sunday and you are leaving the same day.' Möllers found Damien conscious and resigned. He tried to pray, but he could no longer form words. Möllers took his hands and held them for a long time. At 11 o'clock that night, Dutton thought that the moment had come, but again Damien rallied. Dutton walked to the terrace to make a positive sign to the people, who were holding a vigil on the lawn and in the churchyard. Conrardy had organised an adoration of the holy sacrament and the church was full all night. Others came up to see him. At dawn, Sinnett held a consecrated candle near Damien and Conrardy said the prayers for the dying.

Möllers received a message at seven in the morning that Damien was slipping away. On the way to Kalawao, he received another message from a courier that Damien had died in Sinnett's arms at 8 o'clock.

When Möllers arrived, the body was lying on the dining table, clad in a white chasuble with alb, stole and maniple. Conrardy and the brothers had put the vestments on over the soutane. They forgot to empty his pockets and thus it was that Damien was buried with his carpenter's pen in his pocket. He looked at peace, as if he were sleeping before celebrating a festival mass.

The sisters arrived in Kalawao and were greeted by a red-eyed Conrardy. They were struck by the fact that the lawn was covered with silent, weeping people. Sr Leopoldina called them sheep without a shepherd. She was deeply touched and grieved, but Mother Marianne was happy and laughed as she passed Conrardy on her way into the house. Conrardy did not understand her good humour. She said she was come to pay Damien honour and refused to grieve, since he was now demanding his reward.

People were struck by the fact that all signs of leprosy had disappeared from Damien's face and some called it a miracle, although it is a normal feature of leprosy. The sisters posed beside the body and then decorated the rough wooden coffin, which was outside resting on two chairs, with black serge and white satin.

At 11 o'clock, the coffin was carried into the church, where a vigil was held.

The Farewell

On the Tuesday of Holy Week, Dutton flew the flags at half mast and was about to make preparations for who was to participate in the funeral, when Möllers arrived and took over the direction of affairs. He and Conrardy were shocked.

The mother superior and Sr Vincent came with the girls who were well enough and Sr Leopoldina stayed with those who were sick. Möllers allowed only funeral music, out of respect for the dead, in contrast to the usual practice in the settlement, when Damien's band had played.

Möllers celebrated the mass, assisted by Conrardy. Afterwards, the procession made its way to the grave. At the grave, the musicians laid down their instruments. Some climbed into the pandan tree, under which Damien wanted to take his eternal rest. He lay next to the little girl who had been afraid of the dark.

21

After Damien (1889–1995)

Two months before Damien's death, the roof of St Philomena's had been torn off and he never saw his church completed. The tower was still in scaffolding when he was buried. However, he did celebrate mass once or twice at the new altar with the splendid tabernacle. It is not clear what happened to that gift from Fr Hudson. It is well known that the pandan died. Its roots had been damaged during the rebuilding works.

Meyer informed the Board of Damien's death. He was glad that the mother superior was going to look after the boys when she was ready. For the time being, he appointed Conrardy as head of the boys' home, but Conrardy collapsed the day after Damien's funeral. His dysentery was so serious that Dr Swift had him transferred to Honolulu, where he gradually recovered. Meyer therefore appointed Dutton manager of the home, but he lacked authority. On Easter Sunday, during Köckemann's visit, seven boys were so drunk that they were sentenced to fifteen days' hard labour. They were released just as the police surrounded one of the dormitories because three boys refused to hand over their distillery. Meyer reported, 'Kalawao seems to be becoming a really bad place, especially that part where Fr Damien and Conrardy lived.' Meyer, who himself a few months before had sunk the plans for toilets, put the fever epidemic down to inadequate hygiene. 'Poor Fr Damien did not know how to keep anything clean,' he wrote, 'he just could not. Didn't know how to go about it.'

James Sinnett no longer had anything to do with the nursing. He regarded himself as the guardian of the grave. He planted flowers behind the iron fence and, on Easter Day, Köckemann posed there for photographers.

Fouesnel wrote his letter of condolence to the general on Easter Monday, on black-edged paper. His letter was a mixture of criticism and praise for a man who 'cared excessively for his lepers' and 'did not take enough precautions, otherwise he would have lived'. The Hawaiian government had strong feelings about Damien. He had been decorated. His home was his greatest achievement, but he had established it with help from the government and private contributions.

Back in Honolulu, Köckemann thanked Emerson for his condolences. The letter was diplomatic, because he assured the Board of Health that the Catholic mission would continue the humanitarian work, 'in the footsteps of the late Fr Damien, in so far as it is desirable'.

Köckemann put the latest £300 that Chapman had collected in the bank. It is not known how the money was ultimately used. That had already happened by the time he celebrated a pontifical mass for Damien. He was assisted by Evrard and two other priests. Fouesnel had put a lot of effort into the ceremony. The cathedral was elaborately decorated. Symbolically, there was an empty catafalque, with Damien's stole and decoration. These later ended up with the Hawaiian consul in Britain, Hoffnung. Many prominant persons attended.

In his sermon, the bishop spoke of Damien's worldwide celebrity, which was deserved. The two most important titles he had received were 'hero' and 'martyr to Christian mercy'. He said, 'Without ever hurting anyone, Damien, like Christ, has conquered the world by his example.' Meyer was in church, but found some of the pronouncements exaggerated.

On 9 May news of his death reached San Francisco, on 10 May New York, and Pamphile and the Rev. Hugh Chapman read it in the newspaper on 11 May. That day the Prince of Wales was to preside at a meeting in Marlborough House. He had heard of Damien from his personal physician, Dr Stallard, and others. The prince was also in regular contact with Cardinal Manning and other dignitaries connected with the Fund. Prince Edward spontaneously suggested setting up a memorial to Damien. The Damien Fund would promote the study and treatment of leprosy, especially in India and other parts of the British Empire. The *Illustrated Times* devoted a long article to Damien and used information sent them by Dr Arning from Berlin.

A month after Damien's death, Robert Louis Stevenson received a permit to visit the settlement. Emerson had initially refused, but Stevenson had pleaded and the king had also intervened. The author travelled with two new sisters and a married couple, who were to work for the nuns as servants.

There had been a lot of changes in the preceding month. Holes were being dug for the toilets, but it was harder work than expected and Meyer wrote, 'This is silly, impossible.' Nevertheless, it was necessary, because the Board knew that the sisters would only take over the boys' home if it had such facilities. The major clean-up did indeed prove necessary. Another requirement was new dormitories, and there was a search for sponsors.

Dr Swift spent nine days showing Stevenson round the leper settlement. The author also spent a lot of time with the mother superior and wrote a poem for her. He took in the stories that were told about Damien by the English-speakers and wrote to his mother,

> Of good old Damien, about whose weaknesses, and worse, I have perhaps heard everything, I now have a higher opinion. He was a European peasant, dirty, bigoted, lying, foolish, cunning, superb in his generosity, his openness and his fundamental good humour. If you could convince him he was wrong (sometimes after hours of fierce protest) then he would repair his error and appreciated the people who had complained the more. A man of all human grime and insignificance, and yet all the more a saint and a hero for that.

On 30 May he climbed the *pali* and simply dropped in on Meyer. The agent had just written to Emerson not to grant Conrardy an entry permit, at the request of the mother superior. She argued that Conrardy was insufficiently trained in administrative matters to manage the boys' home, and wanted

Möllers to take over. The agent was annoyed because, as he added, 'Conrardy was the best man we have ever had.' Until Möllers was ready to take over, James Sinnett could take over the management.

Julia, the housekeeper at the home, agreed with the mother superior and was willing to work with Sinnett, but she demanded that Meyer guarantee that if Sinnett did not do his work, she could dismiss him. This indeed happened and Sinnett was to be the first of Damien's assistants who left. The Board was happy to pay his fare to Melbourne.

Fouesnel chose his words for his announcement of Damien's death to Edward Clifford carefully. Clifford had published a book about Damien and could make the letter public. The hero had received enormous amounts of money and yet had to be forced to die in a bed, not on a mat. The sisters would take over the boys' home. Everyone was co-operating under Möllers's direction. He did not write that the boys no longer took warm baths every day and that the school was closed.

From the middle of June, the two new sisters, Irene and Crescentia, began to visit the boys' home, which was still managed by Dutton, regularly. The American was gradually becoming famous, because his saying, 'There are Molokais everywhere', caught on. He received piles of letters, each of which he answered with a long epistle, and had less and less time for the 100 boys. Another saying was that working in the leper settlement gave 'a certain entry to heaven'.

The first official anti-Damien attack came on 1 June 1889. Serano Bishop published an article entitled, 'Father Damien's Work', in the Hawaiian Congregational magazine *The Friend*. It was indisputable that Damien was a well-meaning and devout priest, but it was 'an unworthy exaggeration to raise the good priest into a rare and splendid martyr'. He spoke of the gossip about Damien, that did the rounds in Honolulu, as established facts and many would be sorry that he did not publish them. This 'need I say more?' suggested that it was about Damien and women. Meyer saw the danger of such a controversy and contacted Serano Bishop. The agent advised him not to write anything more about Damien, because it would appear underhand. The man was dead. The article was reprinted in several newspapers: *Paradise of the Pacific*, *The Hawaiian Gazette*, *The Occident* and *The Pacific*, published in San Francisco. The Rev. Henry B. Gage of San Francisco asked Charles McEwen Hyde if it was true.

Dr Hyde had for some time thought that the Rev. Mr Hanaloa ought also to be famous, because this man had, as a healthy pastor, followed his wife who had leprosy to the settlement. This was certainly true, for Damien himself had praised the pastor in a letter to Clifford. The only difference was that the Hawaiian knew no English and was not at present a leper. Irritated by the exaggerated praise, Hyde wrote a short letter to the Californian pastor which was to have important consequences. 'I can only reply', Hyde wrote,

> that we who knew the man are astonished at the extravagant praise that a very saintly philanthropist receives in the press. The truth is that he was a coarse, dirty man, stubborn and bigoted. He was not sent to Molokai, but went there without orders and did not stay in the leper settlement (before he got leprosy himself), but moved round freely on the whole island (less than half the island is for the lepers) and often travelled to Honolulu. He had nothing to do with the reforms and improvements. The Board of Health had them carried out when necessary and if there were means for them. He was not a pure man in his relations with women and the leprosy from which he died, he contracted through his carelessness and immorality. Others have also done much for the lepers, our own pastors, government doctors and so on, but never with the Catholic idea of earning eternal life by doing so.

Others, however, wanted to praise him. The general asked Pamphile to gather everything he could find about Damien, with an eye to beatification. The report that the Father Damien Memorial Committee, presided over by the Prince of Wales, had published, strengthened this plan. The Prince of Wales had said, 'The heroic life of Fr Damien has not only aroused sympathy in England, it has forced the situation in the far-flung Indian and Colonial Empire before our eyes and compels us, in part, to follow his [Damien's] example. And this, not for foreigners and strangers, but for our own subjects.'

The Committee wanted to erect a monument to Damien on Molokai, to establish a Fr Damien ward for lepers, attached to the London Hospital and Medical School, and to issue a travel grant for the study of leprosy, especially in India. On 13 January the Prince of Wales presided at the subscription dinner of the National Leprosy Fund.

Pamphile wrote a long letter to the editor of *The Times*, in which he gave information about the family and so on. His most important point was that the honorary title that Damien assigned himself was 'We, lepers . . .'

The superior of Leuven, Maurice Rapsaet, gave a new missionary to Hawaii a letter in which he requested a preliminary inquiry, with an eye to beatification. When he arrived, Fr Valentin Vranckx discovered that Damien, but still more Conrardy, were not popular with the superiors. Damien ought not to have brought Conrardy in, because now they were saddled with a man who only sought honour for himself. It seemed that Damien was a disobedient and difficult man, who could not get on with others, and therefore Vranckx was to refer to him not as Fr Damien, but simply as Damien. Burgerman was the source of this information, yet he had a reputation for being impossible. The superiors repeated that during Damien's life, they had had more trouble with Molokai than with the whole of the rest of the mission. Vranckx asked Möllers, who was then visiting Honolulu, what he thought of Damien. The reply was vague, 'Despite all his money, he died poor. I heard complaints about his chastity.' Dr Mouritz said he was too familiar. He allowed women into his house, which caused gossip.

Köckemann charged Gulstan Ropert with the task of preparing a beatification enquiry. Möllers knew hardly anything about Damien. They had been together for five months on Molokai, but Möllers had been ill almost the whole time. During Damien's death agony, Möllers had sat with him, but had to go back in the mornings to say mass for the sisters. Damien's greatest error was inviting Conrardy to come, because this cast aspersions on the Sacred Hearts Order.

Köckemann sent Rapsaet a copy of his sermon at the memorial service. It contained everything. Damien had his virtues, but these were always interwoven with imperfections. He might be a saint, but a special sort of one. The Order and the Mission were nothing more than 'a backdrop to his own personal glory'. He wanted to close the chapter, because there had already been one unfortunate Protestant article. A month later, Köckemann asked to be relieved of the beatification enquiry, which he called 'unpleasant'. He was convinced Damien was in heaven, but would have to say negative things. Möllers was collecting information.

Because Europe continued to put pressure on him, Köckemann sent Corneille to Kalaupapa to see with Möllers whether a beatification process could be set in train. They were to question under oath people who had known Damien. They prayed for enlightenment during a three-day retreat, while their enquiry took one day. Since they were only going to question *haole* clergy and religious, this seemed to them adequate. Sr Crescentia had arrived after Damien's death and had only seen him during a short visit to Honolulu. Sr Vincent had exchanged a few words with Damien on five occasions. She had eaten at his home at Christmas and admired his generosity. Sr Leopoldina remembered that he had foretold that she would go to Molokai, when he was staying in Kakaako. She had met him twice in Kakaako. She had been struck by his jollity, humility and generosity. She had seen him a few times in Kalaupapa and described one or two simple, endearing incidents. After his death, the disease had disappeared from his face, but, she admitted, that was normal with leprosy. Mother Marianne had first seen him in 1884. His night on the verandah had struck her and after the Christmas incident, he had asked for penance. This had touched her. Möllers concluded that the Christmas incident was a blot on his reputation. Dutton had so much to tell them that they asked him to write it down. None of the patients or *kokuas*, no one on 'topside', Conrardy, Dr Swift,

Meyer, superintendent Reynolds or the people from the Board of Health were heard.

Henry Gage published Dr Hyde's reply. Köckemann called it a 'diabolical and malicious interpretation of Damien's outward faults. De Veuster was touchingly familiar with kings and ministers, men and women, and that caused talk.' Dr Hyde, for his part, reported proudly to his directors that the letter was 'clear and incisive, rather rough than courteous'. He had not thought that Gage would publish it.

When Robert Louis Stevenson read Hyde's letter in the Union Club in Sydney, his blood boiled. It was a cowardly attack on a dead man. He had tears of rage in his eyes. The author of Dr Jekyll and Mr Hyde used his pen as a rapier against Dr Hyde, who had dared to attack such a good person as Damien. He accused Hyde, whom he had met, of 'jealousy, malice and hypocrisy'. He used a well-known technique. He strengthened all Hyde's criticisms of Damien by agreeing with them, and then launched his attack. Yes, Damien was dirty and Hyde was clean, because he had never dirtied his hands, while Damien worked in the 'nightmarish horror' of the leper settlement Hyde had written that Damien was not pure in his relations with women. How did he know this? Was this the sort of conversation that took place in the fashionable house on Beretania Street? Was this the choice language that was used about the poor peasant priest who was toiling away beneath the cliffs of Molokai? He demolished Hyde, sentence by sentence, writing to Hyde as follows: 'You make us sorry for the lepers, who had only this coarse old peasant for a friend and father. Why were you, who are so refined, not there to elevate them with your cultural insights?' This polemic, penned in haste, was a jewel of literary style. Emotion dripped from every sentence. Stevenson hastily had the letter published, not even looking at the proofs. He was not seeking commercial success, he simply wanted to correct someone else. He sent copies to leading figures throughout the world and to several newspapers in various countries. To his friends, he also sent an accompanying letter in which he set out his personal view once again. Hyde also got a pamphlet and an accompanying letter, while the publisher Chatto & Windus was immediately willing to publish the long pamphlet, as was Fr Hudson, who had a copy printed on the *Ave Maria* press.

A few days before he received his copy, Hyde knew that a bomb was about to go off and asked friends, like Meyer, for support. 'If there is one thing I cannot abide, it is an attack on someone's reputation and the demolition of another person's apparent goodness,' Hyde declared. 'I have not attacked anyone. I have simply answered a letter of inquiry. My letter was published without my permission.' He was not asking Meyer to take sides, and wished only to show him his appreciation, which he did not have for Damien. 'I only expressed my pellucid conviction, based on facts that I have got to know.'

Meyer's reply was cautious. 'The extraordinary expressions of praise that Damien has had foisted upon him did not come from people who live on these islands. They were made by foreign visitors, and I fear that their motive was self-interest and that they wished to serve themselves.' Hyde was wrong to attack a dead man, but one thing was certain:

> It was *totally false* that the government neglected the lepers before Damien arrived. Every government did a lot for the lepers and this quite apart from the exhortations or the influence of Fr Damien. In all honesty, I must confess: his advice and help, particularly in the maintenance of peace and order, were very valuable in the management of the leper settlement.

When Hyde had read Stevenson's letter, he groaned, 'I have received the worst blow of my life.' He had been crucified by the world's best-read author because he 'had told the truth about that misleading bigot in Molokai'.

Hyde wrote to Meyer a few days after reading Stevenson's open letter, 'I was attacked because I tried to correct falsehoods. When I defended myself, I was not attacking Damien. I was careful enough not to make public everything that I have been told and that I think I may accept as the truth.'

Köckemann received Dutton's report, which was very strange. Damien played a major role in the author's autobiography. It could be quickly summarised. The patients had preferred the hard-working Damien to the well-paid government doctors. He never finished anything off, was hospitable, met newcomers every week. Not all the changes came from him. He was not entirely clean, but he had a good heart and was it not that that counted? When he had read this, Köckemann decided to close the beatification file. The only trouble was, that Pamphile was persisting. He had even travelled to Manchester to talk about his brother. However, Damien had not performed any miracles.

Meyer was also asked many questions. He described Damien's morals to Captain Julius Palmer.

> For my part, I cannot say anything against him [Damien], but among the Hawaiians, with whom he lived, many rumours about immorality went around. How much value should be attached to these rumours, I leave you to judge, I will only observe that the Hawaiians are people of nature, who judge others by their own standards. They do not regard certain immoral actions as seriously as whites do. Hawaiians do not realise the seriousness of that kind of accusation. Damien was careless and made no attempt to avoid compromising appearances, which explains the rumours. It seems reasonable that your friends in Honolulu never heard anything bad about him, because that is the case with many people. It is also not known how leprosy is transmitted from one person to another. All suppositions as to how Damien contracted the disease and how he spread it further are groundless.

The mud-slinging was not yet over, certainly not after Charles Hyde, in an interview in the *San Francisco Examiner*, declared that Stevenson had confirmed his points, while the *Hawaiian Gazette* suggested a public inquiry into Damien's chastity. A year after he had written the letter to Gage, Hyde published a long article that revived the debate, because once again he raked up the rumours. He gave the name of a lady on Hawaii, but she quickly turned out to be the widow who had filed the complaint against Damien's successor, Fabien Schausten. Köckemann was in a state of panic, because if this woman went on to tell all she knew, the rumour machine on Hawaii would be working for months. The next rumour came from Hong Kong. An English lady, who was on her way from Hawaii to a leper settlement on Robben Island, near Cape Town, had told a certain Rev. Mr Reusch that she had had an affair with Damien during her stay on Molokai. The Board of Health immediately began to examine the records of who had received an entry permit. A Miss Martin had stayed with Dr Mouritz for two or three months, but she had since married and had not travelled to Hong Kong. Sr Gertrude, Dr Swift's senior nurse, had arrived after Damien's death. A Mrs Johnson was working on Robben Island. She had been in Hong Kong and had worked in a maternity home in Honolulu. After questioning, this lady confirmed that she had never had an affair with the priest. Because no trace of this mysterious woman could be found, the case was closed, but the rumour grew to legendary proportions and continued to be mentioned years later.

After two months' sick leave, Conrardy took over the management of the boys' home from Dutton. He still wanted to join the Sacred Hearts Order, but this proved impossible, because the sisters refused to accept him. Matters were bound to end in conflict when the plantation owner Henry Perrine Baldwin imitated Charles Bishop's gesture. He wanted to sponsor twenty-nine buildings for the 100 orphan boys. One of the buildings was a small convent. Sr Crescentia was appointed director in advance and so overrode Conrardy's authority. When the building was almost finished, the mother superior asked for a small house for the small boys near the convent in Kalaupapa. She did not want the children to grow up in the Kalawao churchyard. Mother Marianne had problems with the work in the eastern village, because there were several robberies on the road between Kalawao and Kalaupapa. Because of the general lack of security, she did not want the sisters to spend the night in Kalawao. This meant that every night Conrardy had to take over from Sr Crescentia, while Dutton continued to deal with the administration. Dutton wanted to get rid of Conrardy and he was supported by Möllers.

Things were not going well in Kalawao. A quarrel ended in a fight and Evans, a man who worked for the government, was taken hostage. The rebels allowed Conrardy to go free, because he was a friend. The revolt spread to Kalaupapa, where the girls in the home rebelled. They broke the furniture and threw stones at the sisters, because they wanted freedom and fun, not a conventual life. The sisters and Möllers shut themselves in a room. Möllers kept repeating that they had one another, but that Damien had had to face such uproars alone. The fifteen armed police whom the government sent to the settlement arrested the leaders, who were put in chains.

King Kalakaua wanted to judge the situation on the spot and used the pretext that he wanted to choose the site for the British monument himself. The king wanted to put it in Kalawao, but the sisters asked to have it near their home, so that it could be seen by passing boats.

Damien was not forgotten in Europe. In 1890 and 1891, testimonies were collected for beatification. Bouillon, who was in France, recalled that Damien had gone of his own free will. He was intolerant towards his superiors and stubborn, but what Hyde had said was pure fabrication. Albert Montiton also defended Damien. He was not unchaste, just rather careless. Julia, the housekeeper for the orphans, was the problem. Damien worked much too closely with her and that caused gossip. Köckemann no longer reacted. He shut himself up in his room, refused to hand out relics of Damien and died of a heart attack in January 1891.

King Kalakaua died around the same time. On 20 January 1891 he was succeeded by his sister Liliuokalani. She reigned for nearly two years until, on 17 January 1893, the Reform Party organised a successful coup. The islands became a republic and an annexation treaty was signed with the United States.

Gulstan Ropert was consecrated bishop in San Francisco in September 1892. He was asked to send Damien's possessions to Belgium, because the congregation wanted to open a museum about Hawaii. Dutton was able to find hardly any personal possessions, except a pipe with teeth marks, a photograph of Bishop Maigret, two photographs of Burgerman and photographs of the sisters and girls. There were lots of religious prints, a photograph of the grotto at Lourdes and religious books. He had everything packed for shipment. Damien had kept up to date with his correspondence. The letters from the royal family and the statutes of the Order of King Kalakaua were in a special box. Fouesnel allowed the cases to rust on the quayside and did nothing to get them through customs. After nine months of complaining, Möllers also gave up on the subject. He did not understand this indifference, because Damien worked like a magnet on candidates and benefactors. His only problem was Conrardy, who had now been trying to enter the Order for five years. Dutton lodged three complaints against Conrardy in 1895. Möllers thought two were futile and the third a fabrication. He wondered whether Dutton had not been the cause of many of the difficulties concerning Conrardy in 1888.

When, in September 1893, the sisters had still not taken over the full-time running of the Baldwin Boys' Home, Bishop Ropert invited brothers to come, during a visit to Paris. Pamphile travelled with Ropert and the brothers, finally reaching his destination after thirty years. Once he got to the leper settlement, he saw that he could not cope, and first complained that three priests were too many for such a small community. Moreover, he was ill. When on 26 March 1896 Conrardy lost his permit and had to leave, Pamphile thought two priests too many. The Board's decision was final – Conrardy was not even allowed to stay as a volunteer nurse. Yet he had, as a true child of the Sacred Hearts Order, taught Pamphile and the brothers Hawaiian. He also passed on to them, as best he could, all the knowledge he had acquired during eight years in the settlement. Conrardy defended himself once more, in a newspaper article, and placed the blame for his being driven out on Dutton. He went to Oregon, where he studied medicine. By the time he qualified he was nearly fifty. Thereafter, he travelled through Europe and the United States, in order to raise money for a leper colony near Canton in China. He was in San Francisco when the earthquake struck in 1906 and remained there to treat the wounded and combat epidemics. His colony in China was a great success, although he published nothing about it. It would seem, therefore, that he was not seeking fame. He died in China in 1914.

In Kalaupapa, Möllers dug up his old plans again, and this time he got his new church, which was finished on 4 March 1896. He felt himself to be like Damien during the building, because he also did a lot of the handiwork and boys helped him. The St Francis Church was not consecrated until 29 June 1900, though why it took so long is not known.

Pamphile hated Molokai and experienced temptation. He had nothing to do, either, because five brothers, two lay helpers, five sisters and Fr Möllers now did the work much better than Damien alone. In August 1897, Pamphile threatened to leave the Order if he were not allowed to return to Leuven. In order to avoid a scandal, Ropert allowed him to go. He helped to prepare for Damien's beatification until his death in 1909.

Politics brought the issue of beatification back into question. In 1898, the American marines occupied Honolulu, and Hawaii became American territory. From then on, Dutton raised the American flag in Kalawao every day. Once again, a huge round-up of lepers took place. The number of deaths rose and many people remembered Damien's time. Fr Hudson and Professor Stoddard asked the American government, in the name of the *Ave Maria* movement, to support the beatification of a man who had worked in the newly acquired area. It could be politically useful. Washington agreed. A number of patients and Dr Mouritz were questioned.

Ropert prayed to Damien for a miracle, because this would help the cause, but he admitted to the general that he had reasons to be silent. The general did not urge the point any further, because the advocates of the Order who had to plead the case for beatification in the Vatican Supreme Court cost vast sums of money.

The witnesses disappeared, one by one. Meyer died in 1897 and was succeeded by Charles Reynolds, who had known Damien when he was superintendent. Gerard de Veuster went bankrupt and proposed that the Order should buy the parental home. He moved in 1902 and the house was turned into a novitiate and chapel. The novitiate was plundered during the First World War and things that had belonged to Damien disappeared.

Fouesnel remained provincial until the end of the century, but he became senile and threatened to hang himself. He died on 29 December 1902 from a cerebral haemorrhage.

The new St Francis Church in Kalaupapa was razed to the ground on 12 August 1906. It happened at a time when both villages were undergoing extensive rebuilding. Charles B. Cooper had persuaded the American authorities to carry out scientific research on Molokai. On 3 March 1905 the American Congress approved $100,000 for the building of a hospital with a laboratory and $50,000 running costs for the first year. The Public Health and Marine Hospital was a splendid building, with all the latest facilities, but most patients wanted normality, not a regimented hospital life. The building was closed shortly after the opening for lack of patients, but it had brought two advantages. The leper settlement had received electricity, and everything that could be moved was plundered by the exiles.

Damien's immorality hit the headlines again in 1912. The son of Elijah Bond wrote to the *Advertiser* that his father had transferred the problems that Fabien had had with women to Damien. During the First World War, the exiles held a collection for the Red Cross, when the United States had entered the war. Mother Marianne died in Kalaupapa shortly after the war ended. She is also the subject of a beatification enquiry. Sr Leopoldina died in 1942. Dutton left Kalaupapa once, to die in a hospital in Honolulu in 1932.

The issue of beatification was not taken up again until after the First World War. Ropert's successor, Bishop Alencastre, mentioned Damien during his audience with King Leopold III. The Belgian king wanted to have Damien's remains brought back to Belgium, and asked President Roosevelt personally for permission. He argued that the Hawaiians were neglecting the grave, whereas Damien had not been forgotten in Europe. The Hawaiian Holy Name Society protested against this. It had been Damien's express wish to rest under the pandan. The patients asked to be allowed to keep their hero. A father should stay with his son. They knew what they were talking about, because *kokuas* were no longer allowed in the settlement. On 3 October 1935 it seemed as if only a few parts of the body would be removed but, a few months later, Bishop Alencastre denied this. Everything would be sent to Belgium, because the Belgian government would arrange for canonisation.

On 27 January 1936 a military aircraft crashed on Fort island, one of the Hawaiian Islands, and the six crew were killed. The same day, Bishop Alencastre and the Belgian consul, Lappe, arrived in Honolulu, in order to be present at the exhumation in Kalaupapa. Damien's coffin was packed and transferred to Honolulu, where a service was held in the cathedral with military honours. The remains of the victims of the air crash and Damien were shipped to San Francisco together, on the USS *Republic*. In San Francisco Bay, the captain disappeared in a mysterious manner, and rumours went around Hawaii.

There was another memorial service in the cathedral in San Francisco and then the coffin was taken to Panama by the USS *Republic*, where it was transferred to the Belgian training ship *Mercator*. During the transhipment, the coffin fell into the sea.

Since 1936, Damien's body has rested in the Sacred Hearts church in Leuven. The hand has returned to Hawaii. The day after the beatification, on 4 June 1995, the Hawaiian Bishop di Lorenzo and provincial Bukovski opened the koa wood box, with the remains of the two finger joints that had never developed leprosy, in the Conrad Hilton Hotel in Brussels. The Hawaiians who were present, almost all of them patients, wept and performed rituals that had echoes of their old beliefs. The remains of Damien's hand were reburied on 22 July 1995, in the place he had set aside for himself.

Leprosy is a disease that affects the peripheral nerves, the skin and other tissues. The eyes, muscles, bones, testes and mucous membrane of the upper respiratory tract are all affected. There are two types of leprosy. People with little resistance to *Mycobacterium leprae*, which is related to the bacterium that

AFTER DAMIEN

causes tuberculosis, develop lepromas. These growths are full of bacteria. If leprosy is not treated, the patient gradually deteriorates and his body is overwhelmed by deformities. The tuberculoid form is less malignant. There are fewer bacteria, so that it is less easily passed on. Spontaneous cure does occur, but the nerve damage cannot be reversed. This form affects particularly the skin and the nerves. The incubation period is between six months and fifteen years. Leprosy does not kill, but it reduces resistance and makes the patient susceptible to other, often fatal, infections.

The World Health Organisation estimates that there are roughly fifteen million cases of leprosy worldwide. Fewer than 20 per cent receive regular treatment. Leprosy has become a Third World disease, which, since 1940, has been treatable with the sulphone drug dapsone. From 1947, the patients in Kalaupapa were treated with dapsone, in combination with penicillin and the mycin group of drugs. This stopped the spread of the epidemic, but it was only in 1969 that the segregation regulations were lifted in Hawaii, which by then was an American state.

In the nineteenth century, Hawaii was by no means the only country that used segregation as a means of combating epidemics. As we have seen, Robben Island, later notorious as the high-security prison in which Nelson Mandela was incarcerated, was then a leper colony. In Norway, Australia, Japan, Ceylon and Canada, segregation laws were in force, but Kalaupapa was the first government leper settlement and it served as a model. In order to keep alive the memory of so much pain and suffering, Kalaupapa was created a National Historical Park in 1980.

Mahatma Gandhi wrote of Damien, 'The political and journalistic world recognises few heroes who can compare with Fr Damien of Molokai. On the other hand, the Catholic Church has thousands in its ranks who follow Fr Damien's example in devoting themselves to the care of lepers. It is worthwhile to look for the source of such heroism.'

For this reason, Pope Paul VI declared Damien 'venerable' in 1977, that is, he was declared worthy of veneration. For canonisation, a miracle is required. On 7 May 1984 Mother Teresa wrote to Pope John Paul II,

> As you know, we work among thousands of lepers in India, Yemen, Ethiopia and Tanzania. We set up mobile hospitals and rehabilitation centres on government land. In order to continue this beautiful work of love and healing, we need a saint to lead and protect us. Fr Damien can be this saint. Holy Father, our lepers and everyone on earth beg you to give us a saint, a martyr to love, an example of obedience to our religion.

Mother Teresa had a solution for the absence of a miracle. 'I know a real miracle,' she wrote. 'The removal of fear on the part of the lepers to acknowledge their disease, to acknowledge it and to ask for treatment. The birth of hope in a cure is a miracle.' And she saw a second miracle: 'The change in the attitude of people and governments to the lepers – more care, less fear and the willingness constantly to help.'

The Congregation for the Causes of Saints revived the old miracle of Sr Simplicie Hue, a French Sacred Hearts nun. She was thirty-seven when she started having intestinal problems. The illness lasted for months. On 11 September 1895 she lost consciousness. When she felt her strength ebbing, the sisters began a novena to Damien. The next day she came to. She lay on her side, which she had been unable to do before and she was no longer in pain. This was a miracle, according to the report of the Medical Commission of the Congregation for the Causes of Saints, dated 5 December 1991.

The beatification was due to take place in May 1994 in Brussels, but Pope John Paul II broke his leg a few days before. The celebration was therefore postponed until Whitsun 1995 (4 June). Beatification is the final step before someone can be declared a saint, but miracles are also necessary for that.